The Future of
the International
Monetary System

The Future of
the International
Monetary System

Edited by
Tamir Agmon
Tel-Aviv University

Robert G. Hawkins
New York University

Richard M. Levich
New York University and
National Bureau of
Economic Research

LexingtonBooks
D.C. Heath and Company
Lexington, Massachusetts
Toronto

Library of Congress Cataloging in Publication Data
Main entry under title:

The future of the international monetary system.

Includes index.
1. International finance—Congresses. I. Agmon, Tamir. II. Hawkins,
Robert G. III. Levich, Richard M.
HG3881.F872 1984   332.4'5   83–47657
ISBN 0–669–06721–0
ISBN 0–669–09783–7 Paperbound

Copyright © 1984 by D.C. Heath and Company

Third printing, April 1985

Published simultaneously in Canada

Printed in the United States of America on acid-free paper

International Standard Book Number: 0–669–06721–0 Casebound

International Standard Book Number: 0–669–09783–7 Paperbound

Library of Congress Catalog Card Number: 83–47657

Contents

Figures and Tables

Acknowledgments

This book contains the proceedings of a conference sponsored by the Salomon Brothers Center for the Study of Financial Institutions at the Graduate School of Business Administration of New York University and the Leon Recanati School of Business Administration of Tel-Aviv University. The conference was held on October 7–8, 1982, at New York University.

We are grateful to many people who helped us pull together the resources necessary for this conference. Haim Ben-Shahar, president of Tel-Aviv University, was instrumental in the conceptualization and realization of the conference. Arnold Sametz, director of the Salomon Brothers Center, and Yair Orgler, dean of the Leon Recanati School, provided important organizational resources and support. Administrative arrangements for the conference were executed cheerfully by Marion Epps, Ligija Roze, and Patricia Taylor.

We also wish to acknowledge Pentti Kouri of New York University, Jeffrey Shafer of the Federal Reserve Bank of New York, and J. Richard Zecher of the Chase Manhattan Bank for their contributions at the conference.

Finally, we wish to express our thanks to McGeorge Bundy of New York University and Leonard Silk of *The New York Times*, who addressed the luncheon meetings of the conference. Their remarks were timely and insightful, but, unfortunately, could not be included in this book.

1 Introduction

Tamir Agmon,
Robert G. Hawkins, and
Richard M. Levich

The international monetary system underwent radical changes between 1971 and 1973 and, since then, has continued to evolve. When the United States devalued the dollar (against gold and other currencies) in 1971, it was a major first step toward the existing system of floating exchange rates. Although attempts were made to reestablish a pegged exchange-rate system, albeit with wider bands of permissible fluctuation, at the Smithsonian Accords in December 1971, the first OPEC oil-price increase in 1973 affected international monetary arrangements profoundly, imbuing the floating exchange-rate regime with considerable permanence.

During this transition period, the official international financial institutions—the International Monetary Fund (IMF) and the World Bank—remained almost unchanged structurally. However, their role in setting exchange rates was substantially eroded. Furthermore, the IMF's relative importance as a source of balance-of-payments financing receded as the balance-of-payments shock wave from the OPEC price increases spread among the oil-importing countries.

There were three principal reasons for the radical restructuring of the international financial system in the early 1970s. First, the United States, whose dollar was the key and major reserve currency, unit of account, and source of international reserves, was in a structural balance-of-payments disequilibrium with other major industrial countries. These included Japan, West Germany, France, and much of the rest of western Europe. A realignment of currencies, especially given the relatively high U.S. inflation rates of 1969 to 1971, was unavoidable.

Second, international capital movements had been liberalized during the 1960s. Although current-account convertibility was restored among the major European currencies and the dollar in 1957–58, the 1960s saw a continuing liberalization of international financial transactions as well as of international trade. At the same time, the Eurocurrency and the Eurobond markets expanded rapidly, further deepening the international financial overlay and producing a massive pool of international financial liquidity that could move from one currency to another, affecting the balance of supply and demand in the foreign-exchange markets.

The third reason for the restructuring was the growing magnitude of international shocks to balance-of-payments positions, stemming from the increasing integration of commodity and financial markets. When shocks to balance-of-payments positions are substantial, larger volumes of international reserves and liquidity are needed to finance them if exchange rates remain fixed than if they are allowed to fluctuate. One such shock was the U.S. inflation resulting from the Vietnam War, which exacerbated the U.S. structural imbalance with the rest of the world after 1969. The supreme shock was the first OPEC oil-price increase, in 1973–74, which quadrupled oil prices. Oil-price increases had begun under OPEC auspices in 1970, but they had been minor until the oil embargo of 1973.

The culmination of these events forced massive institutional change on the international financial structure. From 1972 to the present, the international system continued to evolve in detail, but the broad outlines of the present arrangement were already in place by the end of 1973. The chapters in this book attempt to explain various dimensions of that evolving system, the forces that are shaping its evolution, the perceived problems in the current system, and the likely evolution of the system in the future.

Characteristics of the Evolving System

The international financial system that emerged after February 1973, when IMF members agreed that nations need not set parity values for their currencies, is very different from the Bretton Woods system it replaced. Essentially, nations now have individual options with respect to how they set the exchange rates for their currencies. Several of the major currencies are permitted to float relatively freely against other major currencies, with only limited central-bank intervention in the foreign-exchange market. Other nations "peg" their currency to one other major currency, such as the U.S. dollar or the French franc. Several nations peg their currency to some weighted "basket" of foreign currencies, most often the Special Drawing Right (SDR). A few groups of nations have formed currency blocks, the most prominent of which is the European Monetary System. In a real sense, the financial system has evolved into one of currency blocks, with only limited governmental intervention in the setting of exchange rates among the blocks.

As the exchange-rate adjustment mechanism has evolved since 1973, several attempts have been made to place more emphasis upon the coordination of intervention activities of central banks. However, substantial flexing of exchange rates was deemed essential to help absorb the shocks that were jarring international payments balances during the 1970s and early 1980s.

Important by-products of the flexible exchange-rate system and the continuing liberalization of exchange controls over foreign-investment transactions were a wave of financial innovation and the deepening of the foreign-exchange markets. In instruments and markets, innovations such as currency futures contracts, more continuous forward markets, and the like occurred. In the volume of foreign-exchange trading, there was a massive increase among the major market participants. This process of maturation of the foreign-exchange markets was facilitated by the revolution in electronics and communications. One of the major results of this process has been that the foreign-exchange markets can absorb and incorporate, much more rapidly and completely than before, new information about currencies, including projections of future developments and price movements. Thus, not only do exchange rates move more significantly from day to day and week to week, but the public and market participants are now much more aware of those movements than they were prior to the mid-1970s.

With respect to the supply of international liquidity and reserves, the emphasis but not the structure of the international financial system has changed. In the aftermath of the 1973–74 oil-price changes, private financial markets, especially the international commercial banks, were the major sources of lending for international balance-of-payments purposes. They were flush with sources of liquid funds from recycled petrodollars and, unlike multilateral organizations such as the IMF and the World Bank, could respond quickly to the new demands for credit. Thus, the share of international private lending to developing countries in particular rose dramatically from 1973 to 1976.

The pendulum began to swing back after the mid-1970s, as IMF resources were enhanced, IMF quotas increased, and the Arab OPEC countries commenced to relend part of their new financial wealth to selected developing and advanced countries.

Despite these swings in the pendulum, the nature of the international monetary system remained approximately the same. It continued to act as a pool of currencies from which countries in balance-of-payments difficulties borrowed. It continued to be a deliberative body that, together with the Organisation for Economic Cooperation and Development (OECD), provided the principal forum for discussion and coordination of policies between countries. It continued in and strengthened its role as an overseer of domestic economic policies and exchange-rate policies of borrowing countries, and it became more interactive with private borrowers in studying terms and conditions for joint loans to debtor countries.

Through the later 1970s, the share of official international credits began to increase, while private-sector credits in country-to-country lendings continued to rise, but at a slower pace. In 1980, OPEC set an additional 100 percent change in oil prices at a time when some major industrial countries were undergoing sluggish growth or had entered the initial stages of the worst recession of the postwar period. This new price change both contributed to and accentuated the economic slide thereafter. The world again faced major strains, with negative growth in world trade for two consecutive years in 1981–82, record high interest rates in some countries, and the most widespread economic collapse since the 1930s. This situation placed new pressures on international lenders and enhanced the importance of the IMF and the World Bank as international creditors. Many of the oil-importing countries, having expanded their debt to finance the balance-of-payments deficits in the 1970s, were now faced with repayments schedules to which they would not adhere because their export receipts had plummeted due to the recession in the rest of the world. A number of international debt reschedulings resulted from this situation. The worldwide recession radically reduced the demand for energy sources, particularly petroleum, which led to a softening of international oil prices, the erosion of the power of OPEC as supply exceeded demand at the established prices, and a decline in oil-export receipts for several—indeed, all—of the oil-exporting countries. Suddenly, some oil-exporting countries, most prominently Mexico, Nigeria, and Venezuela, became major international debtors with debt-service problems. Thus, the IMF, in union with private lenders, took on an important role in credit renewals, rescheduling, and the supplying of new credits in order to preserve the increasingly fragile structure of international credit and the monetary system that had evolved.

Dissatisfactions with the System

By the early 1980s, there was growing evidence of dissatisfaction with the international monetary system as it had evolved since 1971. The dissatisfaction ranged from concern about unstable exchange rates, to means of avoiding the repudiation of international loans, to concern regarding the fragility of the international financial system and its potential collapse. Among the many criticisms, some of the more specific ones that are addressed in this book are stated in the following paragraphs.

1. The floating exchange rates are too unstable, undergoing wide and reversible swings, which, from time to time, reflect not the true economic forces but the temporary misperceptions of market makers. The instability and unpredictability of exchange rates raise the transaction costs of international trade and investment.

2. Floating exchange rates, or the lack of sanction for currency devaluations and revaluations, do not provide adequate monetary discipline for countries, central banks, and financial officials. Put differently, floating

exchange rates remove a possible source of monetary discipline and encourage the spread of inflation and fiscal laxity from country to country. Rather than being reversed by the monetary discipline (on stable money and prices) that a fixed exchange-rate system provides, inflationary finance is ratified by the devaluation of the currency under a floating exchange-rate system.

3. The current international monetary system is prone to financial and economic crises. The system spreads financial stringency from country to country via the exchange rate or international lending organizations. Any liquid financial institution in one nation has assets and liabilities in financial institutions in other nations, and the default or insolvency of one may spread to the others, affecting the exchange rate and leading to international financial panic and collapse.

4. The current international financial system provides too little credit to those who most need it and cannot accommodate major shifts in demands and needs for loans to particular countries and institutions. There is no organized system to deal with major debt roll overs for borrowing countries that are suffering from declining export markets, for which the countries may not be at fault.

5. The current system provides too much credit and is too competitive, seeking out and attempting to encourage international lending, especially to developing countries that may, in the future, face serious economic difficulties because of their inappropriate economic policies. Competition among financial institutions in a system without exchange controls may lead to their taking too much, rather than too little, risk.

6. Parallel to the previous two criticisms, the current system contains no "true" lender of last resort. Currently, lenders-of-last-resort facilities exist, but only in the form of national central banks. Thus, a true international lender of last resort would coordinate the lending by central banks to private financial institutions that are facing economic difficulties. There exists, however, no such institutional structure to impose or enforce such coordination.

7. The current international financial system is based on multiple national-reserve currencies, which creates the potential for massive international capital movements by official institutions. There is no programmed increase in international liquidity and reserves. Instead, increases are based on the national government's responses to perceived needs or crises and the balance-of-payments imbalances.

8. The current international system gives too little weight, or almost no weight, to the interests of the developing countries. It is inequitable because the international reserves are created mainly for the benefit of the advanced countries.

**Basic Forces of Market Integration and
Government Intervention**

The evolutionary process and current dissatisfactions outlined thus far may
be cast in terms of a conflict between market forces that tend to integrate
world financial markets and government interventions that tend to limit or
resist such integration. International financial integration, brought about
by economic forces and technological improvements, implies greater efficiency in the allocation of world financial resources and closer coordination
of national economic policies, which spreads the burden of international
adjustment.

Market interventions of the state, deriving from its political powers to
issue money, tax, and regulate, generally create barriers to the free movement of goods, capital, and factors of production. This power to intervene
in markets at the national level is a jealously guarded prerogative that
nations cede to international bodies only rarely and reluctantly. When and
how particular nations may use these power, in affecting the money supply,
domestic prices, capital controls, and so forth, are uncertain and may
impede international transactions.

If the short-term political interests of nations are considered explicitly
in the analysis of the international financial system, many of the paradigms
of perfect markets no longer serve as either positive explanations of
national economic behavior or as useful normative guides for making
national or international policy. Changing the international monetary system becomes largely a matter of negotiation in which a variety of economic
and political considerations must be balanced.

Given this conflict between integrating market forces and government
interventions based partially on political objectives, discussions concerning
the operation and reform of the international financial systems may be cate-
gorized in two ways: those that advocate the accommodation of government interventions and those that seek to limit or restrain government interventions and maximize the integrative market forces.

The advocates of the accommodating approach accept the role of the
government in the international monetary system as legitimate. Indeed, they
see that governments have an obligation to devise viable solutions to the system's problems while minimizing the economic cost through direct governmental actions. The chapters by Richard Cooper and Ronald McKinnon are
in this vein, as are Franco Modigliani's comments.

The advocates of the restraining approach acknowledge the role of government in shaping the international monetary system but assign responsibility for most of the system's problems to government interventions and
thus are concerned mainly with determining the most effective way to
restrain governments. Accommodation seeks to improve the effectiveness

and efficiency of government policy; restraint seeks to minimize the discretion of domestic and foreign governments in making economic policy.

Differences between the accommodating approach and the restraining approach are clearly visible in the analyses and prognoses presented in this book. It is widely acknowledged that, in most countries, the exchange rate is a political variable, and the setting of that rate is often among the objectives of a country's government. What is controversial is what can and should be done about this situation. Proponents of the accommodating approach concentrate on the positive aspect of government action. For example, in chapter 2, Richard Cooper argues that any system that does not allow for a sufficient degree of government control may be threatened by complete and direct government control. In this argument, international cooperation is preferred to a design based on free-market principles that will inevitably deteriorate into protectionist disintegration. In chapter 3, on the other hand, Leland Yeager advocates the removal of government from international monetary affairs. One possible means suggested is the adoption of a disciplined international system such as the gold standard.

Some economists who profess to be free marketers advocate systems that remove some policy options (for example, the exchange rate) from the range of choices available to the government. But such a solution to the problem becomes complicated, as Franco Modigliani points out in his comments on chapter 3, by the acknowledgment that there are more markets than the market for money and bonds and there are more variables than national price levels, the exchange rate, and the rate of interest. A system that imposes discipline on these variables may create economically undesirable or politically unacceptable implications for other variables, such as employment and growth.

Accommodation recognizes the balance of political power and its changes through time. As Ronald McKinnon notes in chapter 4, the Bretton Woods Agreement was based implicitly on a strong dollar standard, with the United States pursuing a domestically oriented monetary policy and other countries accommodating themselves to this policy. The central role of the United States carried some benefits (seigniorage) and some obligations (acting as lender of last resort and accepting an additional burden of adjustment). As the balance of political and economic power changes, so must the international monetary system change. The nexus of power in the Western world has become multicountry, and thus it is appropriate that the dollar be augmented by the German mark and the yen as reserve currencies. What is needed is a new international monetary system that reflects the new and evolving situation. The Japanese view, as evidenced in Eisuke Sakakibara's chapter, tends to concur with the general drift of this argument.

The same basic approach can be applied to other macroeconomic and microeconomic issues. For example, the accommodating and the restraining approaches are reflected in the attitudes toward the question of financing developing countries and Eastern European countries. In chapter 6, Carlos Diaz Alejandro presents the problem of international lending in the context of market imperfections. Microeconomic decisions as to who receives loans and how much should be loaned are based on political as well as on financial considerations. Banks have acted as intermediaries for the governments, and they expect some subsidies from their country of domicile if the need arises. The proponents of the accommodating approach accept this implicit arrangement as a workable and desirable solution to the macroeconomic problem of reallocating financial resources in the world. The advocates of governmental restraints, however, would opt for a prescribed, explicit rule of the game and leave the private banks to solve their own lending or loan-rescheduling problems.

Proposed Changes in the System

Dissatisfactions with the existing international monetary arrangements have manifested themselves in a broad range of proposed reforms and solutions. Some of these deal with the process and rules for setting exchange rates; others focus on international lending and liquidity with a view to avoiding financial collapse; and still others are concerned with both preceding subjects as well as with national obligations for balance-of-payments adjustments. The chapters and comments in this book touch upon, at some point, almost all possible alternatives.

A return to a metallic or commodity monetary standard has been seriously advocated by a few economists and several politicians in the United States and abroad, all of whom are proponents of governmental restraint. Adopting such a standard would presumably set exchange rates permanently, enforce monetary discipline, and permit private financial institutions and markets to provide adequate financial resources for temporary balance-of-payments disturbances.

Others advocate further removal of governments and central banks from foreign-exchange-market intervention to allow for a more complete system of flexible exchange rates. This approach is perceived by some as a means of removing the unpredictability of government actions from influencing and destabilizing the foreign-exchange and international-credit markets.

Other proposals of the accommodation type suggest more governmental and official involvement. One proposal advocates more direct, intensive, and continuous coordination of national actions in foreign-exchange markets and of the setting of national monetary and fiscal policies. A second proposal concerns the coordination of national commitments to a supernational fund to provide banks with a risk sharer or to serve as a lender of last resort or to provide a supplemental source of funds for countries in financial distress.

Perhaps the most expansive institutional change advocated by an accommodation-type proposal involves the creation, by national agreement, of an IMF (or other international central bank) with lender-of-last-resort and reserve-creation powers. This would parallel the Triffin Plan, which was supported by many in the early 1960s.

These aspects of the evolving system and alternative future scenarios are examined in some detail in the chapters and comments that follow.

2 Recent History of World Monetary Problems

Richard N. Cooper

This chapter will interpret the recent history of world monetary problems somewhat narrowly. It will discuss international aspects, not by addressing all of the troubles in the world economy that we have seen in recent years, but rather by focusing on monetary relations among countries. In particular, the chapter will look at what is loosely called the international monetary system (to avoid the suggestion that it is systematic, it could be called the international monetary regime). But, to start with, let us recall some not so recent history, because it is useful to remind ourselves of how we got to where we are today. History may be bunk, but it is interesting and relevant bunk.

Designing International Monetary Systems

Awareness of the international monetary system as an international monetary system is a relatively recent phenomenon. It dates from the 1920s. One can find glimmerings of such awareness in the nineteenth-century discussions of bimetallism, but it was not until after World War I that monetary officials first defined the system as a system. World War I had resulted in a very sharp rise in the level of prices, but the rise differed among countries. The problem officials faced was how to restore something close to the prewar international monetary regime, the gold standard, given this large but differential rise in prices. The outlines of their solution are well known. Individual countries were left to adjust to the differential inflation either by deflating or by devaluing their currencies. However, their plan proposed that the prospect of a shortage of gold at the higher world-price level be dealt with by conserving on gold by (1) concentrating gold in the hands of banks rather than the public and (2) encouraging central banks to hold currencies convertible into gold in lieu of gold itself. The system became known as the gold exchange standard. The arrangement was achieved, not by treaty, but by agreement. It was more or less in place, with its participants more or less happy with it, until it broke down in the early 1930s.

The Bretton Woods System

Following the breakdown of the gold exchange standard, the architects of international monetary systems went to work for a second time in two decades. This time, out of the wreckage of the 1930s, they produced the Bretton Woods system. As I stylize it, the Bretton Woods system had five key features.

First, it provided national economic policymakers with a great deal of freedom to pursue national economic objectives, such as assuring full employment, price stability, growth, and so forth. The Bretton Woods Agreement was produced in the same environment that produced the Beveridge Report in the United Kingdom, the Full Employment Act in the United States, and comparable legislation or statements of national policy in other countries. All these acts and statements were derived from the experience of the 1930s and from the determination that that experience should never be repeated.

Second, the Bretton Woods system stipulated fixed exchange rates. It was taken for granted that fixed exchange rates were more desirable than the flexible exchange rates (and the resulting turbulent periods) that prevailed in the early 1920s and again briefly in the early 1930s. It is noteworthy that the architects of the gold exchange standard did not consider leaving in place the de facto regime of flexible exchange rates that existed from 1919 to 1925. So far as I am aware, flexible exchange rates were universally considered a transitory and undesirable state of affairs.

Third, the Bretton Woods system stipulated that currencies should be convertible, one into another, at least for current-account transactions. This feature was conceived against the background of the extensive use—and, many would argue, abuse—of exchange controls by Nazi Germany during the 1930s and the tight wartime restrictions on trade and payments that the architects considered desirable to shed as quickly as possible.

Taken together, these three features—autonomy of national policies, fixed exchange rates, and convertibility of currencies—were in conflict with one another. This conflict was recognized by the architects, who therefore added two further features. They created a new institution, the International Monetary Fund (IMF), to lend money to countries that were in balance-of-payments deficit as a result of the combination of those first three features.

Fifth, countries were allowed, and in time came to be encouraged, to change their exchange rates discretely to correct what was called fundamental disequilibrium, or a payments imbalance that it would be inappropriate to finance indefinitely through the IMF or any other channel.

This, then, was the basic architecture of the Bretton Woods system. There were, of course, many additional details. Interestingly, there was no provision for secular growth in international liquidity, except for a some-what ambiguous provision permitting a uniform change in par values, that is, a deliberate discrete rise in the price of gold. Eventually, the U.S. dollar provided for additional liquidity, as well as emerged as the currency of intervention in a regime in which some operating mechanism was necessary to assure that exchange rates remained fixed.

Thus, the growth of international liquidity—or, more narrowly, of international reserves—was satisfied partly by redistribution of gold from the United States, which had, by the late 1940s, accumulated about 70 percent of the world's monetary gold stock, and even more by the accumulation of dollars by central banks around the world. During the quarter-century between 1945 and 1970, world reserves outside the United States grew by $54 billion, averaging 4.5 percent per annum. Gold provided $13 billion of this increase, $9 billion of which was from the United States and $4 billion of which was from new gold production. Foreign exchange, which was overwhelmingly dollars, provided $30 billion of the growth in reserves. The IMF provided $11 billion, including $3 billion of the new Special Drawing Right (SDR) in 1970. Of course, U.S. reserves declined during this period, because part of its gold stock was lost to other countries (see table 2–1).

One after-the-fact characterization of the Bretton Woods system (that is, a facet that developed as the system evolved, not as it was designed) is that it involved a bargain between the United States, which accounted for

Table 2–1
End-of-Year International Reserves
($ billion equivalent)

	1945	1960	1970	1980
Gold[a]	33.3	38.0	37.2	41.8
U.S. gold holdings	20.1	17.8	11.1	11.2
Foreign exchange[b]	14.3	18.6	44.6	370.8
U.S. liabilities	4.2	11.1	23.8	157.1
Other[c]	—	3.6	10.8	36.5
Total reserves	47.6	60.2	92.5	449.1
Addendum:				
World exports during the year	34.2	113.4	280.3	1844.6

Sources: Data from *Federal Reserve Bulletin* and *International Financial Statistics* various issues.

[a]At official prices of $35 per ounce before 1980 and $42 per ounce in 1980.

[b]Reported assets differ from U.S. reported liabilities by minor differences in concept, by measurement error, by official foreign-exchange holdings other than dollars, and by official deposits in the eurocurrency market.

[c]Special Drawing Rights (SDRs) and reserve positions in the International Monetary Fund (IMF).

about half of the world's industrial production in the late 1940s, and the rest of the world. The bargain was that the United States would maintain domestic economic stability and other countries would fix their currencies to the dollar and accumulate their reserves in gold-convertible dollars. After a period of immediate postwar redistribution, however, they would not actually convert their dollars into gold. In this fashion, other countries would import economic stability from the United States. If a country got out of line with the world norm, it would have to change the par value of its currency. The United States supposedly gained some seigniorage from this bargain, although in my view the question of seigniorage has been greatly exaggerated by academic economists. These reserves were not in currency; they were in assets at market interest rates. It is true, however, that the United States gained financial room for maneuver; that is to say, it did not have to worry as other countries did about how to finance a balance-of-payments deficit. Indeed, under these circumstances, the very notion of balance-of-payments deficit was an ambiguous one for the United States, although year after year the Commerce Department continued to record a figure that it called the deficit.

A result of the arrangement under the Bretton Woods system was that the dollar was overvalued relative to what it would have been without the steady accretion of dollars in the reserves of other countries. This feature permitted some export-lead growth by the rest of the world, which would not have taken place under different monetary arrangements.

In the late 1960s, the United States broke its part of the bargain by inflating too much in connection with the Vietnam War. Some Europeans thought that the United States had too much inflation even in the early 1960s. On this point, however, they would have had much less agreement from Americans. Indeed, the disagreement over U.S. policy at that time indicated one of the weaknesses of the alleged bargain, namely, disagreement over what represented economically stabilizing behavior.

Two Flaws in the System

The Bretton Woods system would have broken down sooner or later, even without the inflation of the late 1960s, because it had two intrinsic flaws. First, the gold convertibility of the dollar was bound to become increasingly less feasible as dollar liabilities rose over time relative to the U.S. gold stock. Yet to halt the accumulation of dollars in reserves would have stifled the growth of the world economy. This dilemma was pointed out by Robert Triffin as early as 1959. To solve this dilemma, in the late 1960s SDRs were created as a long-run substitute for the dollar, but the solution came too late. This part of the system broke down in 1971 with the suspension of the gold convertibility of the dollar. Two points are worth noting. First, throughout this period, after 1954, the U.S. dollar was the only currency that was convertible into gold. Even the Swiss franc was not convertible into gold. Second, after gold convertibility of the dollar ceased, the world continued to accumulate dollars, although that was related to other events as well.

The second flaw in the Bretton Woods system was its reliance on discrete changes in exchange rates to correct imbalances in payments. Once a disequilibrium had persisted long enough to be defined clearly as "fundamental" in nature, the disequilibrium was apparent to everyone and thus the system produced the notorious one-way option for currency speculators. It is interesting to note that the system's architects had appreciated this problem, at least in principle, and they had stipulated that currencies should be convertible for current-account transactions, but not for capital-account transactions. It was envisioned that countries might maintain controls on capital flows under the Bretton Woods system. The United States did not accept that possibility as national policy, but it was allowed under the Bretton Woods system, and, indeed, in a certain sense, it was required by the internal logic of the system. Given the evolving nature of trade, however, it became increasingly difficult to separate capital-account from current-account transactions. Thus, that distinction, which is sharp enough in accounting terms, turned out to be quite blurred in actual economic transactions. In addition to trade credit, the world experienced enormous growth in international direct investment and portfolio capital movements in their own right.

The movement of funds that was associated with anticipated discrete changes in exchange rates became quite enormous and greatly complicated the management of domestic monetary policies. In most countries, they threatened the autonomy of domestic national policy, which was to have been preserved by the Bretton Woods system. For example, in 1969 Germany experienced a 25 percent increase in its money supply in a single week due to the inflow of speculative funds across the foreign exchanges. That was more than the country could effectively sterilize, given the instruments available to the German authorities at that time.

The U.S. inflation of the late 1960s resulted in large dollar outflows in the early 1970s. Fundamentally, free movement of capital, including capital buried in current-account transactions, is incompatible with a system wherein exchange rates are occasionally changed by consequential amounts. As a result of the enormous movement of capital, this part of the Bretton Woods system broke down definitively in 1973, although the breakdown had started earlier with the move to floating rates by Canada in 1970 and by Britain in 1972.

The events of the early 1970s were only the proximate cause of the partial breakdown of the Bretton Woods system. They were not the fundamental cause. The intrinsic flaws in the system would have come to the fore one way or another. They happened to come to the fore in 1971–73.

It is worth remarking that the breakdown of the Bretton Woods system was only a partial breakdown. What broke down were the exchange-rate and liquidity-generating features of the system. The International Monetary Fund is an important survivor, both as a lender and as a forum for managing the international monetary system. The convertibility of currencies and the continuing autonomy of national economic policies—both features of the Bretton Woods system—are still taken as desiderata in well-functioning international monetary systems. It is a measure of the success of that system that we take these features for granted.

Floating Exchange Rates

For the last decade, the world has had floating exchange rates. However, the exchange rates are not freely floating, and for good reason. Governments everywhere are held responsible for the management of their national economies. For most countries, the exchange rate is the most important single price—or rather, because the rate is made up of not one price but several for most countries, the appropriately weighted average exchange rate is the most important single price. Thus, it is inconceivable that a government held responsible for managing its economy could keep its hands off of this particular price. And, sure enough, they have not left it alone.

How are we to assess this period of floating exchange rates? There is considerable dissatisfaction with the world economic performance over the last decade. However, it is difficult to sort out those features that are attributable to the fact that we have had floating exchange rates from those that resulted from the other economic developments that have taken place—oil shocks, more rapid world inflation, two serious postwar recessions, and so on. On the whole, compared to the alternative of attempting to fix exchange rates on a worldwide basis, as under the Bretton Woods system, managed floating has served the world economy well. If we had tried to maintain fixed exchange rates during this period, there would have been much greater resort to restrictions over international transactions, both capital and current transactions, than there has been.

Several observations about our experiences during the period of floating exchange rates can be made. Some of the observations are well known; others are somewhat surprising.

These observations draw on the distinctions between bilateral exchange rates (for example, that between the U.S. dollar and the German mark); effective exchange rates, which represent a weighted average of bilateral exchange rates; and real effective exchange rates, which represent a weighted average of bilateral exchange rates deflated by each national wholesale price index of nonfood manufactures. The discussion on the effective exchange rate and the real effective exchange rate is based on the series published by the Morgan Guaranty Bank, which uses own-country trade shares to weight the bilateral exchange rates, a procedure that seems superior to the frequently used alternative of employing the same (for example, OECD) weights for all national effective exchange rates and more reliable than the IMF procedure of using econometrically estimated elasticities as weights in calculating effective exchange rates from bilateral exchange rates. Thus, in these series, the effective exchange rate of the U.S. dollar is heavily influenced by the bilateral exchange rate with the Canadian dollar, because Canada is an important trading partner, and the effective exchange rate of the German mark is heavily influenced by the bilateral rates with the Swiss franc, the Dutch guilder, and the currencies of other close neighbors, because, taken together, they account for a substantial fraction of German trade.

The first observation that can be made about experience under the floating exchange rates is that variations in real effective exchange rates of the industrial countries, as measured, have been less than the variations in nominal effective exchange rates during the entire period. Britain is the important exception. As predicted, therefore, exchange rates adjust, at least in part, for differential rates of inflation between countries. That is to say, some portion, and that portion varies from country to country, of the movement in nominal exchange rates simply corrects for differential rates of inflation between countries. Some economists have pushed this point further than it deserves to be pushed, but, qualitatively, we have observed the result we expected. Britain is the important exception; the real effective rate of the British pound has moved by more than the nominal rate and in the direction opposite from that differential inflation rates would indicate.

The second observation is that the movements in real effective exchange rates were not especially great until 1981. The range for the United States (on an index of March 1973 equals 100)—and this may be surprising for many—was between 91 and 103. In other words, during this period the maximum range was about 12 percent, with the change in any given year hardly more than 6 or 7 percent, up as well as down. These figures exclude the ranges of the past two years; more on that later. In Japan, the range was a bit greater (also on an index of March 1973 equals 100): from a low of 85 to a high of 116; the range, again with both ups and downs, was about 30 percent over eight years. In Germany, the range was smaller, from a low of 97 to a high of 111, or about 14 percent during this period. Now, these are the exchange rates that are important to the real side of the economy, as opposed to purely financial transactions. They are the exchange rates that influence the profitability of business firms, their capacity to export, the strength of their import competition, and so forth. Contrary to widespread impression, the figures suggest that there have not been wild gyrations in these rates, each country's effective exchange rate being a weighted average, using its own trade weights.

The third observation is that most of the adjustments in real effective exchange rates are readily explicable in terms of macroeconomic developments in each country and its major trading partners. This is especially true of the various rises and declines of the dollar during this period, but it is also true for the ups and downs of the yen. And if one takes into account the fact that Britain has had a major resource development, at least some part of the apparently perverse movements in its real exchange rate and its nominal exchange is also explicable. Thanks to its North Sea oil, Britain switched from being a substantial net importer of oil to being a modest net exporter of oil, with a corresponding improvement in its current-account position.

A fourth point to be considered is that most countries (over 70 percent of the IMF's members in 1982) in this period of floating exchange rates have, in fact, chosen to fix their exchange rates formally to something: to another currency; to a basket of currencies; to the SDR; and, in the case of Europe, to a synthetic European currency, the European currency unit. Many other countries maintain informal ties between their currency and something else. Thus, there is evidence of a widespread urge for greater stability in exchange rates than is afforded by completely free-floating rates. The important exceptions are Canada, Japan, the United States, and the United Kingdom, all important countries that have formally tied their currencies to nothing, although on some occasions they intervened extensively to limit the movements in their exchange rates.

A fifth observation is that the experience of 1981–82 marks an important and troubling exception to this general picture. The yen depreciated further and the dollar appreciated further in real terms and greatly extended the ranges mentioned earlier. The real effective exchange rate of the dollar (again on an index of March 1973 equals 100) rose steadily through 1981 and 1982; in late 1982 it reached 123, a full 20 percent above its previous peak, before receding. The Japanese yen fell to a low of 77 in October 1982, nearly 10 percent below its previous low, before strengthening again. Some European currencies also depreciated sharply (in real terms), especially the Belgian franc and the Swedish kroner. Others, however, remained roughly stable, in real terms, during this period. In late 1982, the German mark, for instance, was slightly lower than it was in late 1979 and slightly higher than it was in late 1980, movements well within its earlier range.

Several developments help to explain the exceptionally strong dollar and the weak yen. First, since late 1980 the United States has produced exceptionally tight monetary policy, and the exchange rate responded to that, as it had to the sharp tightening in late 1979 and early 1980. Japan, in contrast, has pursued a monetary stance that, though tight by earlier Japanese standards, is looser than the policy in the United States. This relationship, however, is not a simple one. The dollar continued to strengthen in the fall of 1982, even after the Federal Reserve had moved to a somewhat more relaxed (though still relatively tight) monetary stance in midsummer.

Another development that might have contributed to the changes in the rates was Japan's substantial liberalization of capital controls in late 1980 and, in particular, its virtual removal of controls on capital outflows. Any pent-up demand in Japan for foreign financial assets would have been satisfied under the new regime, and Japanese financial institutions bought foreign (especially U.S.) securities heavily—an action that surely was also influenced by high U.S. interest rates, which inhibited foreign funds from moving into Japan after the liberalization.

A third possible explanation for the rate changes was the politically motivated capital flight to the United States during this period. The general global unsettlement following the invasion of Afghanistan, the difficulties in Poland, and, in 1982, the financial difficulties in a number of important developing countries, not to mention France, may have led to movements of capital that would not be explained in terms of the usual variables that economists look at, although influences may, in fact, be more important. Sorting out the relative importance of the various factors that strengthened the dollar so much in 1981–82 is work for the future.

Before concluding with a brief look to the future, there are three further points about floating exchange rates that should be mentioned.

The relative stability and explicability of movement in effective exchange rates during most of the past decade was emphasized earlier. Movements in some key bilateral exchange rates have been much more dramatic than movements in effective exchange rates, however, sometimes showing sharp short-run variations not linked in any obvious way to fundamental economic developments. Occasionally, there have been weeks where average daily variations were in excess of 3 percent. Why such great variability? The asset approach to exchange-rate determination emphasizes that stocks of foreign exchange are like any other financial asset, the current price of which reflects all the available information that may have a bearing on the asset's future value. New information, then, may affect market prices (or, in this instance, exchange rates) sharply as the market reappraises the future value in light of this new information.

Understanding the effect of changing information (or news) on market prices represents a valuable insight, and no doubt this relationship helps to explain the abruptness of some movements in exchange rates. However, it hardly explains the sharp variability, up and down, that occurred month after month. Seen from a longer perspective, much 'news' is in fact noise, and one can reasonably expect markets to discount its influence on prices, even in the short run.

Such abrupt up-and-down movements are not, by themselves, likely to affect trade and production much because, unless they are clearly linked to more fundamental economic developments, they will probably be reversed soon. The trouble is that there is another influence at work, and it can cause larger changes in exchange rates than would otherwise take place. This influence is the presence of crowd or band-wagon effects in the trading community. Few know how to interpret noisy news; many use a movement in the exchange rate itself as a source of information about market sentiment. To avoid being left behind, they jump on the band wagon, thus pushing the exchange rate further in the direction it tended to go initially. Expectations feed on expectations. Economic theorists discovered this phenomenon recently and have called it a bubble. It is based on the expectation that prices can rationally be pushed beyond their long-run equilibrium value as long as the participants expect the risk of relapse to be less than the prospect of further gain.

When this is happening, even those who suspect the exchange rate has gone too far still have an interest in holding as long as the prospect for further gain outweighs the probability of reversal. Thus, a secondary judgment, oriented toward market dynamics, is superimposed on the value reassessment that is based solely on the news or information, and this judgment may dominate the movement of exchange rates for a time. This phenomenon would not be troublesome if it had no consequential effects on the real economy. However, in some periods, expectations about the fundamentals may be so weakly held that the rate can be dominated purely by market dynamics for longish periods, measured in weeks. When this happens, the exchange rate may, in turn, produce new information, such as the recorded change in price indexes that include a heavy imported content, or it may set in motion urgent risk-avoiding behavior, such as when multinational firms rush to protect their quarterly balance sheet (at the expense of their operating earnings). Thus, a vicious circle may be set in motion temporarily. In this context, skillful policy actions, including intervention in exchange markets, can influence market dynamics in a way that limits the possible damage to the real side of the economy.

Another observation should be made about floating exchange rates and their effects in recent years. The past decade has been a terrible one for the world economy, with a sharp acceleration of inflation over earlier periods, followed by the two deepest recessions since 1945. There is a strong temptation to attribute this inflationary decade to the breakdown of the Bretton Woods system and the advent of floating exchange rates. Economists will argue for years over the relative importance of (1) fiscal policy mistakes in the United States in the late 1960s that set in motion a wage-price-wage leap-frogging process, not only in the United States, but in other countries as well because of the close linkages under fixed exchange rates; (2) excessive expansion of money supplies in the United States and elsewhere as an autonomous act of policy that was not itself induced by the dilemmas of a wage-price-wage spiral; and (3) supply shortages, real or contrived, originating in the primary sectors of the world economy, notably in grain and petroleum. However these debates come out, it is important to note that the inflation started accelerating in the period before generalized floating was introduced and it continued afterward, so it is difficult to argue that the exchange-rate regime itself had a major bearing on this undeniably important worldwide phenomenon.

A final observation focuses on national economic policy rather than the international monetary policy system. Under floating exchange rates, monetary policy in the United States operates on the domestic economy through a new channel. Traditionally, monetary policy had its heaviest impact on inventories, housing, and those relatively few sectors that are sensitive to consumer credit, particularly the automobile industry. Now monetary policy has a much more pervasive and direct effect throughout the economy. Through the exchange rate, the entire tradable sector is influenced directly by monetary policies. Thus, the consequences of tight money fall directly on many sectors that, in the past, felt them only indirectly through the recession that followed. This change in the effect of monetary policy is not widely understood. In particular, it is not understood by the union leaders and company managers, who see it in the form of declining export orders and stiffer import competition. They attribute the stiffer competition to unfair foreign practices rather than to the Federal Reserve, where the responsibility belongs. Combatting inflation under flexible exchange rates results in stiffer import competition, which helps to keep domestic prices in check. Eventually, people will learn how this new channel of monetary policy spreads the impact more widely. A risk now is that people will mistake the effects of monetary policy via the exchange rate for unfair foreign competition and that they will plead successfully for protectionist legislation and administrative action.

Future Directions

In conclusion, let us consider what we can say about the future, although that is really the subject of the rest of this book. It has already been suggested that free floating is not acceptable and by revealed preference is not generally observed. There is a widespread feeling that exchange rates should be managed even more than they have been. An agenda for the future is:

Can welfare be improved by managing exchange rates and, if so, how should they be managed? Now is the time to begin with formal, even intergovernmental, discussions of what a regime of managed floating might comprise. Proposals involving such things as target zones, indicator rates, reference rates, and so forth should be looked at closely in the light of recent experience. We need not fear that such discussions will mature rapidly. They will not. The difficulties of reaching constructive agreement are formidable and perhaps insurmountable. However, the process of discussing them at this stage would be helpful both in sorting out some of the dissaffection that exists with current arrangements and in improving informal cooperation, even if agreement on a new regime is not possible.

What about that other pillar of international monetary regimes, international liquidity? Liquidity has always been a vague concept and its meaning becomes even less clear in a regime of floating exchange rates and in a world of ready access to private capital markets. There has, in fact, been an astounding increase in official reserves during the 1970s, from $92 billion in 1970 to $450 billion in 1980, not counting the increase in gold reserves if they were valued at market prices. (Paradoxically, the wide discrepancy between official and market prices for gold has made gold less, not more, useful as an international reserve.) The tremendous development of capital markets is not a complete substitute for international reserves, however. Credit has a way of drying up just when it is needed most. It does not provide the same assurance to and protection for countries' actions nor the smooth adjustment that adequate amounts of owned reserves provide. Owned reserves will be necessary and desired as long as we have a regime that is something short of free floating. Another item on the agenda for the future, therefore, is to ascertain how to achieve an appropriate measure of international liquidity and, once we have that, how to go about augmenting it by appropriate amounts.

**Part I
The International Financial
System: Proposals for Reform
and Potential for Crises**

3 Opportunities and Implications of a Return to Fixed Exchange Rates—Is Gold an Answer for International Adjustment?

Leland B. Yeager

The topic and title of this chapter suggests the need for a discussion about institutions. Institutions, broadly conceived of as the environment of rules, constraints, and government practices in which private parties must decide and act, are what policymakers and policy advisors must choose among. It is a mistake to conceive of policymakers as choosing among particular economic magnitudes, such as degress of exchange-rate fluctuation; the sizes of particular items and overall surpluses or deficits in balances of payments; or levels of and changes in countries' international reserves, price levels, rates of inflation, unemployment, and economic growth, and patterns of production and resource allocation. Governments cannot even accurately predict, let alone determine, the levels of their revenues and expenditures or their budget surpluses or deficits. They can influence the magnitudes, of course, but they do so through their choice of institutions. Governments cannot directly choose outcomes.[1]

Conditions That Would Make a Fixed Rate Desirable

This chapter will answer the question posed in its title first with regard to fixed exchange rates and later with regard to gold. Is a return to fixed exchange rates desirable? Briefly, yes—a heavily qualified yes. If we could find a stable money of some other country onto which we would peg our country's money, and if our pegging would not destabilize the monetary conditions and management of that other country, then a fixed exchange rate would benefit us. A fixed rate with a foreign currency of durably stable purchasing power would also give us a fairly stable price level and its attendant advantages.

Our money supply would be regulated automatically and appropriately through the balance of payments. If economic growth or some other development should raise our total demand for cash balances at full employment, the necessary addition to our money supply would flow in, metaphorically speaking, through a payments surplus. As people set about to increase their cash balances, they would exhibit less eagerness to buy goods, services, and securities and more eagerness to sell. These shifts in market behavior would show up not only in domestic but also in foreign transactions, leading to an excess of sales over purchases abroad. Our country's central bank, in buying the surplus of foreign currency offered on the foreign-exchange market to maintain the fixed exchange rate, would be creating domestic base money and so supporting monetary expansion.[2] If some reverse development should initially confront us with an excess supply of money, people's actions to get rid of the excess would show up in a balance-of-payments deficit. To support our currency on the foreign-exchange market, the central bank would remove our surplus money from circulation.

Under a wide range of monetary institutions, a country's real quantity of money tends to accommodate itself to the demand for it (although not in a quick and painless way). Under the imagined conditions, with a fixed link to a stable foreign currency providing a nearly stable domestic price level, our real and nominal money supplies would move in parallel; the distinction between them would be inessential, and the two would be regulated together automatically. No macroeconomic disturbances would arise from the side of money. More exactly, the link to a stable world economy, or the fixed link to a foreign money of durably stable purchasing power, would cushion disturbances. The balance of payments would serve as a kind of buffer. Spurts or slumps of aggregate demand not in accord with the level compatible with full employment and stable prices would be absorbed or filled by payments deficits or surpluses, respectively, especially on current account.

Under the supposed conditions, domestic monetary stability would be compatible with comprehensive financial deregulation. With the domestic money supply automatically adjusting to the demand for it at full employment and stable prices, the government would neither have to manage the money supply actively nor regulate financial practices and innovations out of concern for their influence on the demand for money. No one would even need any definite conception of what constituted "the money supply." Laissez-faire would work.

Speaking of laissez-faire, why not go all the way? Why not abolish the central bank? Why not get the government out of the business of issuing money, so that the question of its pegging domestic to foreign money could not arise? The government might simply define the unit of account employed in its own transactions and recommended for all domestic transactions as one unit of the chosen stable foreign currency. Private parties could express their prices, debts, and contracts in this unit and could agree among themselves on what to use as media of exchange. Plausible candidates would be bank deposits denominated in the stipulated unit of account or equity shares in institutions blending the characteristics of banks, money-market mutual funds, and stock mutual funds against which checks denominated in the unit of account would be written. No government regulation would be necessary or appropriate beyond the usual functions of enforcing contracts and punishing fraud.[3]

The ideas expressed so far presuppose finding an enduringly stable foreign currency on which to base our own monetary system. The ideas apply, furthermore, only to a small country acting almost alone, because if countries that account for a significant part of the world economy were to try to ride piggy back on the ideal foreign currency, the task of the authorities responsible for that currency would be complicated. Gold, as will be mentioned later, does not constitute a good substitute for the ideal but nonexistent stable currency.

Obstacles to Fixed Exchange Rates

Given the preceding requirements, the conditions considered so far cannot be implemented. Contemplating the conditions and what stands in the way of implementing them is one way to arouse interest in the problem we should be considering. The problem facing us is not a choice among rival exchange-rate regimes. Rather, it is one of instituting currencies of stable purchasing power. More broadly, it is one of devising political institutions conducive to the making of sound policies concerning government spending, taxation, and money. The problem is not amenable to a narrowly economic fix.

Even if a stable foreign currency could be found, our country could not peg onto it without sacrificing its national monetary independence. So far, by and large, countries have not been willing to make this sacrifice. More precisely, governments have not been willing to give up their powers to issue money or dominate its issue and to manage it for the sake of government finance and short-run economic objectives.

Continuing insistence on this sovereignty rules out an international system of durably and dependably fixed exchange rates. It was under these circumstances that the world muddled along from World War II until 1973, living with precariously pegged and occasionally readjusted rates. Since then, it has lived with fluctuating rates (with some exceptions, notably the European Monetary System).

Although I have long advocated floating exchange rates, I do not claim that they have worked well since 1973. My chief reason for advocating them was that they can give prudent national monetary management—if and where it exists—a measure of freedom from external disruption; I never supposed that floating rates were either a guarantee of or a substitute for monetary prudence.

The Origin of Floating Exchange Rates

Consider the way in which floating exchange rates came onto the scene. Their predecessor, the Bretton Woods system, never was abandoned intellectually. The short-lived Smithsonian Agreement of December 1971 was heralded at the time as a sound reconstruction of the temporarily interrupted Bretton Woods system. The final collapse of this last-ditch defense for that system left us with what we have had ever since. As Thomas de Vries of the International Monetary Fund (IMF) has candidly written, policymakers stuck to the par-value system during the late 1960s and early 1970s with "almost unbelievable tenacity." "After the considerable disturbances of the 1960s, it took three speculative waves of unimaginable proportions . . . to move the world in March 1973 toward a more flexible exchange-rate regime for an 'interim period,' after which par values were to be gradually reestablished. . . . " The new system came into existence "as a result of *breakdown*" of the old one. For some time, the IMF's Committee of Twenty continued to try to devise a system of "stable but adjustable par values."[4] Our current system, then, is not the result of timely heed to the recommendations of academic economists.

As foreign central banks bought up dollars to keep their own currencies from appreciating against the dollar beyond the prescribed limits, they expanded their domestic monetary bases, much as they might have done by open-market purchases of domestic securities. During 1970–72 and the first quarter of 1973, foreign central banks and governments increased their holdings of U.S. dollar claims (of the types that count as international reserves for their holders) by 346 percent.[5] The biggest increase came in the crisis year, 1971. In that single year, U.S. liabilities to foreign central banks and governments increased by more than their entire cumulative amount through all of history up to the beginning of that year, even counting, in that cumulative amount, the 49 percent increase that had already occurred in 1970. That is, U.S. reserve-type liabilities to foreign monetary authorities more than doubled in 1971 alone. Spurts of the same type of increase recurred in 1972 and early 1973. Supported by the resulting growth of base money, national money supplies exploded.[6] Price inflation followed, reaching double-digit levels in 1973–74.

The depreciation of the dollar after President Nixon "closed the gold window" in August 1971, its official devaluations in December 1971 and February 1973, and its further depreciation until mid-1973 contributed to the unbottling of U.S. inflation, as did the discontinuation of the price-and-wage controls that had been temporarily suppressing inflation. During the long period of pegging, U.S. policymakers escaped the antiinflationary warning or discipline that a depreciating dollar rate might have provided. Because of the dollar's special role in the Bretton Woods system and the country's resulting opportunity to finance balance-of-payments deficits more by running up dollar liabilities to foreign authorities playing the active role in exchange-rate pegging than by losing gold or other reserve assets of its own, the United States also largely escaped the supposed antiinflationary discipline of the balance of payments. Thus, the full consequences of fiscal and monetary irresponsibility were not immediately evident.[7] Then, with the devaluations and depreciations of the dollar, these consequences showed themselves all the more severely because they came in tandem.

To make matters worse, by the time the dollar began falling, it was falling against foreign currencies that were then suffering worsened inflation largely in consequence of the last-ditch defense of Bretton Woods. Foreign price inflation had a further impact on U.S. prices, especially because the dollar prices of foreign currencies had risen at last. To put the point loosely and briefly, the United States suffered a magnified contagion of the inflation that the country, or its overvalued exchange rate, had previously been transmitting abroad. This is not to say, however, that two-way contagion was the main factor contributing to the accelerated U.S. inflation; monetary fundamentals that originated several years earlier were also at work.

Sadly enough, the lessons of the events that led to the speed up of world inflation around 1973–74 are in danger of being forgotten. Numerous published discussions of that period underplay or even ignore how the underlying monetary expansion originated in the last-ditch defense of Bretton Woods. Not even the post hoc premise that places the blame for the inflation on floating exchange rates is valid, by the way, because inflation had speeded up even before floating became general in March 1973.

This speed up also preceded, and by several additional months, the Arab oil embargo and the quadrupling of oil prices in 1973–74. Of course, this event contributed to inflation (as did similar events affecting wheat, soybeans, and anchovies). It is an all-too-familiar error, however, to focus on such newsworthy events to the neglect of the less spectacular fundamentals.[8] Even the emboldenment of OPEC apparently traces back partly to the U.S. State Department's notions about the desirability of financially strengthening anti-Communist regimes in the Middle East and then to Western flabbiness in the face of unilateral modification of existing agreements by some oil countries. Further stimuli to OPEC action came from the boom (around 1972) in wholesale commodity prices (which tend to respond sensitively and early to underlying inflation) and, in general, from the loss of both purchasing power and foreign-exchange value by the dollar, in which

OPEC prices its oil. OPEC predation was partly a consequence rather than entirely a cause of world inflation. A severe inflation develops a momentum of its own. Policymakers hesitate to impose the pains that a cure would require. When policymakers in different countries do attempt a cure, the differing and changing vigor and credibility of their efforts provide a further source of disruption in foreign-exchange markets.

To summarize, the transition to floating exchange rates, far from being the consequence of rational deliberation, came about in almost the worst conceivable way. Policymakers did not adopt floating rates; they accepted them only kicking and screaming, and far too late. They accepted them only after their clinging to fixed rates had wreaked havoc, which the floating-rate regime then inherited. If the advice of the academic critics of Bretton Woods had been taken several years earlier, things would have worked out more happily. Thus I, for one, feel no embarrassment in agreeing that the floating-rate regime has not been working well.

The Performance of Floating Rates

It becomes apparent that the floating-rate regime has not been working well if one takes the width of fluctuations as the criterion of performance. According to Edward M. Bernstein, former research director at the International Monetary Fund, "Fluctuations in the dollar exchange rates for the major currencies have been excessive and disruptive. The rise and fall of such rates by 15 to 20 percent in a few months and by as much as 40 percent in a year cannot possibly reflect changes in underlying economic conditions. With such large fluctuations, the dollar must be overvalued at the top rate or undervalued at the bottom rate, and most likely overvalued and undervalued alternately."[9]

Hans Sieber examined the rate between the dollar and the Swiss franc in five phases of relative dollar weakness and five phases of relative dollar strength from 1973 to the autumn of 1975. The appreciations of the franc ranged from 5 to 32 percent, averaged over 19 percent, and lasted slightly over three months on average. The franc's depreciations ranged from 2 to 23 percent, averaged over 11 percent, and lasted about three months on average. Sieber also examined the spreads between lows and highs of the franc-dollar rate within individual market days and within weeks. Intraday spreads averaged 1.04 percent within 1973 (after the franc began floating, that is, in February through December), 1.06 percent in 1974, 0.69 percent in 1975, and 0.43 percent in 1976. Intraperiod high-low spreads of the franc-dollar rate exceeded 2 percent on 11 percent of the trading days and in 45 percent of the weeks in 1973, on 12 percent of the days and in 58 percent of the weeks in 1974, on 3 percent of the days and in 31 percent of the weeks in 1975, and on none of the days and in 10 percent of the weeks in 1976.[10] As these figures suggest, volatility tapered off after the first two years of floating rates (although it did recur in late 1977 and in 1978). Furthermore, fluctuations were wider for the Swiss franc than for other currencies, probably because of the franc's special role as an investment and refuge currency and the relative thinness of the market for the currency of a small country.

Nonetheless, these figures do illustrate that supporting material is available for those who would want to describe exchange-rate fluctuations since 1973 as wild.[11] They could also emphasize that, in the short run, over periods of up to a couple of years, exchange rates have often moved more widely than (and sometimes even in the opposite direction from) the relative purchasing powers of the currencies concerned. In other words, not only exchange rates in the ordinary sense but even real exchange rates—a confusing term—have been jumpy. (An old and readily understandable phenomenon in times of monetary instability—one repeatedly demonstrated in history, only to be forgotten and then puzzle subsequent generations of economists—is that floating exchange rates respond more promptly and sensitively to actual or prospective changes in underlying monetary conditions than do price levels of goods and services.[12])

Critics perceive overtracking or overshooting on the foreign-exchange market (in the sense expressed by Bernstein, quoted earlier). Of course, it is much easier to make such criticisms with the benefit of hindsight than it is to make the decisions of market operators. It is not clear that the markets have been mistakenly processing the information available to operators at the time of decision making.[13] However, I will not insist on the appropriateness of this line of response to the critics. I will forgo reminding the reader of the elements of outright pegging, inviting one-way-option speculation and so forth, that remain in the exchange-rate systems of many countries. I also will not insist that official intervention may have made the markets jumpier than they would have been under completely clean floating.[14] I readily admit being unhappy with the system we now have.

A Return to Fixed Rates?

Unhappiness with the current system is no reason, however, to return to fixed exchange rates. This is not the remedy. Everyone would agree that a state of affairs in which fixed exchange rates could work would be preferable to the present monetary muddle. Of course, it would be nice if countries could somehow stop their inflations and keep them permanently stopped. However, to advocate fixed exchange rates on the ground that the current system is not satisfactory is like saying, with an air of profundity, that what such-and-such a problem needs is a solution. As was stated at the begining of this chapter, what we have to choose among are alternative sets of institutional arrangements. Bliss is not one of the options.

Sometimes the advocates of what they call fixed exchange rates appear really to be advocating international monetary unification. If so, they should say this clearly. There is a world of difference between, on the one hand, trying to fix exchange rates between distinct national moneys, the quantities of which are still managed or mismanaged by separate national authorities, and, on the other hand, genuine monetary unification. Unification implies the absence of independent national monetary authorities. It implies subordination to and constraint by either a single dominant authority, national or international, or else the more or less irrevocable rules of an international monetary game.

Barring genuine unification, not much in the way of healthy results can be expected from restoring fixed exchange rates of the Bretton Woods variety. (Without an end to inflation or at least harmonization of national inflation rates, a restored Bretton Woods system would tear itself apart again. Given the greater integration of financial markets, the sophisticated financial innovations, and the ways of evading capital controls that have developed in the years since the fall of the Bretton Woods system, one-way-option speculation against suspected exchange-rate adjustments would be even more potent than in the past. Even apart from inflation differentials, real developments—changes in technology and tastes calling for major changes in terms of trade—might well call for exchange-rate adjustments and touch off speculation in anticipation of them.) The supposed antiinflationary discipline of the balance of payments under fixed rates seldom worked as it was supposed to do.[15] The discipline theory is plausible only for countries with an intermediate degree of financial prudence. The least prudent countries will go on inflating anyway, devaluing their currencies from time to time and meanwhile suffering from disequilibrium in exchange rates and probably also controls. The most prudent countries will sometimes suffer discipline in reverse, that is, they will suffer the contagion of inflation imported from abroad or even generated by the exchange-rate system, as has already happened.[16]

Simply to advocate fixed exchange rates, then, reflects either ignorance of what the problem really is—monetary and financial irresponsibility on the part of governments—or a presupposition that this central problem has somehow already been solved. To mistake a symptom for the disease itself and merely try to apply a bandage (that is, to try to fix exchange rates) can do more harm than good and allows the disease to worsen.

Is Gold the Answer?

Does gold and its supposed discipline offer the solution to the problems we are experiencing with the current floating-rate system? I do not think so. The transition to a gold standard would be difficult. The first country or the first few countries adopting it could hardly know the correct price of gold, that is, the correct gold definitions of their monetary units. A price that turned out to be too low or too high would expose them to deflation or inflation, respectively. The early adopters would be tying their moneys to a speculative commodity of unstable value in relation to other goods and services. (Milton Friedman has spoken of pork bellies in this connection; James E. Sinclair has described gold nowadays as "a barometer of world anxieties."[17]) Enlisting the stabilizing properties of a predominantly non-speculative monetary demand for gold would require a coordinated move onto the gold standard by countries accounting for a substantial part of the world economy.

These transitional difficulties need not be overemphasized, however, because other difficulties are more fundamental. A gold standard of the historically familiar type, involving government operation of a monetary system linked to gold, is a particular set of policy rules; and these rules are no more inherently self-enforcing than any other set of monetary rules. The credibility and durability of a particular set of monetary rules depend, among other things, on its having desirable operating properties; and the gold standard seems inferior in this respect to at least a couple of obvious alternatives.

The international gold standard flourished for a few decades because of very special historical circumstances. Mint pars among gold-standard currencies, instead of being arbitrarily chosen, expressed an equilibrium that had evolved gradually between themselves and national price levels. After 1896, mildly rising world prices facilitated relative adjustments of prices and wages, but the uptrend did not last long enough to dissipate its possible benefits by becoming embodied in expectations because war destroyed the system. Relative calm in social and political affairs and the absence of excessively ambitious government programs and excessive taxation all favored confidence in monetary stability. The age of the gold standard was an age of peace, relatively.

The tolerably good performance of the gold standard before World War I hinged on additional favorable conditions that no longer prevail, including: a corps of dedicated gold prospectors working in unexplored but promising areas, a predominantly laissez-faire stance of governments with regard to the economic realm, and, generally, patience with the long and uncertain lags in the response of the gold supply to changing demands for money.[18]

By and large, people (in countries that happened to be on the gold standard, anyway) were freer from government control than in any age before or since—freer to transact business, to make investments, to transfer funds, to migrate, to travel. The civility and internationality prevalent during the brief era of the gold standard have such charm for us nowadays that it seems almost sacrilege to ask whether these benefits resulted from the gold standard or, instead, coexisted with it by mere coincidence.

Restoring conditions conducive to a successful gold standard would include somehow restoring the basis for public confidence in the ability and resolve of governments to adhere to the declared rules of the monetary system; that basis has been shattered by numerous experiences since 1914. It would also include restoring certain attitudes that seem to have been more prevalent in public affairs before 1914 than since that time. Those attitudes favored limitations on the scope of government activity and restraint on the pursuit of special advantage through the instrumentality of government. Broadly speaking, these were liberal attitudes in the nineteenth-century sense. These attitudes have now been undermined in ways analyzed, in part, by Ortega y Gasset in *The Revolt of the Masses*. [19]

Nowadays, we see tyranny in the nondemocratic countries and, in the democratic countries, democracy perverted in such a way that political decisions are made largely in response to special-interest pressures, for the sake of short-run expediency, and without due regard to long-run consequences. But in the gold-standard era, "the democratic system has not been fully developed."[20]

Without a return to liberal attitudes and restraints, a restored gold standard would not work well and would hardly endure. With the required attitudes and with the appropriate institutional restraints on government, the gold standard is not the only set of monetary rules that would function tolerably well. Economists can easily imagine, and have proposed, monetary arrangements that would function better. Enlisting the more desirable operating properties and creating, therefore, greater credibility of a superior system would contribute to the durability of a monetary arrangement.

The Depoliticization of Money

It is instructive to consider monetary systems that are radically different from the ones history has made familiar, even if we decide not to try to implement any of them. We might consider bypassing the central problem of governmental misbehavior by depoliticizing money. A proposal by F.A. Hayek has received much attention: Allow the private issue of competing currencies, each denominated in its own distinctive unit of account.[21] Depoliticization also presumably would allow free banking on the basis of gold—the competitive private issue of notes and deposits denominated in and redeemable in gold. To reduce the possibility of devaluation of currencies defined in gold, governments could be barred from introducing or defining currency units other than units of gold itself. A plausible unit would be the actual gram of gold. (It should be more embarrassing to try to decree a reduction in the gold content of the gram of gold than to decree a reduction in the gold content of the dollar.)

Admittedly, gold coins have some romantic and esthetic appeal, so perhaps coins would be issued in denominations of fifty, twenty, ten, five, and two grams. The fifty-gram piece could be one and two-thirds times the size of the old U.S. $20 gold piece. The two-gram piece probably should be the smallest practical coin. It could be one-third larger than the gold dollar issued from 1849 to 1889, which was an awkwardly small coin. At a price of gold of $400 a troy ounce, the fifty-gram and two-gram gold pieces would be worth $643.01 and $25.72, respectively, in today's dollars. Obviously, if gold had a general purchasing power in the neighborhood of what it has nowadays, gold coins would not circulate very actively. They would serve mostly as reserves in which to redeem the more active circulating medium, probably consisting of bank notes, bank deposits, and token coins. Silver coins denominated in grams might also circulate, but at fluctuating market values in terms of gold. Conceivably, competition between units might result; if the gram of silver emerged as the unit of account, gold could assume the secondary role and be traded at fluctuating prices.

In the spirit of depoliticization, there seems to be no good reason why governments should monopolize the minting of coins or even be allowed to issue them or paper money. The provision of coins, bank notes, and deposits could be left to private enterprise, subject only to the ordinary laws and penalties against fraud and the ordinary enforcement of contracts.

If we are willing to contemplate such an extreme degree of depoliticization of money as has just been sketched out, why not go further? Why not embrace what Robert Greenfield and I have provisionally called the BFH system?[22] That system would have better operating properties than a governmental or a free-enterprise gold standard or a Hayekian system of competing private monetary units. Once it was widely understood, then, the system would enjoy greater acceptability and durability. The government could help launch a new stable unit of account by defining it in terms of a bundle of commodities so comprehensive that its value would remain nearly stable in terms of goods and services in general. The government could conduct its own affairs in terms of the new unit but otherwise would practice laissez-faire toward the monetary and financial system. Private enterprise, probably in the form of institutions combining the features of today's banks, money-market mutual funds, and stock mutual funds, could offer convenient media of exchange. This separation of media of exchange and the unit of account, with the unit defined so as to be practically stable in general purchasing power, would go far toward avoiding macroeconomic disorders and would be conducive to stable prosperity and economic growth.

Interim Advice

It may take a long time before a radically new system is feasible politically. Therefore, let me offer some short-term advice. Countries should continue with floating exchange rates. One reason is that we have no real option under existing circumstances. A reestablished fixed-rate system would succumb to waves of one-way-option speculation even more massive than occurred under the Bretton Woods system. Continued floating will allow the monetarily most prudent governments a chance to achieve currencies of approximately stable purchasing power. Their countries will have a chance to escape being drawn again, as they were in the early 1970s, into inflation transmitted and, indeed, generated by fixed exchange rates. Let these relatively prudent countries experiment with monetarist rules—stable money growth, targeting on nominal gross national product (GNP), targeting on a price index—and with steps toward the depoliticization of money. Do not yoke them at fixed exchange rates to monetarily less prudent countries. (Of course, this is not to say that free exchange rates—or anything else—will provide anywhere near complete insulation from foreign economic disorders.)

In the longer run, scholars should try to cultivate a wider understanding of political economy, including how and why governments tend to operate irresponsibly and what political biases work for inflation. Let us encourage research into those reforms, constitutional or other, that might be desirable and feasible. A more consistently monetarist line of thinking at the Federal Reserve would be welcome, but it is hardly a fundamental reform. Fundamental reform presupposes a major shift in thinking about the proper scope of government and even about economic and social equality and inequality.

Also, for the longer run, depoliticization of money, along the lines of the BFH system, should at least be considered. Even if one does not take its actual implementation seriously, contemplating it is a way of gaining insights into the unsatisfactory aspects of our existing monetary system. (On reflection, it does seem preposterous that our unit of value, analogous to units of weight and length, the unit pervasively used in pricing, contracting, accounting, economic calculation, and business and personal planning, should be whatever value supply and demand fleetingly accord to the paper dollar or even to a quantity of metal demanded predominantly just for monetary purposes.) By contemplating the BFH system, one may become more receptive to radically new ideas. The BFH reform is more feasible than one that presupposes some enduringly stable foreign currency onto which we can peg our own. Also, its adoption does not presuppose coordinated international steps; any major country could act alone in adopting it.

Notes

1. This has long been a persuasive theme of my colleague, Rutledge Vining. See, for example, his "On Two Foundation Concepts of the Theory of Political Economy," *Journal of Political Economy* 77 (March/April 1969):199–218.

2. The bank's passive investment in external reserves ties up wealth at a presumably relatively low yield (as does an investment in gold reserves). It entails some loss of the seigniorage available with the domestic creation of money under floating exchange rates. This point must qualify the remark about the benefit of pegging onto a stable foreign currency.

3. Robert E. Hall has mentioned, if not actually advocated, this arrangement in several not-yet-published papers and discussions. Defining the national unit of account in terms of a particular foreign currency is a variant of an arrangement also discussed by Hall and which is discussed toward the end of this chapter, namely, defining the unit as a bundle of commodities chosen so as to have a nearly stable value in terms of goods and services in general.

4. Thomas De Vries in *Exchange Rate Flexibility,* ed. Jacob S. Dreyer, Gottfried Haberler, and Thomas D. Willett (Washington, D.C.: American Enterprise Institute, 1978), 191–192.

5. Calculated from data in *International Financial Statistics,* November 1974:396, line 4a.d.

6. As James C. Ingram has noted, "in 1970, 1971, and 1972 a veritable explosion occurred in the world money supply. . . . This explosive growth in money supply has been accompanied by rapid price inflation throughout the world. . . . " See "The Dollar and the International Monetary System: A Retrospective View," *Southern Economic Journal* 40 (April 1974):540–541. Figures taken and calculated from Ingram's article show that, between the end of 1969 and the end of 1972, the U.S. dollar value of the total money supplies of countries belonging to the Group of Ten (G–10) increased by 52 percent; there was an 82 percent increase for the G–10 countries other than the United States. For the latter countries, the annual average money growth rate in 1969–72 was more than double what it had been in 1962–69. (To avoid exaggeration from depreciation of the dollar, the last

calculation mentioned refers to money supplies translated into special drawing rights rather than into dollars.)

Accelerated money-supply growth in the major industrial countries at the beginning of the 1970s shows up clearly in the charts in *International Economic Conditions,* published quarterly by the Federal Reserve Bank of St. Louis. Alan Rabin gives a comprehensive survey of the whole episode in his 1977 University of Virginia Ph.D. dissertation, "A Monetary View of the Acceleration of World Inflation, 1973–1974."

7. The fact that rates of monetary expansion and price inflation were lower in the United States than abroad during much of the period in question does not refute the diagnosis that inflation was transmitted from the United States or was connected with overvaluation of the dollar on the foreign-exchange markets. Part of the transmission process was the creation of money abroad as a by-product of support of the dollar. Furthermore, a kind of inflation-transmission multiplier seems to have been at work in the direct-price-linkage aspect of the transmission process. Gottfried Haberler has explained this multiplier in several publications, including *A New Look at Inflation* (Washington, D.C.: American Enterprise Institute, 1973), 90–95.

8. Irving Fisher warned eloquently against making this error more than sixty years ago in *Stabilizing the Dollar* (New York: Macmillan, 1920), 10–17.

9. Edward M. Bernstein, "What Role for Gold in the Monetary System?," in *Report to the Congress,* Commission on the Role of Gold in Domestic and International Monetary Systems, (March 1982), II, 362.

In a recent period of strength of the dollar, from early January 1981 to mid-April 1982, the French, British, German, Japanese, and Swiss currencies depreciated against it by 29, 28, 20, 20, and 12 percent, respectively. See *Annual Report (1981–1982),* (Basle: Bank for International Settlements), 147.

10. Hans Sieber, *Der flottierende Schweizerfranken* (Zurich, Switzerland: Schulthess Polygraphischer Verlag, 1978), especially 32–33, 55–56.

In one period of sixty consecutive trading days early in 1978, the absolute day-to-day percentage change in the rate between the dollar and Swiss franc averaged 1.18 percent. Calculated from data given in Richard M. Levich, *Overshooting in the Foreign Exchange Market* (New York: Group of Thirty, 1981), 10.

11. For a desperately summary measure of exchange-rate fluctuation, the International Monetary Fund has calculated standard deviations of month-to-month percentage changes in monthly average dollar rates and effective exchange rates of the currencies of industrial countries. (A country's effective exchange rate is an import-weighted average of the value of its currency in the currencies of its leading trading partners.) The averages

of these standard deviations of percentage changes for the countries studied, those pertaining to dollar rates appearing first and those pertaining to effective rates appearing in parentheses, were as follows: 1974–77, 1.89 (1.28); 1978, 2.27 (1.44); 1979, 1.37 (0.96); 1980, 2.18 (1.03). IMF, *Annual Report 1981,* 42.

To describe shorter-run fluctuations, the Bank for International Settlements calculated average absolute percentage day-to-day changes of the dollar rates of the mark, pound sterling, and yen. The smallest annual average of these daily changes, about one-fifth of one percent for the mark and one-tenth of one percent for the pound and yen, came in 1976 or 1977. The changes averaged higher in 1981 than in any other year since floating began—somewhat over 0.7, 0.6, and 0.5 percent, respectively, for the three currencies. In the worst months of 1981, the changes averaged nearly one percent for the mark and pound and almost 0.8 percent for the yen. See *Annual Report (1981–1982)* (Basle: Bank for International Settlements), 153.

12. Peter Bernholz, *Flexible Exchange Rates in Historical Perspective,* Princeton Studies in International Finance, no. 49 (International Finance Section, Princeton University, 1982).

13. Richard M. Levich considers three alternative definitions of overshooting: (1) deviation of the actual exchange rate from—its wider fluctuation than—some estimated equilibrium rate (estimated, for example, by purchasing-power-parity calculations); (2) a wider response of the exchange rate to disturbances in the short run than in the long run; and (3) sharper movement of the exchange rate than would occur if market participants had full information about market structure and about disturbances. Levich offers a number of reasons for skepticism that overshooting of any of these types prevails in a way that would have any clear implications for policy. He also observes that, although exchange rates may appear volatile by historic standards, their volatility is not out of line with that of prices in other financial markets that are considered efficient and well-functioning. See *Overshooting,* especially chapters III and IV.

Furthermore, as Sven W. Arndt points out, a floating exchange rate is a flexible auction-market price amidst the inevitably sticky prices of goods and labor. Its relatively wide fluctuations are, in part, an appropriate response to the slowness of adjustments accomplished through those other prices. "Far from representing economic inefficiency, [its] movements serve as early shock absorbers. . . . To the extent that an exchange rate displays greater variability *because* other parts of the system cannot adjust immediately, the fear that other markets will be forced to engage in a series of unnecessary resource reallocations is unwarranted." Commentary in *The International Monetary System: A Time of Turbulence,* ed. Jacob S.

Dreyer, Gottfried Haberler, and Thomas D. Willett, (Washington, D.C.: American Enterprise Institute, 1982), 504.

14. The financial press frequently carries stories interpreting day-to-day exchange-rate jumps as responses to news and correct or incorrect rumors about the presence or intensification or the absence or diminution of official intervention. Headlines such as the following are typical: "Confusion Reigns as Traders Sell Dollars in Reaction to Remarks by Treasury Aide"; "Currency Traders are Disappointed by U.S.-Bonn Moves to Aid Dollar"; Lack of More Moves to Prop Dollar Spurs Profit Taking, Pushing Currency Back"; and "Dealers Devise Special Tactics to Detect When Central Banks Are Propping Dollar." (These headlines were taken from 1978-79 issues of *The Wall Street Journal.*) *Business Week*'s article on exchange-rate instability resulting from what it considered a mistaken switch in intervention by the Federal Reserve and foreign central banks is another example (see "A Blunder Torpedoes the Dollar," 19 February 1979:85.) Such press items hardly prove anything, but they do offer clues to the thinking of people operating in or close to the foreign-exchange markets—and their thinking and reactions are what are at issue here.

There is a pervasive but tacit idea, which seems to be dying harder in its application to foreign-exchange markets than in its applications to other human affairs, that if some aspect of reality is perceived to be unsatisfactory, government intervention will of course remedy it. The unsatisfactoriness counts as argument enough. It is intellectual flabbiness, however, to suppose that a policy is adequately described and argued for simply by reference to its desired results—such as smoothing erratic exchange-rate fluctuations without impeding adjustments to changed economic fundamentals. An expression of hope is no substitute for saying just what interventions the authority should undertake given what currently perceived circumstances and on what scale and with how much persistence the authority should act.

I have tried to assess the case for official intervention, so far as I could intuit what it was, in my *International Monetary Relations,* 2nd ed. (New York: Harper & Row, 1976), chapter 14. It is refreshing to see that skepticism about intervention is being expressed by, among others, Stanley W. Black and Steven W. Kohlhagen. Black, "Central Bank Intervention and the Stability of Exchange Rates," *Exchange Risk and Exposure,* ed. Richard M. Levich and Clas G. Wihlborg (Lexington, Mass.: Lexington-Books, 1980), 137-147; Kohlhagen, "The Experience with Floating: The 1973-1979 Dollar," in *The International Monetary System,* ed. Dreyer, Haberler, and Willett, 142-179.

15. Earl Dwight Phaup, "The Discipline Argument for Fixed Exchange Rates" (Ph.D. diss., University of Virginia, 1974).

16. Not only was the last-ditch defense of the Bretton Woods system inflationary, but the system itself already had a chronic inflation bias. I have tried to explain this in "Discipline, Inflation, and the Balance of Payments," in *Money, the Market, and the State,* ed. N.A. Beadles and

L.A. Drewry (Athens: University of Georgia Press, 1968), 1–34, and in various passages of my *International Monetary Relations*.

17. James E. Sinclair, "Is a Gold Standard Workable?", in *Report, Commission on the Role of Gold* (March 1982), II, 493.

18. Hugh Rockoff, "Some Evidence on the Real Price of Gold, Its Cost of Production, and Commodity Prices," in *A Retrospective on the Classical Gold Standard, 1821–1931,* ed. Michael Bordo and Anna Schwartz (Chicago: University of Chicago Press, forthcoming).

19. Jose Ortega Y Gasset, *The Revolt of the Masses,* (New York: W.W. Norton), 1932.

20. Lars Jonung, "Swedish Experience Under the Classical Gold Standard, 1873–1914," in *A Retrospective on the Classical Gold Standard,* ed. Bordo and Schwartz.

21. F.A. Hayek, *Denationalisation of Money,* 2nd ed. (London: Institute of Economic Affairs, 1978).

22. Named in honor of Fischer Black, Eugene Fama, and Robert E. Hall. Robert Greenfield and I explain the name and describe the system at length in "A Laissez Faire Approach to Monetary Stability" (manuscript, March 1982).

Comment

Anna J. Schwartz

Leland Yeager's chapter offers many instructive points related to institutional choices affecting monetary practices, money growth rates, and international adjustment. Let me note some areas of agreement before turning to a general issue on which I part company with him.

Yeager is right that, for a small country, the best institutional choice may well be unifying its currency with the currency of a larger country with which it has close economic relations and that maintains price-level stability. Such a small country would have no central bank; it would impose no barriers to the movement of money, prices, wages, and interest rates. Thus, unification would provide an effective way to maximize the freedom of the country's residents to engage in whatever transactions they wished. For a small country, a unified currency is likely to reduce the possibility of unwise governmental policy. Its unified currency would have a truly fixed exchange rate, assuring a maximum degree of integration of the country in question with the rest of the world.

Few small countries, however, have refrained from establishing a central bank to conduct national monetary policy and to accept the discipline of a unified currency. For a large country, such as the United States, tying its monetary policy to another country's is not a realistic option.

High and variable inflation rates and interest rates since the mid-1960s and volatile exchange rates since the early 1970s have directed attention to alternative institutional arrangements that might yield a record superior to that of existing monetary arrangements. Yeager examines four alternatives: (1) a return to the Bretton Woods system; (2) a gold standard; (3) Hayek's proposal to depoliticize money issue; and (4) a proposal Robert Greenfield and Yeager have developed that they designate the BFH system, for Fischer Black, Eugene Fama, and Robert Hall. First I will note Yeager's assessments of each of these alternatives and then I will offer my assessments.

Yeager dismisses the notion that we ought to bring back Bretton Woods. He rightly exposes the falseness of the view that the Bretton Woods system was a successful monetary order that should serve a model for the direction in which we ought to head. Bretton Woods, like any gold-exchange standard, had a chronic inflationary bias and, therefore, contained the seeds of its collapse. Given that annual gold production was absorbed by private demand for gold, the provision of additions to international reserves under the system resulted in a U.S. balance of payments in

42

perennial deficit. Under such circumstances, loss of confidence in the value of the reserve currency leads to claims for its conversion into gold, claims that ultimately topple the system.

Yeager correctly notes that a return to a full-fledged governmental gold standard also is not the solution for our current difficulties. Under such a gold standard, governments define the national unit as a specific weight of gold that thus sets the price of an ounce of gold in terms of that unit. There are 480 grains of gold in a fine troy ounce. Dividing 480 grains by the weight of the national unit in gold yields the price. Yeager gives three reasons for rejecting such a standard. The first is the difficulty of envisaging how to manage the transition to gold. The second is that the good performance of the gold standard before World War I was dependent on conditions that cannot now be restored. The final reason given is that there exist operating properties to rules governing monetary arrangements superior to those pertaining to a gold standard.

I agree with these observations, but I do not share Yeager's attachment to a gold-coin standard without national money, a system in which coins of different weights would circulate and prices would be denominated in weights of gold. Yeager designates this monetary order as a free-enterprise gold standard. Private contracts would specify payment in whatever form was mutually agreeable, including the use of electronic transfers of funds that could significantly economize the means of making payments with physical gold or decrease the need to hold gold in physical possession. With the system left to private enterprise, government involvement supposedly would be limited to enforcement of contracts and prevention of fraud. However, when an issuer fails to fulfill his promise to those who entered into a contract with him, third-party effects will occur. Government is then likely to be drawn into the money-creation process to set limits on the size of the fiduciary issue and otherwise regulate promises to pay gold. In addition, all the problems connected with the adequacy of prospective gold supply relative to monetary and nonmonetary demands for gold that arise with more common versions of a gold standard also apply to the free-enterprise gold standard.

Yeager makes only a passing reference to Hayek's proposal to allow the private issue of competing currencies, each denominated in its own distinctive unit of account. Under the proposal, private issuers would be free to produce as much of their money as they wished, and users of money would be free to choose whichever currency suited them best, presumably one with stable buying power. It is not clear how such depoliticization and deregulation, in the absence of a link to gold, would produce a stable price level. In addition, unless brand names were attached to competing private moneys— as a guarantee that private money issuers would not overissue for private gain—government regulation would likely be the end result. Because the money industry is a declining cost industry that is a natural monopoly, currency competition would ultimately self-destruct. At some stage, the money industry would be nationalized.

The proposal that most appeals to Yeager is the BFH scheme, according to which the government would define the unit of account in terms of a comprehensive bundle of commodities with a value that would remain nearly stable relative to goods and services in general. Share titles to bundles and securities financing the commodities would be provided by private-enterprise institutions combining the features of banks, money-market mutual funds, and stock mutual funds. Factors changing the relative price of the commodities in the bundle would merely affect their relative weights within the bundles. The threat of mutual redemption of outstanding shares would serve to limit share issues. Shares would not be convertible into units of the bundles.

I must confess that I regard the new monetary economics, exemplified by the BFH or Greenfield-Yeager scheme, as a disservice to the concept of improving existing monetary arrangements. The use of money evolved as a result of the market's search for an efficient way to reduce transaction and information costs. More efficient financial and monetary institutions than currently exist may well develop in response to market pressures. Imposing a disjunctive system alternative to the present one by fiat—the creation of a system that springs from inventive minds rather than as the expression of market experience—seems to me to misread the evolutionary character of the monetary system.

This brings me to the final point of divergence from Yeager's views. He acknowledges in his conclusion that radical new systems may not be politically feasible for a long time. In the interim, he says, the world should continue with floating exchange rates, while individual countries experiment with monetarist rules, targeting on a price index or gross national product (GNP), and depoliticizing money. His advice for the long run is to be receptive to radically new ideas that will lead to fundamental reform.

To begin with, I disagree with the view that governments should, on an interim basis, be encouraged to target monetary policy on GNP or a price index. That view assumes that we know the unique relation that exists between policy instruments and GNP or a price index, and hence we do not need the intermediate target of monetary growth rates. We are deluded if we believe that we know the economy's response structure in sufficient detail to be able to say that, if we use policy instruments that reduce monetary growth by one percentage point per year, we shall reduce the growth rate of GNP or the inflation rate by some corresponding definite percentage by some definite date. About all the data that are available to the policymaker are the trends in velocity and the economy's normal real growth. Guided by the desire to maintain stability in the price level, and knowing the trends in velocity and the economy's normal real growth, that information can be used to set a bench mark for average monetary growth. Such a procedure is not equivalent to targeting on GNP.

It is with respect to Yeager's advice for the long run that, as I have already indicated, I must take exception. The sweeping changes in the domestic money system that he would support seem to me unwarranted. It is not the use of money by itself that needs to be revolutionized. That is not the cause of instability in the economy, the distortions of inflation, and the volatility of exchange rates. The problems are associated with government regulation and monetary control procedures. I would favor feasible reforms of the present system, such as paying interest on currency and reserves, abolition of interest ceilings on deposits, and constraints on the government's power to manipulate monetary growth. In my view, a constant monetary-growth standard is the monetary arrangement that, given realistic acceptance of the limits of our knowledge of the economic structure, is best calculated to free monetary policy from the uncertainty and excesses that have beset us.

To conclude on a positive note, I endorse Yeager's view that monetary prudence is the recipe for attaining stable foreign-exchange rates. Domestic monetary control is in need of reform. Reform of the current floating-rate international monetary system is not needed.

Comment

Franco Modigliani

When I was invited to comment on chapter 2, I wondered why I was asked. However, upon learning that Leland Yeager was the chapter's author and Anna Schwartz was the other commentator, I understood that my comments were meant to serve as a contrast, in both philosophies and policies to their sections.

I will begin by stating my answer to the great problem before us: how do we achieve price stability (and, I would imagine, stability of employment as well)? My answer is: Pick a world in which a tenfold rise in oil prices is out of bounds and then put stabilization policies in the hands of competent and dedicated Keynesians to whom the president listens. The result will be an indefinite continuation of the golden era of stable employment, stable growth, stable prices, and, incidentally, responsible fiscal policies that characterized most of the fifties and the sixties. Conversely, what you must avoid at any cost is a combination of OPEC (injurious to price stability), monetarism (injurious to employment stability), and pious preachers of balanced-budget amendments who legislate unbounded government deficit (injurious to everything, including common sense).

I must hasten to add that, in fact, I do agree, in part, with Yeager and Schwartz, at least on the negative portion of what they said. That is, we all seem to be against a return to the gold standard. Hankering after the gold standard appears, however, to be limited to a small batch of people—perhaps only those who have invested in gold and a few others, such as the French. Thus, agreement on this issue would not be unexpected.

Why would one want to choose something like the gold standard? There seem to be two quite distinct motives involved. One is the fairly traditional one, that the gold standard would produce price stability because the price of commodities in terms of gold, being a real price ratio, can be counted upon to be rather stable. Thus, the gold standard would enable us to exploit the stability to produce that important social good, the stable price level. The other motive for a return to the gold standard is that it would reduce, if not eliminate altogether, government discretion. For a certain group of people, this is very important—getting the government out of anything is of great value in itself for these people. I do not share this second motive, and I will come back to that later. In essence, my view is that the government should be removed from the things that it does poorly and put into the things that it does well, and I can think of many examples of either kind.

46

Let us look more closely at these two reasons in favor of (or motives for) the gold standard. Consider, first, price-level stability. Yeager did not seem to doubt that a gold standard might produce price stability, or at least that it might have produced it in the past. However, there is plenty of evidence that the gold standard did not produce anything like stable prices. There have been many studies; recently, one by Richard Cooper (1982) summarizes some of the evidence and shows that, by and large, the instability of prices under the gold standard over periods of decades had been, if anything, greater than that prevailing in the period after the abandonment of the gold standard and up to 1982. The difference between price stability under the gold standard and that during the subperiod preceding the great oil shock (a development that has immensely changed the behavior of everything and produced a quantum jump in macroinstability) further supports my contention that the gold standard did not produce stable prices. To make a meaningful comparison, we ought to either leave out the last decade or ask ourselves how the gold standard would have worked with a jolt of that kind. However, the important point is that up to the 1970s—and even including the great inflation of the Vietnam War, which really only reached up to 6 percent—we enjoyed remarkable stability, which the gold standard never achieved. Furthermore, under current conditions, the gold standard could be expected to lead to substantially less stability than past experience suggests, because gold has become a highly speculative commodity. I certainly would not want to live in a world where the price level moves like the stock market, where I could wake up in the morning to discover that the price level had moved down by one and three-eighths overnight.

Thus, there is no reason to think that, even under ideal conditions, the gold standard would produce stability anywhere comparable to that achievable, and achieved, under a fiat standard and by good management of macropolicies. Yeager's hymn to the gold standard includes the claim that that regime was unusually peaceful, leading to the breakdown of national boundaries and freer movement of people. I disagree with that claim, too, because we had a very similar development under the Bretton Woods system and even in the more recent period of floating exchange rates. There has been enormous liberalization of the movement of goods and people. Nowadays, within the European Economic Community people move freely without passports, which is what I remember my parents telling me they could do around the turn of the century. In fact, that liberalization has survived the recent economic turmoil, although I am not sure that it will persist long if we keep heading in the direction the monetarists are leading us. What is attributed to the gold standard is really the outcome of peace and prosperity. Therefore, support for the gold standard cannot be based on the argument that it would provide stability of prices, let alone output or freer movement of goods and people.

Now let us consider the claim that reinstating the gold standard would reduce the role of government. This claim is probably true. First, under the classic textbook gold standard, the government role in monetary matters becomes mechanized. Instead of a computer to compute 3 percent, as Milton Friedman would like, we would have another mechanical rule: buy all the gold that is offered at a fixed price. Thus, the operation is really of a fairly simple kind. And the role of government would be even smaller under the types of gold standard that Yeager describes when he refers to the proposals of Black, Fama, and, particularly, Hall. It has been suggested that, in principle, the government might limit itself to just defining the gold content of the dollar and require that borrowers and lenders pay and accept payment, respectively, in the corresponding weight in gold, unless another form of settlement is agreeable to both parties. That is all that would be needed in order to ensure a determinate price level. As Hall (1981) points out, this conclusion is supported by the U.S. experience in the period up to the Civil War, when there was no treasury money of any kind in circulation, the treasury did not hold gold or engage in any transactions in the gold market, and there was no central bank. All note issue was by private banks, and yet there was a relatively orderly price level. However, that system was probably helped a great deal by the fact that Britain was on the conventional gold standard and hence on a fixed exchange with the United States; presumably, that at least helped to enforce two-way stability between parity and market price of gold.

In any event, as Hall also points out, there were a lot of problems with that system because banks could freely create bank notes, which led to wildcat banking and discounts on notes and resulted in inconvenience and social cost—plus occasional crises during which suspension of species had to be enforced. It is not clear at all that this was such a well-working system.

As for the instability of the price level due to the instability of the price of gold in terms of goods, suggestions have been made for other methods that would take care of the problem, such as the so-called tabular standard. The distinguishing feature of this system is that, in order to maintain the stable purchasing power of the dollar, the gold content of the dollar is changed if the gold price of commodities changes. This system has never been tried, but it is clear that it would run into very unpleasant trouble, because the change in parity can be made only at discrete intervals as the necessary information become available. For instance, the change would be made on the basis of information about the prices that becomes available once a month. The change in the price of gold would then have to be made once a month. If discontinuous changes in gold content were made, however, erratic interest rates and similar sorts of problems would result. Thus, this system also is not completely thought out.

In addition to the preceding problems with the gold standard, there is the old objection that tying the money to gold reserves is a highly irrational and wasteful system because it requires that gold be dug out of the ground and then stored somewhere, both actions entailing costs and serving no real purpose. Presumably, there is nothing that can be done with gold that cannot be done without it, and this assumption applies equally to some other standards that Hall (1981) has proposed. He has told us that you can improve on gold by using a multiple standard consisting of four basic commodities. However, this system would still require the wasteful storing of the four commodities.

To avoid this shortcoming, Hall (1981) has come up with one further suggestion—the reserve standard—that, in the beginning, seems very clever. The idea is that he would use as a backing for the money, or as the object in terms of which the value of money is defined, not gold nor any other commodity, but a piece of paper. The Federal Reserve or some other entity would create something called the reserve unit, and not called the dollar, and then fix the reserve-unit content of the dollar (or the price of reserve units in terms of the dollar). Once the reserve units were created, we would adjust the reserve content of the dollar in order to maintain price stability. For instance, we could make the adjustment on the basis of the cost-of-living index that is produced once a month—if prices go up, the price of reserves would be reduced. If you think about this for a moment, it begins to sound quite similar to what we have now, except that, when we want more money now, we change the quantity of reserves instead of the reserve content. Aside from the formula for determining the change in money, is the difference between this method and our current system very significant? Hall tells us that the great advantage to his system is that the seigniorage would go to the banking system and, presumably, back to the public rather than going to the government. This conclusion, however, is not easily reconciled with the whole literature on optimal taxation. If the government taxes in the form of seigniorage, it will have to raise fewer taxes otherwise. One certainly cannot claim superiority for a system because it eliminates a tax and the counterproducing revenue, especially if that tax may offer advantages.

Actually, having proposed this ingenious method, Hall admits that it is not the best system. Basically, the best method involves going back to where we are now, with the Federal Reserve creating its liabilities, although in this case the liabilities would serve only as bank reserves and currency would be created by banks. However, these liabilities would be managed for the purpose of controlling interest rates. Hall (1981) provides a rule that interest rates are to rise 0.1 percent each month that the cost-of-living index is above some chosen level, for instance, 100. There are, however, problems with this mechanical rule. First, the rule seems to assume that there is a stable long-run relationship between level of interest rates and price level. This makes no sense, because it is the rate of change, and not the level of prices, that is related to (real) interest rates. Given this relationship, applying the Hall rule would result in a very unstable system, one that responded cyclically to shocks. When the price level got back to 100 following an upward shock, the interest rate would be at its highest level, and the price level would continue to fall at maximum speed.

The second problem with Hall's rule is that, with the central bank issuing its liabilities according to the rule, how could you have free banking, including competitive private production of currency, and still issue a stable price level? With the currency created by banks, it is not clear that there would be a well-defined demand for the central-bank-issued reserve, especially given the fact that no one, except possibly banks in making interbank settlements, would have any reason to ask for the reserve units. In fact, one could imagine banks developing all kinds of ingenious devices for economizing enormously on needed reserves, and maybe even getting by without them. Thus, I have serious doubts about whether there would be a stable relationship between the quantity of the reserve money and the overall quantity of money—and hence the price level. At the very least, I think reserve against the issue of currency would be needed.

Next, suppose that Hall's method could deliver some, even if limited, deregulation and price stability? Are these our top priorities? Deregulation is not a value in and of itself. It is only a value if it increases welfare, and why should welfare be increased by wholesale deregulation of the banking system? Competition should be encouraged, but encouraging competition is not the same thing as advocating wholesale abolition of any regulation of the banking system. Thus, I agree with Schwartz that the monetary system is a delicate matter and decontrol should, accordingly, be handled with care.

Another question to be considered is: Is price stability really the only valuable thing in life? Those proposing methods that would produce price stability seem to have forgotten that there are things other than price stability that are important in the world. Stability of output and employment also are important, at least by some measure. Unfortunately, it is hard to measure exactly the relative importance of these things. However, what the proposals imply about output stability must not be disregarded. The whole point of Keynesian theory is that you need to manage money (1) because if you do not manage it velocity changes will result in unstable prices, and (2) because of price-wage rigidities, such changes in velocity, unless offset, will generate output and employment instability.

We seem to have forgotten this point, although there is plenty of fresh confirmation that wages are rigid. If they are not rigid, how do we explain unemployment running at 8, 9, or 10 percent year after year? The unemployment rate cannot be explained by errors of expectations consistent with rational forecasts. We all know about the inflation that is coming; errors from polls of price expectations confirm it. Such errors, however, cannot be the reason we have persistently high unemployment. The reason for this must be sought, instead, in the fact that we have wage rigidity—but not the nominal rigidity described in Keynesian theory. That, of course, was empirically quite wrong. We know that money wages are quite flexible. They can go up 30 percent overnight, as has happened in many countries. Is that rigidity? Not at all; money wages respond quite promptly to recent and anticipated inflation. The problem lies in the rigidity of real wages. Essentially, people do not understand that, under certain circumstances, to reduce inflation they have to accept a lower nominal wage increase, which they regard as a lower real wage, even though, in the end, it may not be. That is why it is so hard to get inflation down. It is only the slack that induces people to accept the slowing down of nominal wages, which is seen as a form of real-wages sacrifice. This view, by the way, has some justification, because, in view of built-in rigidities in the price-wage system (for example, through long-term contracts), whoever is accepting a slowdown may, in fact, initially suffer some real-income reduction, although this may wash out eventually.

It seems to me that, from the point of view of employment stability, the gold standard and related systems are not particularly attractive and, in some circumstances, might be destabilizing. In particular, consider Hall's system and how well it would function if an oil crisis hit. Clearly, when the price of oil goes up, the first thing that happens is that the price level goes up. That cannot be avoided, unless there is a dictator who cuts all other prices and wages overnight to compensate for the higher oil prices. Under Hall's rule, the monetary authority must raise interest rates; because this action clearly cannot initially prevent a wage-price spiral, the interest rate will have to be raised and, presumably, the money supply will have to be reduced. Meanwhile, unemployment is rising. This set of actions amounts to negative accommodation, instead of partial accommodation, which would be hard to defend as optimal. Clearly, therefore, Hall's system would not be good under these circumstances, which really are the only ones that created our current problems. It should be clear by now that, fundamentally, our problems resulted from the oil crisis, although I would agree with Yeager that some earlier developments contributed to the problems. The Vietnam War and some excess creation of liquidity, some but not all of which was sterilized, set the scene for the appearance of problems. But the situation took a quantum jump with the onset of the oil crisis. It should be noted that, with the second oil crisis, when there was no excess creation of liquidity, we still had the same reaction of worldwide inflation.

Having so far been rather negative about various proposals, let me consider about what I am more positive. With regard to the near future, I agree with Yeager and Schwartz that we have no choice but floating. The world economy is much too disturbed at the moment for anything else to work. The currency-block approach is creating strain even within the European monetary union, so it would hardly seem to be the time for extending it, particularly to the United States. We should continue with a system similar to what we have, with minor adjustments. Changing to contemporary reserve requirement domestically will not make any difference, except that it would make interest rates a little jumpier. Moving in the other direction—making interest rates less jumpy—would produce a deterioration of a second order of magnitude.

I quite disagree with Schwartz with regard to targeting on gross national product (GNP). In my view, one should target only on GNP, and any other intermediate target, such as M1 to Mn, should be adjusted frequently to track that final target. Of course, one cannot count on hitting the final fixed target closely. However, there is no use in targeting some magnitude we do not care about simply because it is easier to track. That is like saying: we want to go this way but we will go that way, because the road is bad this way but it is good that way. We choose the good road, then, even though it does not take us where we want to go. It is far better, in my view, to aim in the right direction and be prepared for a rough ride.

On the international front, I think that, in the long run, we ought to aim for a gradual return to a system of fixed exchanges like Bretton Woods, but one purged of the major faults, that have been mentioned (for example, by Cooper in the *Brookings Papers,* 1982). One thing is obvious: adjustable parities would be preferred to rigidly fixed exchanges. Furthermore, big-jump adjustments should be avoided in favor of smaller, more frequent steps, similar to some sort of crawling peg.

Critical in the undoing of the old system (and a big bone of contention) was the convertibility of the dollar into gold and the freedom of the United States to change its parity unilaterally. In my view, the system was born with a congenital defect: on the one hand, the dollar was supposed to be convertible, but, on the other hand, the rate of exchange with the dollar was controlled by everybody but the United States, which had no power over it. This inherent contradiction was bound to cause problems. My proposed reform (Modigliani and Askari 1971) was to let the other countries fix and revise their parity with the dollar but, at the same time, terminate the convertibility into gold (or other assets) at any fixed rate. Under this system, the rest of the world could control the volume of dollar reserves through exchange-rate variations. In addition, I suggested that, in place of convertibility, the United States should offer, for a proper insurance fee, a purchasing-power guarantee for dollar reserves. This guarantee would be achieved by letting the exchange rate between the dollar and the Special Drawing Right (SDR) float with a price index of internationally traded commodities.

This would make the SDR into a constant purchasing-power and medium of exchange. The purchasing-power guarantee offered by the United States would then take the form of denomination foreign reserve in SDR.

References

Cooper, Richard. 1982. "The gold standard: historical facts and future prospects." Brookings Papers on Economic Activity, no. 1, pp. 1–57.

Hall, Robert. 1981. "The Government and the monetary unit." Unpublished manuscript, Stanford University.

Modigliani, Franco, and Hossein Askari. 1981. *The reform of the international payments system.* Princeton Essays in International Finance no. 89. Princeton University, International Finance Section, September.

4

A Program for International Monetary Stability

Ronald I. McKinnon

Pity the poor Board of Governors of the Federal Reserve System. For several years, domestic critics—from Treasury Secretary Regan to Milton Friedman to a full-fledged shadow open-market committee—lambasted them for failing to hit their monetary targets. On June 20, 1982, *The New York Times* reported that the U.S. Treasury was considering curbing the independent power of the Federal Reserve because the Reagan government was unhappy with the volatility in U.S. money-growth rates.

From an entirely different angle, responsible European politicians, such as Helmut Schmidt and the European Economic Community (EEC) Council of Ministers, sharply criticized the unduly tight U.S. monetary policy in 1981 and the first half of 1982 and the projected huge U.S. budget deficits for the 1980s, blaming the U.S. policy for the incredibly high interest rates that depressed European economies and forced a series of unwanted devaluations on European currencies. If the Japanese were not so concerned with the trade war being waged against them—which is merely one consequence of the worldwide depression—they too would complain that, in 1980–82, the U.S. government forced undue monetary deflation on even their robust economy.

Whom to believe and whom to blame? I contend that, for the most part, the Federal Reserve's domestic critics, particularly the monetarists, are wrong, while its European critics have reason to be concerned. The global depression of 1981–82 has a clear monetary origin that is not visible in U.S. monetary statistics but becomes obvious when one looks at the monetary contractions going on in other reserve-currency countries. Figure 4–1 shows the recent sharp slowdown in monetary growth in Germany and Japan in 1980–81.

More generally, over the past dozen years, the Federal Reserve should have considered monetary conditions in other industrial countries when formulating its own monetary policy. Besides accurately explaining the international business cycle, the world money supply (to be defined later) predicted inflation or deflation in the United States itself better than any

This chapter was prepared under the auspices of the Center for Economic Policy Research, Stanford University.

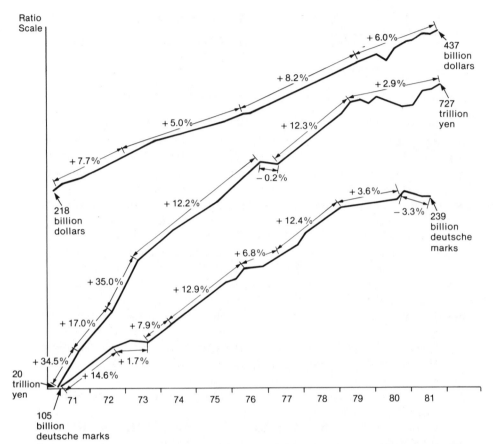

Source: Federal Reserve Bank of St. Louis, *International Economic Conditions,* April 20, 1982.

Figure 4-1. Money Supplies (M1): United States, Germany, and Japan

U.S. monetary aggregate such as M1 or M2.[1] Moreover, the relevant world money supply outside of the United States has fluctuated erratically since 1970: expanding rapidly when the dollar is weak in the foreign-exchange markets, while growing far too slowly or actually declining when the dollar is strong—as at the present time.

In contrast, over the past two years, the Federal Reserve has hit its modest target of 5 to 6 percent growth for domestic M1 rather well—as the 1980–81 quarterly data of the Federal Reserve Bank of St. Louis, shown in the top line of figure 4-1, make clear. Over the past twelve years, the Federal Reserve has succeeded in having much smoother monetary growth (measured annually or quarterly) in the United States than has any foreign central bank in its country (see figure 4-1 and table 4-1, which appears later in the chapter). Yet domestic monetarists have chosen to criticize the virtually uncontrollable weekly or monthly variations in U.S. M1, variations that may have been unnecessarily exacerbated by what could be a technical defect in the Federal Reserve's regulations. Called *lagged reserve accounting,* this possible defect is explained in detail by Friedman (*The Wall Street Journal,* February 1, 1982). Although lagged reserve accounting is commonplace in other countries, in July 1982, the Federal Reserve finally agreed to change to concurrent accounting. This strictly second-order criticism by domestic monetarists is unduly distracting; it seems to suggest that the Federal Reserve has not hit its main monetary targets, when, essentially, it has hit them.

The real problem is that, for the past dozen years, the hapless though all-powerful Federal Reserve has tried to follow the wrong monetary rule. It has focused on purely U.S. monetary indicators—such as M1 or M2 or the federal-funds rate of interest—while behaving as if it were oblivious to the rate of monetary expansion or contraction in the rest of the world.

Because other central banks have been on a de facto dollar standard, their exchange-rate and convertibility obligations have severely circumscribed their control over their domestic money supplies. But the United States, being the center country of the dollar standard, has no exchange-rate obligations and typically does not intervene in the foreign-exchange market. Hence, the Federal Reserve is the only central bank with sufficient power to control the world money supply and, with it, the world business cycle.

This chapter outlines a program for harmonizing the monetary policies of the great industrial economies—principally Germany, Japan, and the United States—in order to bring their collective money supply under control while sharply reducing fluctuations in foreign-exchange rates. The chapter explains why it could be a serious mistake to have more official intervention in the foreign exchanges, as was recently advocated by the Group of Thirty (*Financial Times,* May 7, 1982), before a program of international monetary harmonization is put in place. First, however, the next section makes the case for why control of money growth on an international basis is necessary in the 1980s—although it would have been the wrong strategy during the strong dollar standard of the 1950s and 1960s.

Monetary Isolation in the United States and the Doctrine of Domestic Monetarism

In formulating their monetary policies, the Bundesbank, the Bank of Japan, and all central banks but the Federal Reserve System give some weight to foreign-exchange considerations—albeit on an inadequate and ad hoc basis arising out of a desire to stabilize their individual exchange rates. Since 1945, however, the U.S. Federal Reserve Board generally has followed an isolationist monetary policy—whether based on domestic interest-rate or domestic money-growth targets. While now dangerously obsolete, this philosophy of national monetary autonomy still receives uncritical support from U.S. economists—whether they be Keynesians such as James Tobin or monetarists such as Milton Friedman.

What are the origins of the United States's isolationist approach? In the 1950s and 1960s, the dollar had no significant rivals as a private store of international liquidity or as an international vehicle currency. During this period of the strong dollar standard, U.S. citizens did not even consider holding some of their liquid assets in other currencies. Moreover, the dollar was (and is) the common intervention currency by which other governments intervened to maintain their exchange-rate targets; as is true today, the logical consistency of the dollar standard was best maintained, and conflict was best avoided, if the U.S. government remained passive in the foreign-exchange markets.[2] Hence, the Federal Reserve could well ignore exchange rates and the growth paths of other moneys when estimating the national and international demand for dollars. In the fifties and sixties, it was possible to stabilize the U.S. price level while benignly neglecting monetary conditions in the rest of the world.

After 1970, however, a significant structural change occurred. First the Deutsche mark and now the yen are used increasingly in private international financial markets—although the dollar remains the dominant official intervention currency. (For brevity, the international role of the Swiss franc and hard currencies issued by other small countries is ignored.) Because exchange-rate fluctuations have been so violent, firms, individuals, and a few governments have significantly diversified their liquid-asset holdings away from dollars into other convertible currencies. Although not necessarily an unwelcome development, having multiple reserve currencies potentially destabilizes the demand for any one of them (including the dollar) in response to random political-economic events.

For example, the great appreciation of the dollar since the summer of 1980 (figure 4–2) anticipated the election of a more conservative U.S. president with lower inflation targets—and also reflected political disturbances in Poland and France, where a socialist government imposed a wealth tax and exchange controls. European currencies and, to a lesser extent, the Japanese yen suddenly seemed less attractive as repositories of international liquidity. The dollar, previously battered in 1977–78, surged upward in the foreign-exchange markets in 1980–81.

However, the Federal Reserve was, and is, committed to the doctrine of domestic monetarism: U.S. M1 and M2 should grow within narrow predetermined ranges under the presumption that the demand for them is stable.

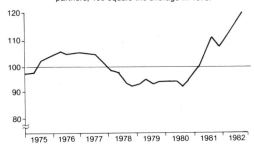

Average trade-weighted value of the dollar measured against seventeen currencies of major industrial trading partners; 100 equals the average in 1975.

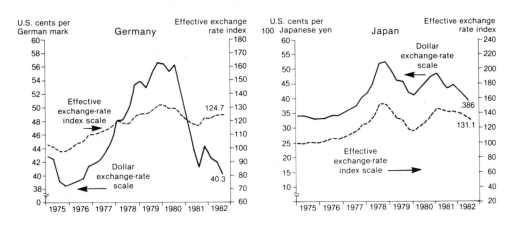

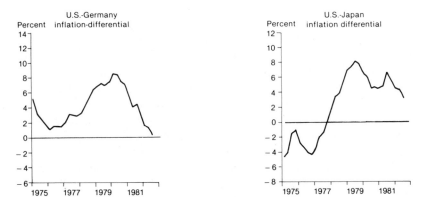

Source: Adapted from the Federal Reserve Bank of St. Louis, International Economic Conditions.

Figure 4-2. The Power of the Dollar

Hence, in 1980–81 the U.S. monetary base was not expanded to accommodate increased international demand. The result was an unduly appreciated dollar, unexpectedly tight money with high interest rates in the United States, and a much sharper recession than the U.S. authorities had anticipated.

This surge into dollar assets in 1980–82 is not the only example of international influences dominating the demand for dollars. In the 1970s, there were two episodes of great bear speculation against the dollar: the traumatic breakdown of fixed official exchange-rate parities in 1971–72 and the run on the dollar in 1977–78 (see figure 4–2) sparked by maladroit efforts by prominent U.S. officials to talk the dollar down in the foreign exchanges. Both episodes were associated with large private shifts out of dollar assets of all kinds into foreign currencies—leading to both direct and indirect reductions in the demand for U.S. M1 (transactions balances) and reductions in the derived demand for U.S. base money. True to their principle of domestic monetarism, the U.S. authorities continued with steady monetary expansion in both episodes (see figure 4–1) when, instead, they should have undertaken a sharp monetary contraction in each case. The result was massive inflation in the United States in 1973–74 and again in 1979–80, with important additional expansionary effects on the money supplies of other countries (described later).

Clearly, with the international demand for dollars so unstable, the doctrine of domestic monetarism has outlived its usefulness in the United States—and never was an operational concept in other countries, as will soon become clear. Yet the Federal Reserve's main critics—particularly those in the U.S. treasury who would usurp the independence of the Federal Reserve—continue to harp on its failure to adhere sufficiently closely to this outmoded and inappropriate doctrine.

Erratic Behavior in World Money

What more international monetary indicator is now relevant? A rather broad definition of world money covers the convertible currencies issued by principal industrial countries; a narrower definition of world money is that issued by the reserve-currency countries. Table 4–1 gives annual growth rates in M1—money in the form of transactions balances as defined by the International Monetary Fund (IMF)—for each of ten industrial countries. The weighted-world-average money growth, in the right-hand column, employs fixed weights based on nominal gross national products (GNPs) as of 1970. Because all the data are annual percentage rates of growth and thus are rescaled every year, they can be aggregated using fixed weights without taking exchange-rate changes into account.

Table 4-1
World Money-Supply Increases: Ten Industrial Countries
(percentage changes between year-end stocks)

	United States	Canada	Japan	United Kingdom	Germany	France	Italy	Netherlands	Belgium	Switzerland	Weighted World Average
(GNP weights 1970)	(0.5174)	(0.0432)	(0.1042)	(0.0648)	(0.0989)	(0.0804)	(0.0491)	(0.0167)	(0.0137)	(0.0115)	
1960	0.6	4.0	36.6	0.4	7.2	14.1	13.6	6.7	1.9	5.0ᵃ	7.03
1961	3.3	12.7	18.4	2.0	14.5	15.5	16.0	7.7	7.7	15.3	8.18
1962	2.5	4.3	16.6	-5.0	6.8	18.1	17.6	7.5	7.2	11.3	6.23
1963	3.2	7.3	34.6	14.5	7.2	14.5	13.6	9.3	9.6	7.3	9.43
1964	4.7	9.4	13.0	3.2	8.5	8.3	7.5	8.0	6.6	6.5	6.57
1965	4.8	14.3	18.2	3.9	7.7	9.4	16.4	10.0	7.1	3.8	7.88
1966	2.4	7.3	13.9	0.0	1.9	7.8	13.3	6.8	6.6	3.8	4.72
1967	7.5	4.0ᵃ	14.1	7.6	10.0	4.8	15.7	6.2	3.2	6.7	8.38
1968	8.1	0.6	13.3	3.9	7.6ᵃ	8.0	11.9	11.4	7.2	11.9	8.26
1969	3.3	-4.2	20.6	0.0	5.3	-2.5	15.9	8.1	-6.0	11.0	4.96
1970	4.3	1.8	16.8	9.3	8.6	11.4	27.4	11.8	7.0	11.0	8.19
1971	6.5	13.1	29.7	15.2	12.8	11.8	19.0	15.0	11.1	18.4	11.77
1972	9.1	12.2	24.7	14.0	14.1	14.9	17.3	17.6	15.2	5.7	12.73
1973	5.7	8.8	16.8	5.1	1.7	9.8	24.3	0.0	7.5	0.0	7.65
1974	3.0	1.5	11.5	10.8	10.7	15.2	9.4	12.2	6.2	-3.3	6.51

Table 4-1 continued

	United States	Canada	Japan	United Kingdom	Germany	France	Italy	Netherlands	Belgium	Switzerland	Weighted World Average
1975	5.5	19.0	11.1	11.0[a]	14.3	12.6	13.4	19.7	15.7	4.4	9.22
1976	5.9	1.5	12.5	11.3	3.3	7.5	18.8	8.2	7.0	10.5	7.36
1977	8.2	10.4	8.2	21.5	12.0	9.3[a]	21.4	13.2	8.3	0.6	10.27
1978	8.2	7.0	13.4	16.4	14.2	11.1	26.6	4.1	5.9	19.7	10.98
1979	8.0	1.4	3.0	9.1	3.2	11.9	23.7	2.8	2.5	−1.3	7.60
1980	5.3	10.1	−2.0	3.9	4.0	6.4	12.9	6.0	0.2	−0.5	4.86
1981	4.1	−2.8	10.0	12.0[b]	−1.6	15.9	4.5[c]	−2.4	2.2	12.7	5.30

Source: All data are noninterest-bearing M1 and are taken from line 34 of the *International Financial Statistics*: data for 1975 to 1980 are from the June 1982 issue, and data for 1960 to 1974 are from the 1981 yearbook.

[a]Implies a discontinuous series where arbitrary averaging was used.

[b]Data break: third quarter of 1980 to third quarter of 1981.

[c]Preliminary data: November 1980 to November 1981.

The first remarkable feature about table 4-1 is the high variance in annual money-growth rates in all countries except the United States, whose M1 growth was relatively smooth. At the other extreme is Switzerland, which provides an alternative reserve currency, the international demand for which is completely unstable. By automatically accommodating this shifting demand through exchange-rate intervention, however, the Swiss authorities alternated between positive money-growth rates, sometimes as high as 18 to 20 percent per year, and negative growth of 1 or 2 percent. Nevertheless, Switzerland's monetary policy was more successful in maintaining stable domestic prices than was that of the United States, as table 4-2 shows. The other industrial countries listed in table 4-1 have erratic annual money-growth rates more akin to those of Switzerland than to those of the United States.

If each of these series of fluctuating national money growth were uncorrelated with the others, there would be no clear-cut implications for world inflation or deflation. Moreover, such statistical independence would imply that the proportional variance (coefficient of variation) in the weighted world average of money growth should be less than the proportional variation in individual countries—as indeed seems to be the case for the figures from 1960 to 1970 (given in the right-hand column of table 4-1).

However, beginning in 1970 with the weakening of the dollar's hitherto unique role as international money, the weighted-world-average money growth began to exhibit much higher variance—as if its components were more systematically correlated. Indeed, as table 4-1 indicates, world money growth increased sharply in 1971-72 and again in 1977-78, when there was speculation against the dollar in favor of almost all other convertible currencies. In both episodes, foreign central banks intervened to slow the dollar's fall by buying dollars (U.S. treasury securities) with their own base money; thus, inadvertently, they collectively increased their domestic money supplies.

Table 4-1 also shows the markedly slower growth in world money in 1980-81, which was associated with massive speculation in favor of the dollar. Unfortunately, this speculation continues to the present (July 1982). This time, foreign central banks have intervened by selling dollars and repurchasing their own currencies, thereby slowing domestic money growth and preventing further exchange depreciation of their own moneys.

Lest one doubts that foreign-exchange speculation and defensive intervention by foreign central banks have dominated this erratic pattern of world money growth, table 4-3 presents the changes in official direct dollar claims on the United States by Canada, Japan, and Western Europe for the period from 1963 to 1981. (The figures for Western Europe are not broken down into individual country components in the International Monetary Fund's statistics.) As table 4-3 shows, these net dollar claims changed rela-

Table 4-2
Wholesale Price Inflation: Ten Industrial Countries
(in percentage changes from past year's period average)

	United States	Canada	Japan	United Kingdom	Germany	France	Italy	Netherlands	Belgium	Switzerland	Weighted World Average
(GNP weights 1970)	(0.5174)	(0.0432)	(0.1042)	(0.0548)	(0.0989)	(0.0804)	(0.0491)	(0.0167)	(0.0137)	(0.0115)	
1960	0.1	0.1	0.1	1.3	1.1	3.6	0.9	-2.5	1.1	0.6	0.6
1961	-0.4	1.1	0.1	3.8	1.5	3.0	0.1	-1.2	-0.1	0.2	0.5
1962	0.2	2.8	-1.6	2.1	3.5	0.5	3.1	1.2	0.7	3.5	0.7
1963	-0.4	1.9	1.7	1.2	0.4	2.8	5.3	2.5	2.5	3.8	0.8
1964	0.2	0.4	0.2	2.9	1.1	3.6	3.2	6.2	4.7	1.3	1.1
1965	1.3	2.1	0.7	3.7	2.4	0.7	1.6	3.5	1.0	0.5	1.5
1966	3.3	3.5	2.4	2.8	1.8	2.7	1.6	4.5	0.6	1.9	2.9
1967	0.2	1.8	1.8	1.2	-1.0	-0.9	-0.1	0.0	0.0	0.3	0.3
1968	2.4	2.2	0.9	3.9	-0.7	1.7	0.3	1.1	1.2	0.1	1.5
1969	4.0	4.7	2.1	3.4	1.8	10.7	3.9	0.0	3.4	2.9	4.0
1970	3.6	1.4	3.6	7.1	4.9	7.5	7.3	6.4	6.0	4.1	4.4
1971	3.3	1.2	-0.8	9.0	4.3	2.1	3.4	1.0	1.9	2.2	3.1
1972	4.5	7.0	0.8	5.3	2.6	4.6	4.1	4.0	4.1	3.6	4.1
1973	13.1	21.5	15.9	7.3	6.6	14.7	17.0	12.4	7.4	10.7	12.9
1974	18.9	22.1	31.3	23.4	13.4	29.2	40.7	13.6	20.1	16.2	21.9
1975	9.2	6.7	3.0	24.1	4.7	-6.1	8.5	7.5	4.5	-2.3	7.5
1976	4.6	5.1	5.0	17.3	3.7	7.4	23.8	7.8	7.1	-0.7	6.6
1977	6.1	7.9	1.9	19.8	2.7	5.6	16.6	5.8	2.4	0.3	6.6
1978	7.8	9.3	-2.5	9.1	1.2	4.3	8.4	1.3	-2.0	-3.4	5.6
1979	12.5	14.4	7.3	12.2	4.8	13.3	15.5	2.7	6.3	3.8	11.1
1980	14.0	13.5	17.8	16.3	7.5	8.8	20.1	8.2	5.8	5.1	13.5
1981	9.0	10.1	1.7	10.7	7.7	11.0	16.6	9.2	8.2	5.8	8.7

Source: Wholesale price indexes from *International Financial Statistics*, line 63, with most recent data from the June 1982 issue.

Table 4-3
Direct Dollar Liabilities of the United States to Foreign Central Banks and Governments
(in billions of U.S. dollars; year-end stocks)

	Canada[a]	Japan[c]	Western Europe[b]	Total	Annual Percentage Change
1963	1.79	1.59	8.51	11.89	
1964	1.81	1.50	9.32	12.63	+ 6.2
1965	1.70	1.57	8.83	12.10	− 4.4
1966	1.33	1.47	7.77	10.57	− 14.5
1967	1.31	1.45	10.32	13.08	+ 23.7
1968	1.87	2.26	8.06	12.19	− 7.3
1969	1.62	2.61	7.07	11.30	− 7.9
1970	2.95	3.19	13.61	19.75	+ 74.8
1971	3.98	13.78	30.13	47.89	+ 142.0
1972	4.25	16.48	34.20	54.93	+ 14.7
1973	3.85	10.20	45.76	59.81	+ 8.9
1974	3.66	11.35	44.33	59.34	− 0.8
1975	3.13	10.63	45.70	59.46	+ 0.2
1976	3.41	13.88	45.88	63.17	+ 6.2
1977	2.33	20.13	70.75	93.21	+ 47.6
1978	2.49	28.90	93.09	124.48	+ 33.5
1979	1.90	16.36	85.60	103.86	− 19.9
1980	1.56	21.56	81.59	104.71	+ 0.8
1981	2.40	24.72	65.22	92.34	− 11.8

Source: *International Financial Statistics* (*IFS*) of the International Monetary Fund. Most recent data from June 1982 issue.

[a]From line 5aad, *IFS* (United States).

[b]From line 5abd, *IFS* (United States).

[c]Because direct U.S. liabilities to the Japanese government were not available, the virtually identical series on total Japanese reserves in foreign currency was used. Data from line 1dd, *IFS* (Japan).

tively little in the 1960s, escalated rapidly in 1970–72 and again in 1977–78, and exhibited net negative growth in 1979–81.

These worldwide monetary explosions in 1971–72 and 1977–78 accurately predicted worldwide inflation—with about a year-and-a-half lag—in 1973–74 and again in 1979–80, as shown by the average wholesale price indexes in table 4–2. And the contraction in world money growth in 1980–81 predicted the marked slowdown in world commodity-price inflation that began in 1981 and became much sharper in 1982.

Using formal statistical regression techniques, a Stanford student confirmed that this broad definition of world money predicted U.S. GNP and U.S. prices over 1970 to 1981 better than did any purely U.S. monetary aggregate.[3] The superiority of this indicator becomes more evident intuitively if one compares the limited variance in U.S. money-growth rates in table 4–1 to the high variance in U.S. rates of price inflation in table 4–2. In most other countries, world money also predicted national price inflation and deflation better than did any purely domestic money-growth series.

In short, in the 1970s and 1980s, the system behaved as if the demand for world money was quite stable, whereas the demand for each national currency—including that for the U.S. dollar—was not. To dampen the international cycle of inflation and deflation, therefore, the feasibility of stabilizing world money growth would seem well worth investigating.

The Exchange-Rate Trap

If the industrial countries, acting independently, smoothed the hitherto erratic fluctuations in each of their domestic money supplies, would they thus indirectly stabilize world money growth? Unfortunately, no. Exchange-rate fluctuations would become even more violent in response to international shifts in the demand for each national currency.

Consider the plight of the Bundesbank and Bank of Japan in July 1982, when the dollar was very strong in the foreign exchanges. Both Germany and Japan had depressed domestic economies and domestic money growth below desirable long-term trends. The authorities in both countries knew, however, that any substantial domestic monetary expansion would immediately spill into the foreign-exchange markets and depreciate their undervalued currencies even more. Imagine the protectionist hue and cry in the United States if the yen were to depreciate by another 20 percent and make U.S. industry even less competitive in world markets!

Recently, a prestigious international commission, the Group of Thirty, called for even more official intervention in currency markets—urging the United States in particular to stabilize the dollar (*Financial Times*, May 7, 1982). As was stated in the Group of Thirty's recent report: "A high exchange rate can promote de-industrialization, undermine credit-worthiness, and impart a deflationary bias to national policies. A low exchange rate involves welfare losses and renders the economy more vulnerable to inflationary impulses coming from high import prices and strong export demand."

While agreeing fully with this assessment of the adverse consequences of large exchange-rate fluctuations, I believe that the group's emphasis on increased official intervention to smooth exchange rates is seriously misplaced. If, as posited here, the great swings in the dollar exchange rate (shown earlier in figure 4–2) merely reflect direct and indirect shifts in international monetary demand from one currency to another, official stabilizing intervention cannot be successful unless the domestic and/or the relevant foreign monetary base adjusts by the full amount of the intervention.

That is, the monetary consequences of the official intervention will not be sterilized. And, as long as the United States continues to maintain fixed growth in U.S. M1 irrespective of events in the foreign-exchange market, foreign money supplies will continue to do all the adjusting.[4] The consequence of such intervention is the erratic pattern of world money growth, as was shown earlier in table 4-1: the world money supply expands when there is speculation against the dollar and reserve accumulation by foreign central banks, and the world money supply contracts when there is speculation against the dollar and reserve decumulation by foreign central banks.

Thus, we are in an exchange-rate trap. With U.S. money growth fixed, official foreign intervention to smooth an exchange rate can be successful only if that country's money supply is forced to fluctuate. In addition, when foreign central banks intervene in concert for or against the dollar, the world's money supply spirals out of control, with unfortunate implications for world inflation or deflation.

The Financial Importance of Germany and Japan

Clearly, the Federal Reserve System should consider money growth abroad and the dollar exchange rate when deciding on the rate of U.S. monetary expansion. When the dollar is unusually strong in the foreign-exchange markets, U.S. monetary growth should increase automatically to offset the tendency for money growth abroad to contract; similarly, U.S. money growth should contract sharply—perhaps becoming negative—if the dollar is unusually weak, as happened in 1971-72 and again in 1977-78. Most importantly, these desirable features should be incorporated into an easily understood international monetary rule that stabilizes expectations regarding future inflation; the discretionary powers of the monetary authorities should be limited without strait-jacketing them with technically infeasible operating procedures.

Besides the United States, what other countries should be brought into a monetary pact for stabilizing the world system? What is a relevant limited definition of the rest of the world for the reformulation of U.S. monetary policy? From time to time over the past twenty years, one or another of all ten currencies in table 4-1 have been alternatives to the dollar as repositories of international liquidity. Recently, however, some of the major European currencies have become less attractive: British and Italian rates of price inflation in the last decade (see table 4-2) have been too high and unstable to satisfy international investors. Some countries, such as Italy and France, impose unusually tight exchange controls on capital account, which makes their moneys distinctly less convenient international stores of value.

As of 1982, therefore, the deutsche mark (DM) remained the principal hard European currency that provides portfolio alternatives to dollar assets. Clustered around Germany are a number of small countries that have exchange rates more or less fixed to the DM—and whose monetary policies tend to be very similar to Germany's. Indeed, figure 4-2 (presented earlier in the chapter) compares the great fluctuations in dollar/mark exchange rates to the relatively mild movements in Germany's effective exchange rate—and these mild movements relate to the fact that the trade weights are dominated by Germany's European trading partners. (The Swiss franc is a more independent reserve currency, but Switzerland is too small a country to have much impact on the world system.) Henceforth, then, the deutsche mark may be identified as the key European hard currency in international portfolios.

Japan's huge economic size, importance in world trade, and rapid growth make it an obvious candidate for any international pact. Also, the yen has become increasingly important as an international currency. Although it suffered from very high price inflation in the first monetary explosion of the early 1970s, the purchasing power of the yen has been relatively stable since the mid-1970s (see table 4-2). Over the period of 1978 to 1980, Japan virtually eliminated the detailed exchange controls on capital account that had prevented Tokyo from becoming an international financial center. Foreigners may now hold Japanese financial assets, sell yen-denominated bonds, or borrow directly from Japanese banks. (To be sure, the Bank of Japan still exercises some guidance in these respects.)

Consequently, there has been a marked increase in invoicing of international trade in yen. Euroyen trading is developing rapidly, and the yen is being used more widely as a standard of value in capital-market transactions outside of Japan than ever before. Central banks in other Pacific-Basin countries are relying increasingly on the yen—to some extent instead of the dollar—as a convenient method of establishing the foreign-exchange value of their currencies. Thus, the yen may be identified as the dominant Asian reserve currency.

The yen and deutsche mark do not experience the ebb and flow of the demand for dollars fully in concert. One is not entirely representative of the other. The movements in the dollar/yen and dollar/DM exchange rates are related but, nevertheless, somewhat differentiated (as was shown in figure 4-2). Because of official foreign-exchange intervention, both Japan and Germany have experienced more erratic annual growth in their domestic money supplies (M1) than has the United States. Nevertheless, deviations in the German and Japanese money-growth rates from trend have not been perfectly correlated—as figure 4-3 makes clear.

In summary, although the deutsche mark and yen are each important reserve currencies and potential alternatives to the dollar, each should be recognized as independent entities in any international monetary pact. On

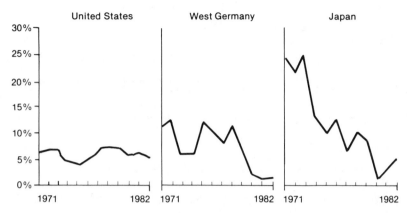

Source: Adapted from the Federal Reserve Bank of St. Louis, *International Economic Conditions*.

Note: The growth of the U.S. money supply has been much steadier than the growth in either West Germany or Japan. Annual percentage changes in M1 for the three countries are shown in this figure. M1 comprises currency in circulation plus checking-account deposits.

Figure 4-3. Swings in Money Supply

the other hand, harmonized monetary relationships among the triumvirate—Germany, Japan, and the United States—should be sufficient to stabilize the international monetary system as a whole. No other substantial sources of international money are in prospect. The remainder of this chapter, then, will focus on this narrower definition—the sum of yen, deutsche marks, and dollars—in developing a rule for stabilizing growth in world money.[5]

A New International Monetary Standard

Let us start with the proposition that percentage growth in the nominal money stocks, M1, of each of our three reserve-currency countries should have a fixed weight in the determination of percentage growth in world money. Let us suppose further that this weighting system is independent of any arbitrary starting set of exchange rates that link the three currencies. Thus, our international rule must be of the form:

$$\% \, M1^W = 0.45 \, \% \, M1^{US} + 0.35 \, \% \, M1^G + 0.20 \, \% \, M1^J \qquad (4.1)$$

where % denotes percentage change in the succeeding variable; $M1^W$ is the relevant world money stock; and the other superscripts refer to the United States, Germany and Japan, whose M1s are measured in dollars, deutsche marks, and the yen, respectively. The substantial but merely illustrative weight of 0.35 assigned to Germany reflects its disproportionate importance in the European monetary system. In practice, the exact weighting system would be negotiated by the three central banks, taking the relative size of GNPs into account. As long as their sum is one, the precise weights chosen, and whether other hard currencies are included in the definition of $M1^W$, are not critical. (Indeed, the rate of growth in the broader definition of world money, as was given in table 4-1, is calculated in a similar fashion.)

The preferred procedure is to calculate the sum of M1s for the United States, Germany, and Japan on a monthly basis and then to instruct the three participating central banks to aim for annual growth in this sum, $M1^W$, of, say, 6 percent. For example, a target range for growth in world money stock of 5 to 7 percent for the following year could be announced jointly while, at the same time, individual official targets for each of the three countries' M1s would be discarded. In this example, 6 percent was chosen to approximate expected real GNP growth in the triumvirate—taking into account that Japan with its high saving rate may reasonably be expected to grow faster than Germany or the United States.

Technically, it is much more difficult for the three countries to achieve national money-growth targets separately than it is to smooth aggregate money growth for the group. The reason for this is straightforward: the ebb and flow of international monetary demand among the three currencies implies that if any one of the countries (say, the United States) succeeds in hitting its separately specified target, the other two are unlikely to do so (see figure 4-3). And, in an integrated world, it is the group's collective money supply that determines aggregate demand for goods and services. Hence, the new rule should be more credible.

Note that, in equation 4.1, percentage growth in $M1^W$ is a well-defined monetary indicator easily calculated from the sum of our three national money-growth rates; paradoxically, however, the exact units and composition of $M1^W$ itself have yet to be defined. Indeed, the readers or central bankers who follow equation 4.1 need never know the precise definition of $M1^W$. The rule governing percentage growth in world money would still be fully operational. To assuage intellectual curiosity, however, let us integrate equation 4.1 to obtain:

$$\log M1^W = 0.45 \log M1^{US} + 0.35 \log M1^G + 0.20 \log M1^J + \log S \quad (4.2)$$

where $\log S$ is the constant of integration. However, S does have an economic interpretation. It is a scale factor—an unknown and unneeded amalgam of hypothetical or actual exchange rates. To see this more clearly, take the antilog of equation 4.2 to obtain:

$$M1^W = S \cdot (M1^{US})0.45 \cdot (M1^G)0.35 \cdot (M1^J)0.20 \qquad (4.3)$$

If the absolute level of $M1^W$ as defined by equation 4.3 were to be used for any analytical or policy purpose, the relevant exchange rates linking $M1^{US}$ to $M1^G$ to $M1^J$ would have to be specified. For example, if we decide arbitrarily to express our monetary index, $M1^W$, in dollars, then some current, base-period, or purchasing-power-parity dollar/mark, S^G, and dollar/yen, S^J, exchange rates would have to be determined to replace the undefined S in equation 4.3. The absolute value of world money in dollars would then be:

$$M1^W = (M1^{US})0.45 \cdot (S^G M1^G)0.35 \cdot (S^J M1^J)0.20 \qquad (4.4)$$

Fortunately, however, our monetary rule is concerned only with linking the percentage growth rates in $M1^{US}$, $M1^G$ and $M1^J$, without making any assumptions about exchange rates. Henceforth, we will work only from equation 4.1 and ignore all the exchange-rate complications associated with equation 4.3 or 4.4. This methodology is valid not only because of its simplicity but also because the desired world money growth should, in the deeper economic sense, be independent of exchange-rate fluctuations. Otherwise, our rule would not provide an independent and unambiguous monetary anchor—nor would the world price level be determinant.[6]

Implementation: Controlling Each Country's Monetary Base

How could the three individual, and perhaps highly variable, national money-growth rates be manipulated to assure a preassigned growth rate of 5 to 7 percent in world money stock? Without separate national targets for each M1, how would the three participating central banks divide up their responsibilities for creating money?

In the steady state under this new international standard, each of the three central banks' domestic money-market transactions would remain practically unchanged. That is, the Federal Reserve would continue to buy enough treasury bills and bonds to keep $M1^{US}$ growing at a hypothetical 5 percent rate. The Bank of Japan would buy Japanese treasury bonds (or rediscount private loans) so that the $M1^J$ would hypothetically grow at 9 percent, reflecting the higher average GNP growth in Japan. With a projected GNP growth closer to that of the United States, the Bundesbank would choose a monetary growth rate closer to the U.S. level from the domestic component of its monetary base.

Borrowing the variables from table 4-4, A^{US}, A^G, and A^J define the domestic components of the U.S., German, and Japanese monetary bases, respectively. Let us suppose that world money growth reaches its desirable long-term trend path under our new monetary agreement. (The transition to equilibrium money growth is discussed later.) Let M_0 denote the starting monetary base of each country after the new system is introduced and when it enters steady-state growth. Then, the predetermined growth paths taken by the domestic components of each country's monetary base at any time (t) would be:

$$A^{US} = M_0^{US} e^{0.05t} \qquad (4.5)$$

$$A^G = M_0^G e^{0.05t} \qquad (4.6)$$

$$A^J = M_0^J e^{0.09t} \qquad (4.7)$$

The coefficients 0.05 and 0.09 are merely illustrative of the estimated long-term money-growth rates in each country that could be calculated to yield long-run stability in the prices of tradable goods. Under the further (but unnecessary) assumption that the income elasticity of the demand for base money is unity, 0.05 and 0.09 would reflect the desired average growth in nominal GNP in the United States (and Germany) and in Japan—again consistent with secular stability in the prices of tradable goods in each country. With these internationally compatible price-level targets, there need be no persistent tendency for exchange rates to change in one direction or another.

Fortunately, targeting growth in the domestic components of each country's monetary base, as described by equations 4.5 through 4.7, is a straightforward procedure and not that much different from current operating procedures. Each central bank would use some combination of open-market operations in domestic government bonds and controlled rediscounting of domestic bank loans to achieve its prespecified target for domestic-credit expansion.

In so controlling the domestic component of its national monetary base through open-market operations or rediscounting, each central bank would set up its monetary accounts to make a sharp distinction between the domestic and foreign components of the base. This would be done most easily by having Germany and Japan keep the working part of their exchange reserves on deposit with the Federal Reserve Bank of New York at a short-term market rate of interest; this would replace their current practice of holding nonmonetary U.S. treasury bills or bonds. Stripped down to essentials, this system would leave the balance sheets of the three central banks as they appear in table 4-4.

Table 4–4
Foreign and Domestic Components of the Monetary Base: United States, Germany, and Japan

Assets	Federal Reserve System (dollars)		Liabilities
Domestic assets: government bonds and loans to commercial banks	A^{US}	M^{US}	U.S. monetary base: currency plus reserves of U.S. commercial banks
		FR^G	Deposits of Bundesbank
		FR^J	Deposits of Bank of Japan
Assets	Bundesbank (deutsche marks)		Liabilities
Domestic assets	A^G	M^G	German monetary base: currency plus reserves of German commercial banks
Foreign reserves held with the Federal Reserve	FR^G / S^G		
Assets	Bank of Japan (yen)		Liabilities
Domestic assets	A^J	M^J	Japanese monetary base: currency plus reserves of Japanese commercial banks
Foreign reserves held with the Federal Reserve	FR^J / S^J		

Notes: S^G is the average historical exchange rate for dollars/deutsche marks, whereas S^J is the exchange rate for dollars/yen. Thus, current or future exchange-rate fluctuations would have no direct effect on the German or Japanese monetary bases.

Note that the foreign component of the monetary bases of both Germany and Japan would simply be reserves held directly on deposit with the Federal Reserve Bank of New York. Under the proposed system, Germany and Japan would be the only two countries in the world that hold their working-dollar reserves as direct deposits with the Federal Reserve. (All other countries would continue to hold their official dollar-exchange reserves in U.S. treasury bonds or bills, Eurodollar deposits, or other non-monetary financial instruments that are independent of the U.S. monetary base.) Moreover, these German and Japanese reserves held with the Federal Reserve would define the foreign component of the U.S. monetary base that varies with the ebb and flow of the international demand for dollars.

The greatest departure from present practice would be in the Federal Reserve's reactions to the foreign-exchange interventions in dollars by the other two central banks. For example, when the Bundesbank enters the foreign-exchange market to repurchase base money in DM to prevent the dollar from appreciating further against the mark, the monetary base in Germany would contract and that in the United States would expand automatically so as to leave total base money unchanged for the system as a whole. In table 4-4, this situation would be reflected in a decline in FR^G with all the A's held constant. In effect, as the demand for dollars increased against deutsche marks or the yen, the U.S. portion of the joint monetary base would expand while the German and Japanese portions would contract.

If, for example, the Bank of Japan is buying dollars—as it did massively in 1978 to prevent the dollar from depreciating too fast—the resulting sales of the yen would expand the Japanese monetary base above its trend. Under the new regime, however, the Federal Reserve would allow these official Japanese purchases of dollars to contract the U.S. monetary base below its trend so as to leave their joint money supply unchanged. (If the sharp increase in world money that occurred in 1978 had been prevented, the great price inflation of 1979–80 would have been ameliorated.) Referring again to the variables in table 4-4, the sharp increase in FR^J would automatically contract Federal Reserve liabilities (monetary base) in the hands of the U.S. banking system and nonbank public. In effect, the Federal Reserve would agree not to sterilize the monetary consequences of these interventions. Hence, the rate of growth in world money would be, in the first approximation, invariant to official interventions in the foreign exchanges.

If all the national money multipliers linking base creation to growth in each M1 were known with certainty, controlling domestic credit expansion by each central bank according to equations 4.5, 4.6, and 4.7 should be sufficient to keep M1^W growing within its hypothetical range of 5 to 7 percent. However, money multipliers may vary. (Much of the unexplained variance in the U.S. money multiplier may be related to foreign-exchange disturbances.) Let us suppose that the triumvirate of central banks found that, after a few months, M1^W was growing at only 4 pecent per year and there was no net pressure on one currency or another in the foreign-exchange markets. Growth in the domestic components of their monetary bases, then, would be increased proportionately (by mutual agreement) to return to the 6 percent growth in M1^W. If one of the three currencies seemed to be weak in the foreign-exchange markets, then only the other two countries would step up the rate of expansion in the domestic components of their monetary bases in order for the system to return to 6 percent growth in M1^W.

Notice the dichotomy in how disequilibrium exchange rates enter the operating procedures of our hypothetical international monetary board. On the one hand, the joint target for monetary growth, M1 ^{W}, as defined by equation 4.1, is independent of any exchange-rate fluctuations that might occur. In the absence of fixed official exchange parities, this independence is necessary if smooth growth in M ^{W} is to become an operational concept. On the other hand, suppose adjustments in the rate of domestic-base-money creation for the system as a whole are necessary because, say, the money multipliers are variable. Then, whichever currency is strong or weak in the foreign exchanges is best taken into account in deciding how the domestic components of each country's monetary base are to be adjusted.

In summary, our program for international monetary harmonization would use growth in M1 ^{W}—the collective money supply held by non-banks—as the single target variable, for which the domestic component of each country's monetary base would be the discretionary control variables. Foreign-exchange interventions would always be symmetrical, so that one country's monetary base would be reduced by as much as the others' increased—leaving M1 ^{W} largely unaffected. Because these foreign-exchange interventions would accommodate much of the ebb and flow of international demand from one currency to another by allowing each national money supply to vary accordingly, exchange-rate fluctuations—whether measured on a daily, weekly, or yearly basis—should be much less than those experienced over the past dozen years. If exchange-rate over-shooting is largely eliminated, fluctuations in short-term rates of interest should also be greatly dampened in each of the three countries.

Notice that this proposal does not mandate that the Bundesbank or the Bank of Japan must intervene in the foreign-exchange markets. Hence, any international agreement need not (and best not) specify any exchange-rate norms or parities. Rather, if the Bundesbank or Bank of Japan chose to intervene to iron out sharp exchange fluctuations (as they have done inten-sively since 1970, usually with very good reason), the new system ensures that the critically important world money supply would not inadvertently spiral out of control. Indeed, if this system of international harmonization had been put in place in 1970, the two great inflations of the 1970s would have been largely ameliorated and the great deflation of 1981–82 would not have been so unexpectedly severe.

Transition

How would the new money standard have worked if it had been introduced in, say, mid-1982, when growth in the joint money supply was far below its desirable trend? An international monetary board would have quickly cal-culated that the German and Japanese M1s were below their trends and that both currencies were undervalued. Although the U.S. money supply was close to its trend, the Federal Reserve would have begun expanding the U.S. money base, nudging the dollar down in the foreign-exchange markets and reducing short-term U.S. interest rates. This would have allowed the other two central banks to expand their monetary bases, in part by eliminating their need to intervene in the foreign-exchange markets to prevent their currencies from depreciating. Once the aggregate money supply of the group was on its preassigned trend of 6 percent growth from a mutually agreed-on base, the Federal Reserve would have desisted from any further expansion. To stabilize expectations regarding future inflation, this eventual termination of the extraordinary U.S. expansion would have been well advertised.

The system would then have reverted to its steady state: domestic monetary expansion of 5 percent in the United States and Germany and 9 percent in Japan, with ongoing symmetrical (and offsetting) adjustments in support of any further stabilizing foreign-exchange interventions by the Bundesbank or Bank of Japan. In effect, I am suggesting that the Friedman rule for smooth monetary growth be shifted from a national to a carefully defined international level.

It would be sad if the current unduly sharp deflation in the world at large, and in the United States in particular, forced the Federal Reserve to increase its money-growth rate in a purely ad hoc fashion: neither formally abandoning the old rule of domestic monetarism nor officially adopting a preferred international monetary standard as previously outlined.[7] An unarticulated monetary policy would upset the already jittery financial gnomes regarding potential price inflation in the future and would leave money markets in disarray. The effectiveness of any short-term monetary expansion for alleviating the worldwide slump would be reduced.

Notes

1. See my "Currency Substitution and Instability in the World Dollar Standard," *American Economic Review* (June 1982):320–333.

2. A more complete rational for how the world dollar standard works is provided in chapter 2 of my *Money in International Exchange: The Convertible Currency System* (New York: Oxford University Press, 1979).

3. Kong-yam Tan, "World Money, Income and Prices: Some Preliminary Evidence" (Unpublished paper, April 1982).

4. A full model of this asymmetrical adjustment process with the United States as the center country is provided in my "Currency Substitution and Instability in the World Dollar Standard."

5. Although the technical details were not worked out fully then, this basic idea for controlling world money goes back to my "A New Tripartite Monetary Agreement or a Limping Dollar Standard?," *Essays in Interna-*

national Finance, no. 106 (International Finance Section Princeton University, October 1974).

6. As Mr. Kong-yam Tan has pointed out to the author, there is a consistent definition of the absolute level of world prices that corresponds to the absolute level of world money given by equation 4.4. From an operational viewpoint, however, this can be safely ignored.

7. Over the past year, the Bank of England seems to have adopted an informal exchange-rate target without formally abandoning its domestic money-growth target. This is not the best way to reduce apprehension in the financial markets. For a more complete analysis of Britain's misfortunes with the doctrine of domestic monetarism, see my article, "The Exchange Rate and Macroeconomic Policy: Changing Postwar Perceptions," *The Journal of Economic Literature* 19 (June 1981):531–557.

Comment

Edward M. Bernstein

Ronald McKinnon has provided an imaginative chapter regarding the international monetary system under floating exchange rates. It ought to end the delusion, which is still widely held, that floating exchange rates give national monetary authorities great freedom in policymaking. About two years ago, at a meeting in New York, I expressed the view that national monetary authorities have less freedom in policymaking with floating rates than they had with fixed parities that properly reflected the relative international economic position of the large trading countries. At that time, the vice-president of the Bundesbank, Helmut Schlesinger, said that he and his colleagues held the opposite view—that Germany had regained its monetary freedom only after the fixed dollar rate was abandoned.

The principal problem with floating exchange rates in the past ten years is that changes in rates have been dominated by enormous capital movements, mainly to and from the United States and usually but not always initiated by changes in interest rates. Under fixed parities, where the exchange market had confidence in the rates, a rise in the interest rate brought the desired inflow of funds, but not on a virtually unlimited scale. In 1860, the Bank of England adopted the rule that the bank rate should be raised in steps of one percent if the object was to affect the exchange rate. The one-percent rule was said to be necessary because it would compensate foreign bankers for the cost of shipping gold to London and returning it to the continent after the interest rate was reduced (Bagehot, *Lombard Street,* pp. 181 and following).

This illustrates the basic difference in the effect of changes in interest rates under the two exchange systems. With appropriate fixed parities, a higher interest rate could of itself draw in funds from abroad, but only until the exchange rate reached the top of the range. Thereafter, bringing funds into the country to earn the higher interest involved the risk that they would have to be returned at a lower exchange rate. With floating rates, however, an inflow of funds in response to higher interest rates results in an appreciation of the exchange rate, but without a known limit. As a consequence, when the exchange rate rises, the inflow of funds accelerates in expectation of a further rise in the exchange rate rather than because of the higher interest rate. After a time, the excessive rise in the exchange rate becomes apparent, the risk of holding a long position in the currency that has appreciated becomes too great, and the capital flow is reversed, with a consequent fall in

78

the exchange rate. This has happened repeatedly in the dollar rates of exchange for the currencies of the Group of Ten and Switzerland.

In the ten years of floating rates, there has been nothing so astonishing as the appreciation of the dollar since the end of 1979. In the thirty-three months thereafter to the end of September 1982, the dollar rose by an average of 45 percent against the currencies of the Group of Ten and Switzerland, weighted by their exports in 1973-75. Such an enormous rise in the foreign-exchange value of the dollar cannot be due to changes in underlying economic conditions. It means that the dollar was either undervalued (relative to these ten currencies) at the beginning of the period or overvalued at the end of the period, and most likely it was alternately overvalued and undervalued.

The behavior of the exchange rate is an integral part of monetary policy. An undervalued currency is like a too-easy monetary policy. It tends to stimulate output through its effect on exports and imports, but it also causes prices to rise more than they would on the basis of domestic factors. And an overvalued currency is like a too-tight monetary policy—it tends to restrain output and to hold prices down to less than they would otherwise rise. If the central bank intervenes in the exchange market to moderate excessive fluctuations in exchange rates, however, it is engaging in open-market operations that may not be called for by the behavior of domestic prices, output, and employment. The effective exchange rate—the weighted average of the dollar rates for the currencies of its trading partners—is significant for determining the effect of changes in exchange rates on a country's exports and imports, but the dollar rates for the currencies of the other large industrial countries are of primary importance for determining the effect of changes in exchange rates on the prices of basic commodities.

At different times, countries have different attitudes toward changes in the foreign-exchange rates for their currencies; sometimes they are more concerned with the effect on output, at other times they are more concerned with the effect on prices. In recent years, the Group of Ten and Switzerland generally have been much more concerned with the unfavorable effect of the appreciation of the dollar on their prices than on its favorable effect on their trade balance. That is why some of these countries have intervened to support their currencies by selling dollars in the exchange market. If one of the large industrial countries, say, Germany, intervenes, it becomes essential for other countries to do the same or the foreign-exchange value of their currencies will fall even more. Intervention in the exchange market, however, affects the monetary base in the same way that open-market operations do.

McKinnon points out that, as a consequence of intervention, in 1980-81 the money supply (M1) fell in five of the ten countries of the Group of Ten and Switzerland and rose very little in the other countries. In these two years, the weighted average increase of the money supply (M1) in the Group of Ten and Switzerland, excluding the United States, was lower than in any of the previous twenty years, if not longer. In the meantime, the growth of M1 in the United States in 1980–81 was the smallest since 1974. Thus, we had a conjuncture of exceptionally slow monetary growth in the industrial countries in these two years. In my opinion, McKinnon is right in maintaining that the present worldwide recession is due mainly to the tight monetary policy of the United States and its restrictive effect on the money supply of the other large industrial countries that intervened in the exchange market to limit the depreciation of their currencies relative to the dollar. However, the growth of the money supply in Europe, Canada, and Japan could become excessive and stimulate an acceleration of inflation if the dollar were to fall and these countries intervened to moderate the appreciation of their currencies relative to the dollar.

McKinnon proposes to deal with this problem by having the United States, Germany, and Japan agree on the rate of growth of the money supply in each country to achieve a target for the growth of their aggregate M1s, which he regards as indicative of the world money supply or at least the total money supply of the large industrial countries. Each central bank would undertake domestic reserve-creating transactions that would be consonant with an agreed rate of growth of its own money supply. Germany and Japan would keep reserve balances with the Federal Reserve Bank of New York, which they would use for intervention, if necessary, to maintain a presumably agreed-upon range for the dollar exchange rates for the DM and the yen. Thus, if the dollar were strong and Germany and Japan intervened by selling dollars, the monetary bases in these countries would be reduced, but the base in the United States would be increased by the same amount the others' were reduced. If the M1 coefficient of the monetary base were the same in the three countries, the growth of the total of their M1s would be unaffected by the intervention of the monetary authorities in the exchange market.

McKinnon emphasizes that this new system would result in a regular growth of the world money supply. Such growth would be in contrast to the large variations that have occurred since 1971 as a consequence of the intervention of the monetary authorities in the exchange market: an excessive rate of growth when Europe and Japan bought dollars to limit the rise in the dollar rates for their currencies and a deficient rate of growth when they sold dollars to limit the fall of their currencies in terms of the dollar. Intervention by drawing on dollar reserves at the Federal Reserve would mean that the monetary base in each country would grow more or less than at the agreed rates for domestic reserve-creating transactions, but the aggregate growth in the three countries would be close to the target they had set. Presumably, this would not only minimize year-to-year variations in the behavior of prices but would also tend to moderate fluctuations in exchange rates, except in response to changes in relative prices and costs.

What McKinnon is proposing is the restoration of the classical gold standard without gold parities and without gold reserves. According to this proposal, intervention by the monetary authorities with dollars held at the Federal Reserve would serve to keep exchange rates within an acceptable range, thereby performing the same function that gold flows performed prior to World War I. Under the classical gold standard, surplus and deficit countries shared in the adjustment process in inverse proportion to the size of their economies. The adjustment became one-sided, however, when surplus countries neutralized the expansionary effect of a gold inflow, while deficit countries were compelled to follow a restrictive monetary policy in order to protect their gold reserves. As Keynes pointed out, this was a change in the rules of the classical gold standard. In *A Tract on Monetary Reform* (p. 198), he wrote:

> The theory on which the Federal Reserve Board is supposed to govern its discount policy, by reference to the influx and efflux of gold and the proportion of gold to liabilities, is as dead as mutton. It perished, and perished justly, as soon as the Federal Reserve Board began to ignore its ratio and to accept gold without allowing it to exercise its full influence, merely because an expansion of credit and prices seemed at that moment undesirable.

The asymmetrical response of monetary policy was even greater under the gold-exchange standard when the reserve-currency country could virtually ignore its balance of payments. It is interesting to note that the Gold Delegation of the League of Nations, which was concerned mainly with a possible shortage of gold, recommended that countries on the gold-exchange standard should hold their reserves with the central bank of the reserve-currency country. Nevertheless, the general rule in the 1930s was that countries should insulate the monetary system from changes in reserves by conducting reserve transactions through an exchange-equalization account outside the central bank. McKinnon wants an international monetary system under which the monetary base would respond to intervention in both the country holding currency reserves and the reserve-currency country. This could require enormous variations in the growth of the U.S. money supply from year to year.

McKinnon asks us to abandon domestic monetarism for international monetarism. He supports his case by citing "the massive inflation in the United States in 1973–74 and again in 1979–80," which he attributes to the U.S. monetary expansion of the two preceding years "with important expansionary effects on the money supplies of other countries" as a result of their intervention in the exchange market. These are not the best years to illustrate the effect of monetary expansion with a two-year lag, nor is the wholesale price index the best measure for this purpose. As table 4C-1 shows, the U.S. wholesale price index rose by 13.1 percent in 1973 and by 18.9 percent in 1974. Over these two years, the price of wheat rose by 158 percent and the price of oil rose by 419 percent. The U.S. wholesale price index rose by 12.5 percent in 1979 and by 14.9 percent in 1980. Over these two years, the price of wheat rose by 35 percent and the price of oil rose by 126 percent. The sharp rise in the wholesale price index in these years was due more to developments in Russia and the action taken by members of OPEC than to the growth of M1 in the United States two years earlier.

A better measure of the inflation in the United States is the price deflator of the domestic non-farm-business product. This index rose considerably in 1974–75 and in 1979–81 because of the large increase in wages and the lag in productivity. That is not to imply that the rise in this price deflator and the increase in wages were independent of the expansion of the money supply. U.S. monetary policy has changed in the past two years and the expansion of the money supply has slowed. The average hourly earnings index rose by 6 percent over the twelve months preceding September 1982 and the implicit price deflator of the non-farm-business product rose by 6.9 percent over the year to the second quarter of 1982. Incidentally, the wholesale price index rose by 1.4 percent over the twelve months preceding September 1982, partly because of the recession, but mainly because of the appreciation of the dollar in the exchange market.

I agree with McKinnon that we must take an international view of monetary policy. I cannot agree, however, that the world money supply should be managed by reproducing the effects of the classical gold standard, with the United States accepting huge changes in its monetary base due to intervention by Germany and Japan, to say nothing of the intervention by other countries in the Group of Ten and Switzerland. I do not think that the capital flows of recent years can be explained as flows from countries with a relatively excessive money supply to countries with a relatively deficient money supply. The reason for capital flows is to acquire assets denominated in dollars, not disequilibrium in cash balances. A full response of the money supply to official intervention would result in disruptive changes in the monetary situation.

Managing the world money supply, particularly M1, seems to me a one-dimensional monetary policy on an international scale. I think monetary policy should be concerned, not only with the money supply, but with interest rates and exchange rates as well. I agree that it is necessary to have greater conformity of monetary policy among the large industrial countries, although I would add Britain and France to McKinnon's three in order to include the five currencies that comprise a unit of Special Drawing Rights. We should ask the International Monetary Fund to take the lead in making

Table 4C-1
Changes in Prices and U.S. Hourly Earnings, 1972–1981

	Percent change from previous year									
	1972	1973	1974	1975	1976	1977	1978	1979	1980	1981
Wholesale prices, United States	4.5	13.1	18.9	9.2	4.6	6.1	7.8	12.5	14.9	9.0
Wholesale prices, world	4.1	12.9	31.9	7.5	6.6	6.6	5.6	11.1	13.5	8.7
Price of wheat, United States	13.1	100.5	28.6	−17.1	−10.8	−22.4	23.8	25.3	7.8	1.3
Price of oil, Saudi Arabia	15.2	42.1	261.5	9.8	7.4	7.7	2.4	33.6	68.9	13.4
Non-farm-business deflator[a]	3.0	3.8	9.7	9.9	5.0	5.8	7.0	8.6	10.1	9.6
Hourly earnings index[a]	6.2	6.2	8.0	8.4	7.2	7.6	8.1	8.0	9.0	9.1

Source: *International Financial Statistics*, various issues.

[a]Both the deflator of the gross domestic non-farm-business product (from Bureau of Economic Analysis) and the hourly earnings index, which reflect total private nonagricultural payroll employment, have been adjusted to eliminate the effect of shifts in the proportion of employees in high-wage and low-wage industries and of over-time pay in manufacturing (from Bureau of Labor Statistics).

the present system of floating rates work better before attempting to devise a new international monetary system.

References

Bagehot, Walter. 1876. *Lombard street: A description of the money market.* New York: Scribner, Armstrong & Co.

Keynes, John Maynard. 1923. *A tract on monetary reform.* London: Macmillan and Co.

Comment

Jacob A. Frenkel

Ronald McKinnon's paper is highly innovative and, like many original contributions, it is unsurprisingly controversial. I believe that he draws an important distinction between closed- and open-economy perspectives for the analysis of macroeconomic theory and for the design of macroeconomic policy, and I agree with his overall recommendation that both theory and policy could be improved by the adoption of the open-economy perspective. My comments deal with some of the conceptual issues that he raises as well as with his policy recommendations.

One of McKinnon's important claims is that U.S. inflation can be explained better in terms of the world money supply that in terms of the domestic U.S. money supply. The implication of this observation is that policies that are designed to control U.S. inflation should attempt to control the world money supply. McKinnon goes on to assert that the evolution of the world money supply can account for the international business cycle and that the proper policy should aim at harmonizing the monetary policies of the major industrial economies, principally Germany, Japan, and the United States. Although I am sympathetic to the notion that global policies are responsible for the evolution of the world economy, I find the emphasis on monetary policy a bit excessive. Specifically, the business cycle of the 1970s is explained more by real than by monetary shocks. Because the origins of the business cycle include important real factors, the questions to be considered are: How much can harmonized monetary policies do? And what role should fiscal policies play in this context?

In McKinnon's framework, one of the important policy variables is the world money supply. It is critical, therefore, to define this central variable very carefully. McKinnon uses great care in defining the index of the world money supply, but I confess that I still have significant conceptual difficulties in dealing with such an index when exchange rates are flexible. Specifically, although the meaning and the theory of the composite index of the world money supply are perfectly clear when the relative prices (exchange rates) among the various national moneys are fixed, the meaning of such a composite index is less clear when the relative prices (the exchange rates) among the components of the composite index are variable.

One piece of the interesting evidence that is presented by McKinnon is the high correlation among changes in the various countries' money-growth rates during the 1970s. In interpreting this fact, he suggests that the correlation reflects the weakening of the dollar's role as international money, a weakening that induced an increased variance of the growth rate of the weighted world money supply. According to an alternative hypothesis, however, the high correlation need not reflect the characteristics of the international monetary system but rather the nature of the shocks and the resulting policies of individual countries. Thus, because the most prominent shock during the 1970s was the oil shock, which was common to most countries in McKinnon's sample, it is not unlikely that these countries, facing the common external real shock, attempted to defend themselves by following similar monetary policies, which resulted, in turn, in the measured ex post facto correlations.

Observing the pattern of correlations, McKinnon proposes that the Federal Reserve alter its orientation from looking only at domestic statistics toward looking also at foreign data. In evaluating this general policy prescription, one needs to be aware that the reaction of foreign policymakers, which is reflected in the ex post facto correlations, was based on their knowledge that the Federal Reserve's policy is based mainly on the value of domestic data. It is not clear that, once the Federal Reserve shifts its orientation, foreign-policy behavior will remain intact. This problem is characteristic to policy recommendations that are based on past reduced-form relations rather than on structural parameters.

I turn next to the recommendation that the monetary policies of Japan, Germany, and the United States should be harmonized. McKinnon's criterion for the choice of these major countries was their ability to control the world money supply and thereby the world price level and maybe also the world real economic activity. One of the questions that might be asked, however, is whether these countries also satisfy the various criteria for the formation of a currency area, because, as is well known, economies that join a currency area need to coordinate their monetary policies, while economies that do not belong to that currency area need not coordinate their policies.

Another question concerning harmonization is whether it is realistic to presume that these countries are likely to harmonize their monetary policies. Put differently, even if such harmonization were desirable from the viewpoint of the world, is it likely to be adopted? When considering this question, it is instructive to recall John Stuart Mill's analysis in his *Principles of Political Economy,* written more than a century ago. In that book, he regretfully concluded:

So much barbarism, however, still remains in the transactions of the most civilized nations, that almost all independent countries choose to assert their nationality by having, to their own inconvenience and that of their neighbors, a peculiar currency of their own.[1]

In predicting the future course of events, Mill believed that, eventually, the international monetary system would evolve into a unified currency area, a process that would be brought about by, what he termed, "the progress of political improvement."

Mill's prediction clearly has been refuted by the actual trend of events. This outcome may be regretable, but it is typical of government policies. As a general rule, governments tend to discount the future heavily, because their time horizon is relatively short. Consequently, faced with a conflict between internal and external targets, elected officials (who wish to be reelected) typically will sacrifice external obligations to domestic goals by renouncing previous commitments to the international rules of the game. Because such a breakdown of those rules could be very costly from the global viewpoint, it is extremely important that the design of policy does not depend in critical ways on harmonized policies, given that such harmonization may not be sustainable.

I believe that McKinnon makes his most important contribution with regard to the more general issue of the role of international considerations in the design of domestic monetary policy. His prescription recognizes that, in an interdependent world, it is clearly suboptimal to ignore external considerations. It further recognizes that, even if the exchange rates are flexible, the international mobility of capital does not enable complete insulation from foreign shocks. Recognizing the interdependence of the world economy, McKinnon proposes a monetary rule by which the Federal Reserve would alter the monetary growth rate according to whether the dollar is unusually strong or unusually weak in the foreign-exchange markets. According to McKinnon, "the discretionary powers of the monetary authorities should be limited without strait-jacketing them with technically infeasible operating procedures." McKinnon argues that these discretionary powers can be implemented whenever the exchange rate is out of line. The considerations that would trigger a modification of the course of domestic monetary policy would stem from the *external* sector.

It is of interest to compare McKinnon's criterion for discretionary policies with the criterion established by the Committee on Financial Distress, which examined the financial crisis in Britain during 1847. That crisis occurred against the background of the famous Peel's Act of 1844, according to which monetary policy had almost no discretionary powers because note issue required, at the margin, 100 percent gold reserves. The financial crisis of 1847 resulted in a severe crisis of confidence of internal convertibility of deposits into notes. To alleviate the crisis and to restore confidence, the Bank of England had to suspend Peel's Act. Subsequently, the Committee of Inquiry decided to modify the rule and concluded:

The Committee are of opinion, that the Principle on which the Act of 1844 should be amended is the Introduction of a discretionary relaxing Power;

such Power, in whomsoever vested, to be exercised only during the Existence of a favorable Foreign Exchange.[2]

Thus, the recommendation also linked fiat issue and the state of the foreign-exchange market, but, in contrast with McKinnon's rule, the amendment to Peel's Act introduced discretionary powers in order to restore internal financial confidence rather than to restore external imbalances. Therefore, when the exchange rates were not favorable, the amendment did not allow for discretionary policy.[3]

As for McKinnon's rule, I see no difficulty in linking the rate of monetary growth to the conditions in the foreign-exchange markets if the main shocks to the system are of a monetary origin. If, however, the shocks are of real origin, then we may observe variations in nominal and real exchange rates that reflect fiscal imbalances, and, under such circumstances, it is not clear that the proper policies would link the rate of monetary growth to the state of the exchange rate.

I wish to conclude with a final remark on implementation. The success of a new program and a new monetary arrangement depends on the adoption of a consistent set of policy tools and on a reasonable understanding of the implications of each course of action. It might be very costly to experiment with a new system just to learn how it works. In these matters, the cost of delaying the adoption of a new international monetary arrangement until its full implications are understood is likely to be small relative to the cost of a premature implementation. McKinnon's proposal is very attractive. However, because it is so novel and unconventional, prudence is clearly called for. More discussions and critical evaluations would be highly desirable. In view of the controversy that this proposal has already stirred, it is worthwhile to conclude by recalling John Maynard Keynes's remarks in his closing speech to the Bretton Woods Conference:

> I am greatly encouraged, I confess, by the critical, skeptical and even carping spirit in which our proceedings have been watched and welcomed in the outside world. How much better that our projects should *begin* in disillusion than that they should *end* in it.[4]

Notes

1. John Stuart Mill, Principles of Political Economy, (Boston: Little, Brown & Co., 1848).

2 .T.E. Gregory, ed., *Select Statutes Documents, Reports Relating to British Banking, 1832-1928,* vol. II (London: Oxford University Press, 1929), 40.

3. For further discussion of the 1847 crisis and Peel's Act, see Rudiger Dornbusch and Jacob A. Frenkel, "The Gold Standard and the Bank of England During the Crisis of 1847," in *A Retrospective on the Classical Gold Standard, 1821-1931,* ed. Michael Bordo and Anna Schwartz (Chicago: University of Chicago Press, forthcoming).

4. R.F. Harrod, *The Life of John Maynard Keynes* (New York: Augustus M. Kelley Publishers, 1969), 583.

5 The Potential for Financial Crises

Hyman P. Minsky

The topic of this chapter, the potential for financial crises, could suggest either a discussion of the current (late 1982) status of world economies or an analysis of the determinants of the potential for crises. The former interpretation of the topic would lead to a review of the current weak spots in the national (U.S.) and international economy, whereas the latter would require an examination of what there is about capitalist economies that makes an embryonic financial crisis occur with some regularity and how such embryos may be aborted. Therefore, the topic is two sided and provides the option of choosing one side over the other. What follows will lean toward the development of a theory of financial crises in an open economy with the institutional structure that now rules. However, this exercise in theory will be related to stylized facts about world economies in this epoch.

First, the chapter will examine the determinants of the potential for financial crises within a closed economy that has institutional features (such as the United States's). At this stage of the discussion, financial instruments that cross national lines will be ignored. However, the chapter will go on to include international financial connections. This initial emphasis on a closed United States makes sense, even in the context of an argument that looks toward an examination of the stability of the international financial structure, because the U.S. dollar is the dominant currency of denomination for international debts.

Stylized Facts about Financial Crises

To develop a theory to explain the potential for financial crises and why the potential may not lead to a realized crisis, we need to agree on what has to be explained. What we have to explain is the emergence of intermittant threats of financial crises since the mid-1960s, after a lengthy period in which such threats did not occur.

Since the middle 1960s, we have experienced the following embryonic financial crises:

1. The credit crunch of 1966.

2. The Penn Central/Commercial Paper liquidity squeeze of 1969-70.
3. The Franklin National/Commercial Bank Real Estate Investment Trust (REITs) debacles of 1974-75.
4. The summer and autumn of 1982, with continuing perils of the savings and loan associations (the thrifts), the drama in Mexico, problems of domestic banking (of which Penn Square is a dramatic example), and widespread deterioration of corporate financial strength.

Each episode is associated with (1) the Federal Reserve fighting inflation by taking steps to constrain monetary growth; (2) financial innovations that, for a time, offset the impact on the flows of credit of the Federal Reserve's acts aimed to constrain inflation; (3) a threatened financial crisis; and (4) the Federal Reserve's intervention (as a lender of last resort) to abort the embryonic financial crisis.

The first twenty years after World War II were an era of financial tranquility and economic expansion. During these years, the Federal Reserve (and other central banks) did not need to intervene as a lender of last resort. Since 1966, a pattern has developed in which accelerating inflation has led to the Federal Reserve's efforts to constrain growth of the money supply. This has resulted in a credit crunch, liquidity squeeze, financial debacle or the like, that is, a breakdown of financing and refinancing through normal channels has either taken place or has appeared to be imminent. This, in turn, has led the Federal Reserve to intervene as a lender of last resort by either refinancing endangered units on concessionary terms or announcing that such refinancing is available. In as much as the breakdown of market refinancing has taken place because high interest rates weakened financial structures, the Federal Reserves has accompanied its spot interventions to refinance particular organizations with general market interventions that increased the availability of credit through ordinary financing channels. In the aftermath of a crisis, the Federal Reserve has abandoned monetary constraint and shifted to accommodating market needs.

An apparent change in the economy's behavior took place in the mid-1960s, a change that was related to changes in underlying financial relations. These underlying conditions, which determine whether financial tranquility (such as ruled between 1946 and 1965 or so) or financial turbulence (such as has ruled since 1966) dominates, are the cash-flow commitments in the debt structure.

U.S. economic history since 1966 can be represented by a six-stage cycle: (1) accelerating inflation, (2) monetary fiscal constraint leading to a financial crisis, (3) a sharp downturn, (4) intervention, (5) a bottoming out, and (6) recovery.[1] The liability structures that are conducive to the periodic emergence of a financial crisis still exist and the capacity to innovate in finance, which makes for inflationary expansions, is still in place.[2] It must be emphasized that the prerequisites for cycles with crises are in place.

There is a coincidence in time that is really not a coincidence, once financial relations are integrated into the theory of system behavior. Since 1966, stagflation as well as financial and economic turbulence have characterized the economy's performance. The inflation has been fueled, in good part, by financial innovations. The climate for such innovation has been favorable partly because the lender-of-last-resort interventions by the Federal Reserve have effectively contained the downside systemic risks from exposed financial positions. A dilemma for Federal Reserve policymakers has been to effectively increase the downside risk from financial adventuring without simultaneously risking the triggering of a serious or even a runaway systemic debt deflation.

Robust and Fragile Financial Structures

Our economy is a capital-using capitalist economy with a complex and evolving financial structure. Because of this, there are two sets of interrelated linkages among our yesterdays, today, and tomorrows. One set is the relations among the capital stock, investment, and profits; the second set is the commitments stated in the outstanding financial instruments and those being created. Linkages between the two sets of interrelations are found in the way financial instruments finance investment spending and affect asset prices and in the relationship between business profits and the validation of business debts.[3]

We also have an evolving structure of financial institutions that sit between and among households, businesses, government units, and other financial institutions and that borrow, endorse, lend, and invest to the linkages in production and finance. Considered as a whole, then, what we have are a financial structure and financing activity that are essential determinants of the performance of the economy. In our economy, only that which is financed takes place; the level of employment is what it is because only so much demand for labor has been financed.

If we ask why the financed demand for labor falls short of the full-employment level, the answer is that bankers and businesspersons do not visualize sufficient profit opportunities in the economy to warrant financing any greater demand for labor. The question of the economy's ability to provide full employment comes down to the existence, in the projections that guide businesspersons and bankers, of sufficient profitable investment opportunities to generate full employment. The profitable investment opportunities need to be viable at available and anticipated financing terms.

Financing contracts were entered upon in the past, and these past contracts determine the payments that have to be made today. The payment commitments falling due today are on account of both principal and interest. The funds to fulfill these commitments can be obtained by (1) cash on hand or the sale of superfluous assets, (2) gross profit flows, and (3) issuing new debts (that is, refinancing).

The key relations in a similarly sophisticated system are between gross profit flows and maturing cash-payment commitments over a relevant (short) time period. It is useful to distinguish three cases. If gross profit flows (defined as gross capital income net of taxes on income) exceed maturing cash-payment commitments, then in the terminology being used here, the unit is a "hedge" financing unit. If gross profit flows fall short of maturing cash-payment commitment, but the interest portion of the cash-payment commitments are equal to or less than the nondepreciation part of the gross profit flows, then the unit is a "speculative" unit. If the gross profit flows fall short of the maturing cash payments and the interest due exceeds the net-income part of gross profits, then the unit is a "Ponzi" unit. Whereas speculative units roll over their debt, Ponzi units both roll over the principal of maturing principal and capitalize at least part of the interest that is due.[4]

If a unit is a hedge unit, then the relations between cash flow and cash-payment commitments on account of debt can deteriorate only if the relation between cash flow and gross profits deteriorates. If a unit is a speculative unit, then its financial position can deteriorate either because interest rates rise or because gross profits deteriorate. If a unit is a Ponzi unit, then its financial position can deteriorate because interest rates rise, gross profits deteriorate, or the capitalization of interest leads to a sufficient deterioration in the margin of safety provided by equity so that the unit's credit worthiness evaporates.

It is clear that the overall robustness or fragility of the financial structure—when robustness or fragility reflects the magnitude of the cash-flow shortfalls or interest-rate changes that can be adsorbed without causing a rupture in financing channels—depends on the mix of hedge, speculative, and Ponzi units. The aggregate debt/profit flows of business, the mix of short- and long-term debts, the holding of cash and liquid assets relative to debts, and the trend of interest rates show that the weight of speculative and Ponzi finance has increased since World War II. In addition to the evidence from corporate and household finance, nonperforming loans at financial institutions and the high cost of funds to the thrifts have made many banks and thrifts Ponzi-financing organizations. The growth of the commercial-paper market and the shutting down of the new-issue market for long-term bonds by interest-rate peaks imply a systemic shift toward speculative finance. Market evolution provides evidence that a shift toward fragility in financial markets has taken place.[5]

The data on financial institutions that stand between business as debtors and households as asset owners show that there has been an increase in intermediate layering (REITs, money-market mutuals, futures and options markets). One of the important changes has been the decreasing weight of core (demand and passbook-savings) deposits relative to bought money in banks and thrift institutions. This implies that the vulnerability of financial institutions to money-market changes has increased. Furthermore, the leverage on equity of major financial institutions has increased even as the apparent need for equity has risen because of the greater volatility of interest rates and the increased exposure to intermittent losses of liquidity. The implicit dependence of financial institutions on supportive behavior from the central bank has increased as their equity ratio has decreased.

We have ignored households in this quick survey of the determinants of the robustness or fragility of the financial structure, even though a not insignificant proportion of households are now vulnerable to a deflation of asset values. Ignoring households is appropriate because, on the whole, household fragility rests on the sensitivity of households to a decline in income, rather than to adverse financial-market developments.

The significant difference between hedge financial units and speculative and Ponzi financial units is that the viability of a hedge unit—that is, its ability to meet financial commitments—will not be directly affected by financial-market developments that lead to run ups of interest rates, whereas the viability of speculative and Ponzi units will be so affected. For hedge units, a run up of short- and long-term interest rates can affect only the expenditures (if any) that involve debt financing, whereas for speculative and Ponzi units, a run up of interest rate affects the ability of such units to fulfill payment commitments. The cash flow on debts for speculative and Ponzi units can rise relative to the cash receipts on account of assets because of financial-market developments.

The Determinants of the Position and the Shape of the Demand for Financing (and Refinancing)

One characteristic of the financial crises of the turbulent era that began in the mid-sixties is the peaks of both short- and long-term interest rates. These peaks occurred even though, at times, the supply of finance, from the evolving institutional structure as well as from the banking system, increased rapidly. As everyone knows, an economist has been taught to say supply and demand in response to any question, so the analysis of any price is reduced to the study of the behavior of supply and demand in markets. Thus, to explain interest-rate peaks, we have to examine the demand and supply for the financing and refinancing of positions and activity.

Demand for financing had to have been shifting outward and have been inelastic with respect to interest rates for the observed explosion of interest rates to have occurred. Because current-market demand for financing is a summation of various demands, the behavior of market demand depends upon the behavior of particular demands. Among the component demands for financing are the demands because of: (1) ongoing investment, (2) current losses, (3) the rolling over of maturing debt (refinancing speculative positions), and (4) capitalization of interest (Ponzi finance). Since World War II, the weight of these components in the aggregate demand for finance has changed as the structure of business liabilities has changed. A rise in the weight of short-term debt financing in total financing has increased the weight of items 2, 3, and 4 in determining the demand for financing. Furthermore, changes in the composition of the demand for financing, between long- and short-term financing, has occurred. The peaks in long- and short-term interest rates in the financing cycles since 1966 have been accompanied by a decrease in new issues of long-term private debt. During the recessions that followed the various credit crunches, the volume of private long-term debt that was issued increased very rapidly, exceeding the current pace of external financing of investment. As a result of these shifts, the liability structure of business has deteriorated by more than the current demand for financing indicated during high interest-rate periods and has improved by more than the flow of internal funding indicated during the lower interest-rate periods that followed the credit crunches.[6]

The contribution of the components of the demand for financing to the total demand depends on the liability structure. The relative significance of the components has varied over the postwar era. The particular financial problems of the 1980s will center around the impact of debt burdens and the increase in speculative and Ponzi finance in liability structures on the economic system. Each of these components will be examined separately.

Investment Programs as Payment Commitments

The creation of capital assets is a time-consuming process, especially because technology has evolved so that expensive special-purpose plant and equipment is a large proportion of investment. Each step in an investment program involves costs—not only on the site of the prospective plant but also for the inputs manufactured off the site. These costs have to be financed. Some of the finance comes from external sources. An investment boom is accompanied by a demand for finance. The total demand for finance due to investment increases even after new starts decrease.

The putting together of investment outputs is a sequential process. Each step in the process involves interest-inelastic demands for finance. Furthermore, the total amount tied up in financing investment increases as an investment boom matures, because of new expenses and the compounding of interest on prior debt-financed expenses. Demand for finance because of investment in process is inelastic with respect to current short-term interest rates.

The financing of investment can be visualized as a two-step process, in which short-term borrowings are used to finance investment in process and internal funds and longer-term debts are used to finance the holding of the capital assets that result from investment. (This generalizes the relationship between construction financing and take-out financing in the construction industry.) If an investment boom is associated with high and rising short- and long-term interest rates, the borrowers' reluctance to fix high interest rates into their payment commitments and the lenders' reluctance to take long positions in the light of the capital losses they experience as interest rates rise lead to a decrease in the funding of short-term debt into long-term debt. Thus, the component of demand for financing in short-term markets due to investment will be both increasing and inelastic. An implication of an investment boom for financial markets is that any shortfall of the rate of increase of available short-term financing below the accumulating demand for financing because of investment will lead to sharp increases in interest rates. Such a shortfall can occur either because an inflationary expansion leads to the demand for financing outrunning a growing supply of finance or because the central bank constrains the rate of growth of bank reserves.[7]

The Cost of Corporate Bureaucracy as a Financial (Payment) Commitment

A shortfall of business receipts relative to costs leads to a need to borrow or sell assets to acquire cash to meet payments. Recent examples include firms that made enormous losses even though they were not initially burdened with debt. The necessary payments on investment are not the only income-related payments that are not readily adjustable as output and sales revenue decrease.

Myron J. Gordon recently examined the cost of corporate bureaucracy over the postwar period.[8] Although issue can be taken with some details of Gordon's analysis, his data indicate that the cost of corporate bureaucracy as a ratio to the nominal value of output has risen from 14.6 percent in 1942 and 13.2 percent in 1950 to 26.5 percent in 1972 and 26.2 percent in 1977.[9]

In the United States, management is able to lay off blue-collar workers and decrease the inflow of purchased materials quite rapidly when sales decrease. Management, however, does not shrink (or increase) corporate bureaucracy with every change in sales proceeds. In fact, some dimensions (sales efforts, advertising, and product development) of what the corporate bureaucracy does seem to react perversely in response to a drop in sales that is deemed transitory. The multimillion-dollar losses that lightly indebted corporations have experienced are due mainly to a decline in sales receipts, because the payroll and purchased services that are not directly due to the production of output do not decrease. For a firm, costs due to corporate bureaucracy and business style are determinants of the potential for large-scale losses. With large-scale losses, a quick deterioration of the liability structure may occur; that is, debts, especially short-term debts, can rise rapidly. In the aggregate, the greater the proportion of costs that are not readily adjustable downward, the greater the likelihood that a systematic deterioration in financial positions will occur when sales decline. Business style, which is reflected in the cost of corporate bureaucracy, can lead to rising and interest-inelastic demands for short-term financing when sales fall.

The Impact of Liability Structures

The roll-over demand for financing due to maturing debts for speculative and Ponzi financial units constitutes an inelastic demand for short-term finance. The net interest that is capitalized by Ponzi financing units constitutes a rising and interest-inelastic demand for finance. This net-interest component of the demand for financing is perverse, inasmuch as higher interest rates increase the need for such financing. A rise in interest rates will increase the demand for financing due to speculative and Ponzi liability structures so that a further rise in demand, which implies a further rise in interest rates, will take place.

Ongoing investment projects are financed by a mixture of internal funds and borrowings. Whereas unfavorable financing conditions affect current decisions to start investment programs, they do not affect investment programs that are under way, unless they force the abandonment or delay of projects into which costs have been sunk. Inasmuch as investment programs are financed by a combination of internal and external funds, if units that are part of investment programs are also speculative or Ponzi financing units, then a run up of interest rates will lead to a decrease in the availability of internal funds to finance ongoing investment programs; this will lead to a rise in the external financing required by investing units. The higher the interest rates, the greater upward shift in the demand for financing.

Losses due to business style or corporate overhead lead to an inelastic demand for finance. Such losses occur when sales revenues fall. A decline in sales revenue leads to an interest-inelastic and -rising component in the demand for financing.

It is the existence of inelastic and upward-shifting demands for finance that can transform a decrease in the rate of increase of financing available through banks, which the Federal Reserve can induce, into a sharp run up of interest rates. Volatility of interest rates depends on the mix of liability structures, the pace of ongoing investment activity, and the potential for an explosive increase in business losses when sales revenues decrease.

The extent to which interest rates are volatile depends on the mix of hedge, speculative, and Ponzi financing. The mix of hedge, speculative, and Ponzi financing depends on voluntary decisions and the volatility of interest rates, especially their volatility in response to monetary constraints. This is so because the mix of financial structures determines the extent to which there are borrowers who cannot reduce their demand for credit as interest rates rise and because high and rising rates that shut down the long market cause units that prefer hedge financing to be speculative and speculative financing units to be Ponzi, even as Ponzi units exhaust their capacity to borrow. Once the ability to borrow is exhausted, then nonperforming loans on the books of a financial organization grow rapidly. Nonperforming loans shift the affected financial organizations toward the Ponzi end of their financing spectrum. Unless government or central-bank intervention (such as deposit insurance) occurs, nonperforming assets lead to refinancing crises for financial institutions.

The structure of financial relations in the 1950s was such that an initial rise in financing terms (caused by an increase in the demand for or a fall in the supply of financing) did not lead to further increases in the demand for financing. In other words, the system of financial relations was not conducive to instability.

In recent years, the structure of financial relations has been such that an increase in the demand for financing and a rise in financing terms are likely to lead to further increases in the demand for financing and further rises in financing terms; the system has become unstable. In the structure that ruled in the 1950s, movements were damped out; in the structure that now rules, movements tend to feed upon themselves until barriers, such as are exemplified by refinancing crises and threats of widespread default, are reached. The reaction by governments and central banks at the barrier determines what follows; these reactions are policy reactions.

Sometime between the 1950s and today, the financial structure passed an imprecisely demarcated border between a structure in which initial deviations were offset and damped out and a structure in which initial deviations are amplified. Hindsight enables us to place the time at which the border was passed in the mid-1960s.

Lender-of-Last-Resort Interventions

With Ponzi financing, the margin of safety provided to lenders by equity decreases; furthermore, with high and rising interest rates, the capitalization of interest becomes an open-ended sink of lender's funds. The ability of private lenders to carry Ponzi units is limited. Furthermore, because lenders buy their funds on markets, they are vulnerable to runs. Deposit insurance protects eligible deposits in banks, but banks have become increasingly dependent on funds that exceed the insured limits or that, although insured, yield market-determined rates. When the asset structure is heavily weighted with nonperforming or concessionary loans, either runs or interest-rate premium on liabilities result. As financial positions in general begin to deteriorate, a small rise in interest rates above market will push some particular set of financial institutions, whose equity or profitability has been largely compromised, into acknowledged liquidity or equity shortfall. For such institutions, the ordinary channels for refinancing and placing new debts are closed.

In these circumstances, the Federal Reserve or central bank (and deposit-insurance organizations are best considered as part of the central bank) is confronted with a choice of letting liability holders suffer losses or of refinancing the threatened institution on concessionary terms (that is, below market rates). Presumably, the Federal Reserve's decision is based on whether the problem is systemic or special. If it is special, the Federal Reserve is supposed to stand aside and allow the individual unit and its uninsured creditors to take their losses; if the problem is systemic, the Federal Reserve is supposed to intervene. The decision is a judgment call.

Intervention as a lender of last resort by a central bank has three aspects:

1. Refinancing of threatened units.
2. Fixing money markets so that financing terms ease for all units.
3. Setting regulations and proposing legislation that imposes serious barriers to financial developments deemed disruptive so that they will not occur again.

The financial crises that have occurred since 1966 have not led to a debt deflation because the Federal Reserve and cooperating agencies (Federal Deposit Insurance Corporation (FDIC), major banks, etc.) have intervened as a lender of last resort to refinance threatened organizations and to ease general financing conditions. However, the embryonic crises have led to declines in investment and, therefore, to prospective declines in profits. In the postwar era, the prospective decline in profits has not been fully realized because the effect of investment on profits has been offset by government deficits.

Profit Flows: The Other Side of
Liability Structures

A liability structure of any date can be separated into dated, demand, and contingent payment commitments. The dated and demand commitments can be transformed into a time series of payment commitments. Offsetting these payment commitments are sources of cash. These sources are cash on hand, profit flows (the profit concept has to be made precise), and the sale of assets or new borrowing.

Inasmuch as the price that can be obtained by selling capital assets depends on the profits these assets are expected to yield and borrowing ability depends on expected future profits, the ability to pay debts depends on cash on hand, current profits and expected future profits. The renewable or roll-over part of the ability to pay debts is determined by profit flows, and the synchronization of profit flows with payment commitment determines where an economy is positioned on the hedge, speculative, and Ponzi axes. What determines profit flows is the question to be addressed now.

Profits are earned by capital assets, not because they are productive but because they are scarce. This is a paraphrase of a view central to Keynes's theory. It is demand relative to productive capacity that makes business profitable and capital assets valuable. Steel and automobile plants and airlines would be more profitable now (in 1982) if the financed demand for their outputs were such that they were producing at or close to capacity levels. It is insufficient demand for output that has led to the low profits of industry. Supply-side economics fails because investment does not take place unless it is deemed profitable, and the profitability that guides investment depends on expected future demands as well as on the anticipated tax laws and financing situation.

What determines the scarcity, that is, the profitability, of capital assets? Here Keynes and Kalecki, rather than neoclassical theorists, are helpful.[10] Neoclassical theory tells us that capital's income is the marginal productivity of capital multiplied by the stock of capital. As every economist who has ever understood Joan Robinson knows, the concept of capital in neoclassical theory is obscure and hazy. The neoclassical synthesis makes sense only if the economy is assumed to be in equilibrium yesterday, today, and tomorrow.[11]

Thus, neoclassical theory does not deal with the shifting aggregate profitability of business. However, the Kalecki view does deal with this. In the Kalecki view, under strict limiting assumptions, gross capital income (profits, for short) equals investment. Under looser assumptions, profits equals investment plus the government deficit; and, under quite general conditions, profits equals investment plus the government deficit plus the balance of trade surplus plus consumption financed by profit income minus savings financed by wage income.[12]

These Kalecki equations reflect quite simple ideas: for example, that workers who produce investment goods have to eat. The output of consumer goods has to be allocated by price among the workers who produce consumer goods and those who produce investment goods. This implies that there will be an aggregate mark up on labor costs in the sales proceeds of consumption producers equal to the wage bill in investment-goods production. The Kalecki equations also reflect a well-known phrase: workers (in consumption-goods production) cannot buy back what they produce.

The validation of business liability structures—that is, the fulfillment of expectations about both the ability to meet payment commitments and the ability to refinance (fund or roll over) debts—depends on current and expected profit flows. If the economy has no government sector or a small government sector, the potential for a profit-sustaining government deficit is small. If we ignore the looser or more realistic Kalecki profit equations, a decline in investment leads to a fall in profits.

In a no-government or small-government capitalism, wherein the consumption coefficient out of profits is zero, the savings coefficient out of wages is zero, and international trade is small (this roughly conforms to the U.S. economy in the 1920s), a fall in investment leads to an equivalent fall in profits. However, profit flows are allocated by the liability structure and dividend conventions to debt validation, dividends, and retained earnings. In a system with momentum, dividends are maintained so a shortfall of profits results mainly in a squeeze on retained earnings. If the system is highly indebted, with debt coverage deteriorating, the planned leverage on retained earnings in the financing of new investment programs will decrease. As a result, with a lag, investment activity will decrease, and then profits also will decrease. Deteriorating financial coverages will lead to increasing roll over and new external debt; the burden of outstanding debt, that is, the ratio of debt-servicing charges to cash flows, will increase. This is a broad-brush characterization of one aspect to the interactions that lead to a deep depression.

However, if government is big—so that the potential for a large government deficit is built into the economy—then a deterioration of profits need not occur when investment declines. The automatic stabilizers built into the tax and spending programs as well as discretionary fiscal-policy actions along orthodox Keynesian lines can sustain and even increase profit flows during a recession. The burden of the debt does not rise because a decrease of investment does not lead to a profit decline when an offsetting increase in the deficit sustains profits.

The viability of business liability structures depends on the behavior of the determinants of the flow of profits. If the reaction of the flow of profits to a run up of the carrying costs on debts and mounting debts is such that profits decline, then initial problems in validating debts will lead to a cascade of problems. However, big government and the deficits it can generate provide support for profits when investment declines. The ability to contain and control financial crises is due to the stability of profits, in the face of the financing problems that lead to lender-of-last-resort interventions, and the stability of profits reflects the offsetting effect that big government has on profits.

Financial Relations of an Open Economy

For the first twenty years after 1946, financial stability and economic expansion in the United States were sufficient to assure the stability of the international financial and monetary system. This was so because of three factors:

1. The U.S. economy was open and able to maintain a close approximation of full employment in spite of rising imports. Sustained U.S. demand assured markets for the rest of the world and made for favorable profits in the export-surplus economies.
2. The U.S. financial system was robust in the sense that overall private indebtedness was low, indicating that the speculative and Ponzi components of the financial structure were of minor importance. This robustness meant that the interest-rate response to monetary constraint was not unstable, so that explosively high interest rates did not occur. Instead, moderate interest rates were the rule.
3. The rest of the world had a relatively low level of international indebtedness. Only a small portion of export earnings went to debt servicing. Furthermore, any shortfall of revenues to finance debt servicing or imports was offset by additions to debt.

Today, each of these factors has changed. For almost a decade, the U.S. economy has not been able to achieve the low rates of unemployment that characterized the 1950s and 1960s. Twice in the past decade, the U.S. financial system has experienced serious threats to its stability. Financing charges on the external debts of many countries are now a large ratio to exports; this means that for these countries the usual bundle of imports can be financed only if much of the interest due is capitalized.

Analysis of international financial relations discloses that large external debts now rule for much of the world; these debts are, to a large extent, to banks; and the debts are, to a large extent, denominated in dollars. For some of the bank debts denominated in dollars, neither the debtors, the banks, nor the owners of the bank's liabilities are U.S. citizens.

Banks manage their books so as to avoid open positions. If a bank has dollar liabilities, it aims to have dollar assets; however, the dollar assets of banks include dollar-denominated debts of businesses and governments that earn their income or collect taxes in a currency other than the dollar. The owners of capital assets that will be used to earn profits in, say, pesos may have dollar-denominated debts. Similarly, taxes are collected in local currencies, and the servicing of government debts may call for dollars. Even though bankers do not have open positions, their debtors do. The cash-flow commitments by such debtors to banks can be fulfilled only if their profits and taxes in the local currency can be transformed into dollars at favorable terms.

In a closed economy, if liability structures impose payment commitment that are too great for profits flows, then, in the aggregate, the situation can be resolved by a combination of government deficits and central-bank interventions to refinance defaulting institutions. However, in an open economy, such interventions by a local central bank and treasury cannot assure adequate profit flows and refinancing in the foreign currency in which debts are denominated. Only the Federal Reserve can refinance dollar debts without limit, and only the U.S. Treasury can sustain dollar profits by its deficit.

Today, the main problem with the international financial structure is that a great deal of debt is denominated in dollars. It takes dollars to validate dollar debts. The sources of dollars to units outside the United States, however, are existing dollar balances, the trading balance, and additional loans and investments by holders of dollars.

The existing dollar balance of the critical debtors are low relative to their overall debt positions, so the existing holdings are not a meaningful source of dollars. International investments and loans depend on the perceived prospects of payments, which mean that they reflect expectations of future dollar earnings. The ability to borrow dollars depends on the lender's belief that the dollars will be repaid—that is, that the borrower will earn dollars. A combination of current and expected deficits in the U.S. balance of trade is necessary if current debts are to be serviced by a combination of dollar surpluses on trade account and new loans denominated in dollars.

The balance of payments of a country can be conceived as consisting of four tiers.[13]

Tier I: The current balance of trade.

Tier II: Tier I plus interest and dividends on financial assets.

Tier III: Tier II plus capital movements (loans).

Tier IV: Tier III plus equilibrating flows of international monetary reserves (dollars).

In a world where there is a large amount of international debts denominated in dollars, the willingness of creditors to hold such debts depends on the debtor's being able to earn dollars or to earn something that can be exchanged for dollars: the United States must run a global deficit on tier I.

If the United States were to conform to the pattern of international financial relations that ruled when Britain was dominant, then there would be a U.S. deficit in tier I, a surplus after tier II, and a deficit after tier III (capital exports lead to a deficit).[14] The deficit after tier III would result in an increment in the holdings of the rest of the world in the New York money market; that is, there would be a rise in the rest of the world's liquidity. This final deficit in the U.S. balance of payments would be a desired increase in liquidity; if it were not desired, the holders of money-market assets would be able to reduce the incremental debt component used to finance their long-term capital inputs.

Implications of International Financial Linkages

The existence of a significant body of debts denominated in dollars creates the problem that the international financial system must resolve. The basic open positions in the international economy are of those units—be they governments or businesses—that earn their profits in a local currency and need to make payments in dollars on account of debts. These units need to earn a sufficient income in their domestic currency, and they need to be able to exchange these profits for dollars at an exchange rate that is consistent with the profitability of their business. An immediate implication of the relationship between dollar debt and local currency earnings is that the price of dollars cannot rise significantly faster than the domestic inflation rate allows profits in the local currency to rise. If a depreciating local currency leads to monetary-fiscal policies that depresses activity and, therefore, profits, then the ability of debtors to meet their obligations can be impaired because of the course of aggregate profits. Sustained aggregate profits in the domestic currency plus a dollar that is not appreciating too fast are required if the foreign dollar-denominated indebtedness is to be validated.

For the dollar not to appreciate too rapidly, it is necessary that the supply of dollars on exchange markets equals the demand for dollars due to the sum of trade and financial payments. A creditor country in whose currency debts are denominated needs to run a deficit on trade account. One obstacle to the United States's running a large enough trade-account deficit is that the imports hurt U.S. domestic employment. A trade-account deficit lowers profits in the United States even as it raises profits in the countries with a trade surplus. After the scare of 1978–79, the United States is afraid of the potential for financial instability due to a large-scale balance-of-payments deficit. The distinction between a necessary deficit level and an excessive deficit level has to be drawn—and the measure of the necessary deficit is found in the interest-servicing "nut" that the rest of the world has to make.

The institutional fact that a large part of the dollar-denominated debts are at floating interest rates, together with the present size of international indebtedness, has implications for the operations of monetary policy within the United States. It was argued earlier that, if there are (1) large-scale ongoing investment programs, (2) a large speculative and Ponzi component to the financial structure, and (3) significant and growing nonfinancial corporate overhead costs, rising interest rates will tend to increase rather than decrease the demand for financing. This implies that a program of monetary constraint to contain inflation will lead to explosive interest-rate increases.

The Eurodollar interest rate moves with the U.S. interest rate, because each holder of Eurodollars has the option of investing in domestic U.S. assets. An explosion of U.S. interest rates will lead to a large increase in the dollars needed to service dollar-denominated debt. If the sum of dollar earnings minus the nonfinancial need for dollars is not sufficient to meet debt-servicing charges, then the amount of the current account that needs to be capitalized into debt increases as interest rates increase. That is, international indebtedness denominated in dollars exacerbates the instability of interest rates. If borrowing in order to fulfill financial contracts continues for several years, then there will be a large increase in dollar-denominated debt, even though no acquisition of productive assets will be financed by the additional debt. One side effect of the experiment with monetarist precepts by U.S. authorities has been a sharp increase in the burden of debt for economies that have significant quantities of dollar-denominated debt: Mexico and Brazil, among others, are paying part of the price for the United States's experiment with monetarism.

If the current monetary system is to be viable in that (1) no large volume of international debt repudiation takes place and (2) the international financial and trade system is not repressed by variants of beggar-thy-neighbor policies, then the United States must maintain a large deficit on trade account, even after the trade deficit becomes palatable, because of that close approximation to full employment that exists in the United States. Furthermore, U.S. monetary policy must be sensitive to the level of interest rates. Explosive interest rates (such as those that ruled almost throughout 1979 to 1982) increase the absolute burden of indebtedness of the rest of the world, even when there is no improvement in the capability of the rest of the world to increase net dollar earnings. This implies that Federal Reserve policy must always accommodate markets, which means that monetary policy is available to fuel an expansion but not to constrain an inflation. Inflation must be constrained by other than monetary measures.

The massive indebtedness denominated in dollars that now exists has a special property—that the ultimate owners of much of the international dollar indebtedness are not U.S. citizens. In the nineteenth century, when Britain was the center of the world's financial system, the ultimate holders of pound-denominated debts were, to a large extent, British. Today, U.S. citizens are the holders of dollar-denominated debt to a much lesser extent. Whereas the profits in offshore countries that the British trade deficit engendered became, in good measure, income of British subjects, the profits that a responsible U.S. policy would engender around the world would not, to the same extent, become income of U.S. citizens. This may make the United States less willing and perhaps less able to cope with the unemployment and lower domestic profits that the necessary chronic trade deficit implies. New dimensions in U.S. domestic policy as well as new levels of international understanding are necessary if the current international financial structure is not to lead to a serious crisis.

Although the massive growth of dollar-denominated debts does constrain U.S. policies, these massive debts have given the United States a very large degree of fiscal autonomy. Monetary and fiscal policies to achieve and sustain full employment may be undertaken now without fear that they will trigger a run from the dollar such as seemed imminent in 1979. In particular, the aggregate validation of the international financial structure—that is, the avoidance of an international financial crisis—depends almost exclusively on U.S. policies. An adequate flow of dollars through a deficit on the trade account should avoid a generalized crisis, especially if the Federal Reserve stands ready to offer sufficient dollar accommodations to the central banks of the home countries of banks that have significant dollar-denominated liabilities.

Although the potential for a financial crisis exists, a financial crisis is not inevitable. The avoidance of a crisis depends on the rest of the world's earning sufficient dollars to fulfill their financial commitments. For the United States to tolerate such permanent deficits on trade account, trade deficits must be compatible with the country's first achieving and then sustaining a close approximation to full employment. Any effective action by the United States to close U.S. markets to the rest of the world will only increase the potential for a full-fledged crisis.

Thus, although the international financial situation is serious, it is not hopeless. All that is needed for stability to be sustained is for the United States to devise and put into effect policies that achieve and sustain full employment with relatively stable prices, while accepting a large deficit in its balance of trade and keeping its interest rate high enough so potentially "hot" balances stay invested in dollars. Now that what needs to be achieved has been identified, the next step is to set up a structure that allows what needs to happen, to happen. Putting it into place is, admittedly, more difficult than knowing what needs to be done. As Portia remarked in *The Merchant of Venice,* "If to do were as easy to know as what were good to do, chapels had been churches and poor men's cottages prince's palaces."

Notes

1. Hyman P. Minsky, *Can "It" Happen Again?* (Armonk, N.Y.: M.E. Sharpe and Company, 1982), chapter II, "Finance and Profits." Initially published in joint Economic Committee, Congress of the United States, *The Business Cycle and Public Policy 1929-80* (Washington, D.C.: U.S. Government Printing Office, 1980).

2. Henry Kaufman, *A Difficult Transition* (New York: Salomon Brothers, Inc., 1982). See also Kaufman's *Forces Affecting the Near-Term Financial Behavior* (New York: Salomon Brothers, Inc., 1982).

3. Minsky, *Can "It" Happen Again?*, chapter 10, "An Exposition of a Keynesian Theory of Investment."

4. Minsky, *Can "It" Happen Again?*, 22-33.

5. U.S. Congress, House Committee on Banking, Finance, and Urban Affairs, Subcommittee on Domestic Monetary Policy, *Employment Risks from Present Credit and Business Liquidity Conditions,* 97th Cong., 2d sess. (Washington, D.C.: U.S. Government Printing Office, 1982), see statements by J. Charles Partee, governor, Federal Reserve Board, pp. 81-118.

6. Allen Sinai, "Economic Policy and Business Liquidity," in House Committee on Banking, Finance and Urban Affairs, *Employment Risks,* pp. 91-123.

7. In the past, the constraint on the supply of bank credit would have resulted from an external drain or an internal drain of reserve money. See J. Viner, *Studies in the Theory of International Trade* (New York: Harper and Brothers, 1937), chapters VI and VII.

8. Myron J. Gordon, "Corporate Bureaucracy, Productivity Gain and Distribution of Revenue in U.S. Manufacturing 1947-77," *Journal of Post-Keynesian Economics,* Summer 1982, 483-96.

9. Similar results were reported by P. Sylos-Labini, "Prices and Income Distribution," *Journal of Post-Keynesian Economics,* Fall 1979, 3-24.

10. M. Kalecki, *Essays in the Theory of Economics Fluctuations* (London: Allen and Unwin, 1939).

11. J. Robinson, "The Production Function and the Theory of Capital," *Review of Economic Studies* XXI (1953–54):81–106. See also Robinson's *The Accumulation of Capital* (London: Macmillan, 1956) and G.C. Harcourt, *Some Cambridge Controversies in the Theory of Capital* (Cambridge: Cambridge University Press, 1972).

12. Minsky, *Can "It" Happen Again?*, 37, 38. See also Robert Dixon, "Aggregate Non-Wage Income in the U.S., 1948–1980" (Paper presented at the Annual Meeting, American Economic Association, December 27–30, 1982).

13. Hyman P. Minsky, "Financial Interrelations, the Balance of Payments and the Dollar Crisis," in Jonathan Aranson, *Debt and the Less Developed Countries,* (Boulder, Colo., Westview Press, 1979).

14. R.S. Sayers, *Bank of England Operation 1890–1914,* (London: P.S. King and Sons, 1936).

Comment

Robert Z. Aliber

We are indebted to Hyman Minsky for his continued concern with the cyclical instability of the market economy and, especially, its financial sector. His argument is intuitively compelling, as a set of stylized facts especially in the context of the surge in business failures and the widespread concern with the stability—or the fragility—of the U.S. financial system and the international monetary arrangements. The United States appears to be subject to a sequence of inflationary and deflationary shocks following changes in the rates of money-supply growth. At the beginning of the sequence, a shift toward monetary expansion leads to increases in the inflation rate—as the monetary expansion continues and the economy grows, the yearly inflation rate increases. At some stage, the authorities shift to a contractive monetary policy to cope with the increases in the excessive inflation rate. This shift results in a turnabout and decline in the anticipated inflation rate and in more and more firms being caught between declining equity values and rising interest rates. Business failures and bankruptcies increase. Finally, the authorities feel compelled to shift back to an expansive monetary stance to protect the system against a financial collapse.

In this sequence, the rate of price increase at the peaks of each inflationary cycle is higher than in the previous cycle—and so are the rates of price increase at the troughs. The unemployment rate appears to be higher at the same stage of successive cycles.

Minsky's chapter deals with two distinct but related themes. Most of the chapter is a restatement of Minsky's hypothesis about the inevitability of the financial cycle in the domestic context. At the end of the chapter, Minsky explores the implications of the cycle for the international monetary and financial arrangements.

The Minsky Theme in the Domestic Context

Minsky's analysis of the fluctuations in the international economy involves a study of the reaction of the economy to a variety of shocks and the problems encountered by the monetary managers as they seek to prevent a financial collapse. Shocks may lead to a decline in asset values and an increase in business failures. If a shock is sufficiently severe, bankruptcies may be pervasive. Some financial institutions may experience funding problems

110

because their loan losses are high. To prevent the bankruptcies from escalating, the authorities must take measures to float off the crises. These measures seek to increase equity values and the net worth of various firms. If the measures taken by the monetary authorities succeed, then the economy will expand and the inflation rate will increase. The increase in the value of real assets and the increase in production and employment will lead to declines in the rate of business failures and bankruptcies. Some of the non-performing loans held by banks will again become performing.

Minsky argues that increases in the amplitude of these swings in the inflation rate, the unemployment rate, and the rate of business failures are inevitable in the structure of the economy. Certainly, these swings have been larger as one cycle has followed another over the last several decades. What must be determined is whether the observed increases in the amplitude of these cycles are due to chance or are inevitable given the structure of the economy. The chance argument states that the odds are one in two that the second cycle in a series of two will have an amplitude greater than the first and the odds are one in four that the third cycle in a series of three will have an amplitude greater than the second if the second had an amplitude greater than the first. Minsky asserts that the increasing amplitude is systemic rather than by chance, but he does not explain his argument fully. Does the heart of the inevitability argument lie in the behavior of the financial markets, the goods market, or the labor market? Does the case for the inevitability of larger swings depend on the way the system is managed? What would happen if the monetary-expansion phase were shorter in the second cycle—would the unemployment rate be higher than when the previous cycle peaked? Does the increase in the inflation rate occur because some actors in the system must be surprised or fooled? Does Minsky believe, then, that there is some sort of money illusion? Or does he believe that the inflation rate must be higher than anticipated because the participants caught on to the losses in real value from the previous and lower inflation rate? Minsky might argue that a more rapid increase in the price level is necessary for the monetary expansion to have the same impact on reducing the unemployment rate. He might argue this—but he does not. And so the question of why the amplitude of cycles must necessarily increase remains unanswered.

The Minsky Theme in the International Context

The real task for Minsky's chapter is to deal with the role of lenders of last resort in the international context. The argument in favor of their presence is by analogy: if domestic lenders of last resort were established to cope with domestic financial crises, then should not an international lender of last

resort be established to cope with international financial crises? Lenders of
last resort are needed to protect the financial system because of the externalities associated with the failures of individual institutions, especially those
triggered by changes in investor-asset preferences. A shift toward higher-
quality assets—toward currency and away from demand deposits—might
automatically prove contractive because the reserve requirements applicable
to currency are much higher than those applicable to deposits.

Some analysts suggest that the Great Depression was intensified by the
absence of a lender of last resort. Consider the stylized facts. The Credit
Anstalt in Vienna incurred significant liquidity problems when its credits to
banks in various countries in Eastern Europe went sour. Credit Anstalt had
borrowed from banks in Germany and Great Britain; it was one bank in a
chain of banks. In addition, the German banks had borrowed from banks
in Great Britain. Thus, there was a tiering of international credits. The failure of Credit Anstalt caused a ripple of illiquidity to move through north-
western Europe. There were runs on banks because of a concern that the
banks might not be able to redeem their liabilities at par, and there were
runs on countries in anticipation that the countries might be obliged to
break the link between their currencies and their gold parities.

According to one theory, if there had been an international lender of
last resort, the availability of credits might have forestalled the acceleration
of the credit collapse. The Austrian monetary authority might have reduced
the likelihood of the failure of Credit Anstalt by rapidly increasing the supply of reserves or, perhaps, by designing monetary policies to increase the
price level in Austria. Such measures, however, might have exacerbated the
flow of funds from Austria to Germany and to Great Britain, depleting its
own gold and foreign-exchange reserves. The availability of an international lender of last resort might have enabled Austrians to cope with the
external drain—but only if the drain had been due to a reversible shift in
currency preferences of investors rather than to an overvalued currency.
The access to an international lender of last resort would not have enabled
Great Britain to maintain its traditional parity for sterling in terms of gold,
given that sterling was overvalued—unless the price levels of its trading
partners would have increased. Once the link between sterling and gold was
severed, the pressure on the U.S. gold position was inevitable. Then, after
the increase in the U.S. dollar price of gold in January 1934, the pressure on
the French and Dutch gold parities was inevitable. The conclusion to draw
from this historical experience is that an international lender of last resort
would have been of modest use in forestalling the crises in the 1930s because
the financial flows were undertaken to cope with inappropriate gold and
foreign-exchange parities.

Over the last several decades, the scope or purpose of the lender-of-last-
resort arrangement in the international monetary system has changed. The

International Monetary Fund (IMF), established in the 1940s, was viewed as an international lender of last resort. Member countries would have access to the resources of the IMF under the General Arrangements to Borrow.

The analogy between the lender of last resort in the international context and in the domestic context is weak, because, in the domestic context, the need for such a lender is to cope with a systemic crisis and a shortage of reserves at the global level. In contrast, in the international context, the concern is with country-specific rather than systemic crises. If there is a shift in investor demand from one currency brand of deposits to another, funds might have to be recycled to enable the country that is losing reserves to cope with its payments deficit or the depreciation of its currency. However, there would be no need to increase the reserves of the system, because the reserves lost by one country would be acquired by some other country.

In the 1960s, the confidence problem was one of a trilogy of international monetary problems along with the reserve adequacy and the balance-of-payments adjustment problems. The dominant source of the confidence problem was the shift by national monetary authorities from dollar-denominated reserve assets; the concern was that the international reserve base would be eroded. The analogy with the domestic system was that gold was the quality reserve asset. However, the increase in the demand for gold could not be satisfied because of restrictions on its supply due to the depletion of U.S. gold reserves. The gold miners were caught between higher production costs and a fixed selling price as long as the U.S. authorities maintained the $35 parity. The secular gold shortage resulted from the inflation associated with World War II and the Korean war, not from a shift in central banks' preferences toward holding a larger proportion of gold in their reserves. Access to an international lender of last resort might have enabled the United States to delay a change in the dollar price of gold, but such access would not have postponed the need for this change indefinitely.

In the mid-1970s, the lender-of-last resort issue reappeared following the failures of Herstatt and the Franklin National. There was concern regarding the adequacy of lender-of-last-resort arrangements for the "stateless" Eurobanks and the extensive tiering that existed. If there were a run on a Eurobank in Zurich, would the Swiss National Bank be obliged to provide reserves to the Eurobank? Where would the reserves come from if the Eurobank was in Luxembourg or in Panama, countries without central banks? By itself, tiering generally involves either extensive interbank transactions or a long chain of loans or deposits from one offshore bank to another. If the bank at or near the end of the chain is unable to repay, the demands for repayment, which would fall on other banks in the chain, would increase sharply. The process would be energy expanding, like the chain of falling dominoes. Moreover, as investors shift funds from deposits in offshore banks to deposits in domestic banks, the credit contract would be automatic—on a worldwide basis, there would be an increase in the effective reserve requirement.

Whether it would be appropriate for an international lender of last resort to deal with the liquidity needs of Eurobanks depends on how the off-shore banks are related to domestic banks. Most offshore banks are branches of the major international banks; nearly all of the deposits in off-shore banks are in branches of major onshore banks. Each commercial bank is responsible for the liquidity needs of its offshore affiliates, both branches and subsidiaries. In addition, the central bank in each country is responsible for the liquidity of its commercial banks. Because Eurobanks have parents that are important in the country where they have their head-quarters, the ultimate source of liquidity to a Eurobank is the central bank of its parent.

Most recently, concern with the need for a lender of last resort in the international context has centered on the large credits from banks in the United States and elsewhere to Mexico, Argentina, Brazil, and Venezuela. In the aggregate, loans to these countries make up a large part of the capital of the specified banks. If one or two of the countries were to default, the ability of these banks to survive would be seriously handicapped. Concern has arisen because these particular countries have had severe problems in meeting their debt-service payments on time, in part because of a decline in their export earnings.

One interpretation of these recent events is that developing countries used the occasion of a decline in real interest rates to borrow more abroad. To transfer the real assets, a real appreciation of their currencies was neces-sary; otherwise, the real transfer could not be affected. Subsequently, when the real interest rates increased, it was inevitable that the real value of the increase in the external debts would decrease and that a real depreciation of the currencies of the borrowers would be necessary. To the extent that the countries have resisted the real depreciation, they have had foreign-exchange crises. These crises are like traditional foreign-exchange crises, except the countries face large volumes of external debt. (Once the country appears unable to repay on schedule, the supply of external funds declines, and so the ability of these countries to refinance their external debts declines. The public-policy issue involves the extent to which public or gov-ernment funds should be made available so that the borrowers can repay their private debts according to schedule.)

The need for institutional arrangements to facilitate recycling should be distinguished from the need for an international lender of last resort. The current problems the developing countries are having in managing their external debt either would not have arisen or would have been much less severe if the countries had not permitted their currencies to become overvalued. If the externalities associated with the countries' inability to repay on schedule are severe, then there may indeed be a need for agents to help refinance. However, such agents need not be lenders of last resort, whose role is to protect the stability of the entire system, not individual components.

**Part II
Regional Issues and
Distributing the Burden of
Adjustment**

6

Some Financial Issues in the North, in the South, and in Between

Carlos F. Diaz Alejandro

From the Wild West of the United States and unregulated Hong Kong, to prudent Bogota and born-again Santiago de Chile, during the early 1980s, banks and other financial intermediaries have been experiencing discomfort and even failure. Companies and countries, big and small, announce almost daily their incapacity to meet their financial obligations. From the financial repression and too little intermediation in the 1950s and 1960s, both national and international markets now appear to have swung to bubbly excess, or so the financial press tells us. Mocking bankers and teasing borrowers, common practices during the early 1930s, have once again become popular sports across the ideological spectrum. This chapter will probe explanations for this state of affairs, focusing on issues of interest to less-developed countries (LDCs), particularly semiindustrialized Latin American nations, but also highlighting themes common to the analysis of any financial market. Much discussion on the external debt and financial liberalization of LDCs has neglected those themes, often with seriously misleading consequences.

The major topics to be discussed are: (1) international, private financial markets and their alleged imperfections, and how they favored or penalized different types of LDCs during the 1970s; (2) international exchange-rate and liquidity arrangements and how they impinged on LDCs (experiments in the exchange-rate policy carried out by Southern Cone countries in Latin America, and their interaction with international capital markets, will also be discussed); and (3) the role of international financial institutions, particularly the International Monetary Fund and the World Bank.

Many related topics, such as concessional finance, direct foreign investment, export credits, and the future of Special Drawing Rights (SDRs), will receive little or no attention. The most shocking omission is the lack of discussion of the financial (and real) plight of the poorest LDCs, a plight that was particularly acute during the early 1980s and is without likely remedies for the rest of the decade. Reflections on easier problems will close the chapter.

The following persons provided useful comments during the preparation of this chapter: Edmar Bacha, Sidney Dell, Jonathan Eaton, Gerald Helleiner, Charles Kindleberger, Cristian Ossa, and John Williamson. Virginia Casey expertly and speedily typed the manuscript.

International (Private) Financial Markets

The stylized facts regarding the 1970s upsurge of private lending to some LDCs (primarily the newly industrializing countries, NICs) are fairly well known, so they will not be discussed here. For a discussion of those facts, see *International Financial Intermediation: A Long and Tropical View* (Bacha and Diaz Alejandro 1982).

The focus will be on the following questions:

1. What is wrong, if anything, with the present arrangements of private financial markets? Are bankers, as is often alleged in the financial press, shortsighted lemmings (or burros), or are they maximizing agents as clever as the average businessperson, taking advantage of flaws in market mechanisms? Both microeconomic and macroeconomic considerations will be included in the discussion.
2. If flaws in market mechanisms exist, who gains and loses from them at international and national levels, particularly among (and within) LDCs?

Imperfect Markets and Clever Agents

A central argument is that financial markets are quite different from spot commodity markets. The spot market for homogeneous apples can be modeled as one where price summarizes all relevant information for atomistic buyers and sellers. This textbook idealization captures the essence of certain types of real-world competitive spot markets. Any individual can buy or sell all the homogeneous apples he wants at the going market price. Everyone is a small price taker.

There are no small lenders or borrowers in the sense that no one can borrow all he wants at going market rates, even when most borrower's transactions would not affect standard market rates. No one will lend simply on the basis of the highest price offered for the loan. Once apple quality is established and sound cash is produced on the spot, apple buyers and sellers will care only about price. Every loan, however, will necessarily involve considerations other than price, which includes risk premia: the size of the loan will be a matter of discussion (that is, there will be some rationing) and other conditions may be attached. Why? Lenders can never be quite sure whether borrowers intend to repay, and there is no completely credible way for borrowers to persuade lenders of their honorable intentions. There is no simple way around these informational asymmetries. Acknowledging such a

simple fact is a start toward understanding why lending nations want gunboats, the Mafia breaks thumbs, and bankruptcy laws exist.

A lender contemplating an international loan will have well-known concerns regarding the soundness of the project and the willingness and ability
of borrowers to translate project earnings into foreign exchange. Without
grossly departing from the usual rules of the game nor taking leave of his
senses, however, the loan officer may also think:

1. The project may not be particularly good, but the borrower is likely to
   have plenty of foreign exchange from other national sources. (The loan
   is more likely to get the green light if the bank has many other lucrative
   links with the borrowing country.)
2. Neither the project nor the prospects for the borrowing country look
   good but:
   a. Somebody will bail the country out in the future either because it is
      too strategic or because its failure to service debt would create an
      international panic.
   b. Even if the country is not bailed out, the bank cannot be allowed to
      fail, and so it will be difficult to show that the lending was not wise.
   c. Even if the bank fails, the loan officer's responsibility in the event
      will be difficult to establish. A loan officer will never go far by let-
      ting other banks take a larger share of the business; risks must be
      taken, especially when blame for failure may be difficult to assign.
      The money, after all, is not the officer's (in contrast with direct for-
      eign investors) and, anyway, some of the depositors are insured by
      the government.

It should be noted that some of the lenders are either nationalized (for
example, French banks) or are said to be closely attuned to signals emanating from their governments and their exporting or foreign-policy concerns
(for instance, German and Japanese banks). It has been argued that the failure of most LDCs to sell bonds or floating-rate notes to individual investors
shows how much more sensitive those individuals are about LDC risk than
are the banks that manage their deposits. Public utterances of those bankers
will tend to project an optimism that may or may not be warranted.

Most of the preceding considerations apply to national and international lending as well as to lending to sovereign borrowers or to large companies. This is why central banks have prudential regulations covering commercial banks and other financial intermediaries, particularly when deposits
in those institutions are insured. Few laissez-faire enthusiasts would go as
far as eliminating all prudential regulations concerning national financial

systems (although in some Latin American countries ill-conceived experiments in financial liberalization came very close to that, with lamentable consequences). In general, regulations for domestic lending seem greater than those for international lending occurring from offshore centers, for example, the Eurocurrency market.

Although a lender's concerns as to whether borrowers really intend to repay loans lead to rationing of credit and presumably to less lending than under full-information circumstances, the other thoughts a loan officer may have may lead to more lending than is socially desirable. Socially desirable loans are defined here as those financing activities that yield a rate of return higher than a hypothetical interest rate generated by fundamental thrift and productivity data for the world economy, both adjusted for risks that could not be avoided even by the wisest cosmopolitan planner. (See Goran Ohlin [1976] for an early discussion of moral hazard and expectations of public subsidies in international lending.) As a result of market imperfections, some induced by governments, others intrinsic in capital markets with incomplete information, some borrowers may be shut out, while others are showered with loans, depending on the specific characteristics of lenders and borrowers, as well as the stage of the business cycle.

On the borrowing side, public agents signing up the loan may not always be high minded and patriotic and often do not face much of a liability if things go wrong. Private agents on the borrowing side typically will have their loan repayment guaranteed by the public sector. In some cases (which will be discussed later), exchange-rate policy may induce private agents to borrow abroad, insuring them against devaluation risks either explicitly or implicitly. The incentive structure for both public and private agents often contains strong inducements to borrow abroad more than is socially desirable, in the sense defined previously. To check these tendencies, and to avoid making the terms of borrowing unduly onerous, many countries attempt to exercise central control over external borrowing.

Even before the "Great Fear" of August-September 1982, there was considerable discussion in the United States about the optimal regulation of banks and other financial intermediaries. The dangers of combining generous explicit or implicit deposit insurance with the lifting of supervision over portfolios have been generally recognized. A strong case can be made that the deregulation of financial intermediaries in any country must be accompanied by the substantial reduction in deposit insurance and the requirement that those intermediaries provide the public with information about their portfolios. Under those circumstances, it is conceivable that depositors could pick and choose among banks according to their preferences in their risk-return trade off; a weakened deposit insurance would not allow depositors to think that one bank is as good as another. Whether a more transparent and less regulated banking system would be a reliable supplier of the public good, money, remains a moot point. This discussion involves macro-economic considerations, to which we now turn.

Macroeconomic Considerations and Some History

The consequences of the informational and moral-hazard imperfections listed earlier can be found in an Indian village as well as in Bogota or New York, in national as well as in international credit markets. They go on all the time, in spite of supervision by central-bank authorities, without unduly exacerbating the pains of the human condition.

However, financial markets have also been found both to aggravate and initiate macroeconomic instability. Charles P. Kindleberger (1978, especially chapters 1 and 2) has provided a masterful description of a typical financial crisis, as insightful for 1982 as for earlier years. As a consequence of shocks of sundry nature, "the temptation becomes virtually irresistible to take the money and run" (Kindleberger 1978, p. 10). Such behavior by individual lenders, of course, aggravates the crisis, which can only be stopped by someone's acting as lender of last resort. At this aggregate level, there are complementary informational and practical game-theoretic considerations making central banking more of an art than a science: "the lender of last resort should exist, but his presence should be doubted" (Kindleberger 1978, p. 12). One may note that, not only is economic history full of examples of financial manias, panics, and crashes, but there is also a growing industry of model building that shows that markets composed of perfectly rational agents can generate bubbles with dramatic bursts. Those markets could be for foreign-exchange or for other financial assets (including future claims on apples). See Rudiger Dornbusch (1982) for a survey of bubbles, runs, and peso problems. Both the new theories and the historical record are open to various interpretations. Discussing the need for a lender of last resort, Robert M. Solow (1981, p. 241) cautiously notes:

> All the theorist can say is that there is a potentially sound argument that rests on the unstable propagation of disturbance through the financial system, beyond the bounds of what ordinary prudence can be expected to cope with. . . . One could argue, with some justice, that a confidence-worthy and confidence-inspiring monetary-financial system is a public good.

Do crashes result mainly from the accumulation of inevitable microeconomic imperfections or mainly from macroeconomic mismanagement by foolish governments? The problems experienced in the 1920s and 1930s are very much in the mind of today's financial actors, and it may be useful to dwell briefly on those experiences, which included massive defaults by Latin American LDCs. The literature is replete with stories of microeconomic imperfections in the financial markets of the 1920s, which, in many instances, are overly polite descriptions of what went on between bond salespersons and borrowing tyrants. Yet, when all is said and done, one comes back to sharing the conclusion of the young Henry Wallich: "If the depression of the 1930's had been mild, and if the steady expansion of world trade and capital exports had continued thereafter, defaults probably would have been infrequent and could have been settled without much difficulty . . . " (Wallich 1943, p. 321). This, one may add, seems quite plausible, even though in those days there was not an International Monetary Fund. There were plenty of mechanisms intermediating between bond holding "widows and orphans" and borrowing countries, which were used to carry out what today we would call debt-rescheduling exercises and stabilization plans. These included the Ottoman Public Debt Administration, the Financial Committee of the League of Nations, and the several ad hoc financial missions to Latin American countries, representing bondholders' associations, but closely linked to authorities in lending countries. See Jeff Frieden (1981), Winston Fritsch (1979), and John R. Ruggie (1982) for more information on these organizations.

The similarities and differences between bond lending in the 1920s and bank lending today offer a promising field for research. Price-level expectations then were, of course, different from those of today, encouraging longer-term contracts denominated in dollars and pounds. Inflation in key currencies has eroded even domestic bond markets in major countries, and indexing has proven to be a far from adequate substitute for stable price-level expectations. In the 1920s, news about major borrowers were quickly translated into changes in open-market bond questions; today, bank secrecy helps to hide such news or at least delay its dissemination (the secrecy also fuels rumors and fluctuations in the prices of bank shares, which may be more destabilizing than fluctuations in bond prices). Borrowing by issuing securities restricts the risk of default to the specific investors who bought the bonds; bank financing creates a situation richer in externalities, where the repercussions of any default could go well beyond the defaulting country and its creditors. Bonds, of course, offer the more sensible arrangement of financing long-term investments with long-term debt, while bank financing engages in remarkable feats of maturity transformation.

It remains to be seen whether the present regime of bank lending coupled with discreet scheduling to handle unforeseen shocks will prove more resistant to defaults and repudiations than the old bond system and whether the avoidance of educative crunches and bankruptcies is a slippery slope leading down to widespread state support for, and bailing out of, the banking system (see Colchester 1981; Cooper and Truman 1971; Diaz Alejandro

1981; Eaton and Gersovitz 1981; and Sachs and Cohen 1982). The stability of the present regime was tested during 1982, but the circumstances were different from those in the period from 1928 to 1933. It is ironic that the shift toward bank lending was induced partly by the regulations introduced during the 1930s to avoid abuses in bond and security markets. Also interesting to note is that, during 1982, bankers and their supervisors were nervous not only about the situation in Mexico and Poland but also about what was happening with International Harveser, AEG-Telefunken, and Dome Petroleum.

Gainers and Losers

Assuming that lenders of last resort exist, that real interest rates are at their normal long-run levels, and that the rules of the game for trade and credit are steady and allow substantial international flows of goods and bonds, who gains and loses from informational imperfections in credit markets? In particular, do LDCs gain or lose from them? And, within LDCs, who reaps the gains or bears the costs?

The 1970s showed that most LDCs did not receive significant amounts of medium-term private credit. In some cases (for example, India), it has been presumed that government authorities chose not to borrow at commercial terms. In others, even if demand existed (at less than astronomical interest rates), the presumption has been that lenders simply rationed out those borrowers they did not regard as credit worthy—that is, no private loans were forthcoming at any price for those LDCs. It is difficult to believe that, in these LDCs, there were no projects yielding sufficiently high social rates of return, including suitable calculations for the foreign exchange needed to service loans, to justify commercial borrowing. Here is a prima facie case that either informational imperfections, or other types of imperfections, clog up lending channels. One can imagine that organizational flaws among potential borrowers, including misguided economic policies, are some of the other types of imperfections. On the lending side, one might conjecture that information gathering could have significant economies of scale, and the potential market of some LDCs may not be large enough to justify the necessary allocation of loan officers' time.

Other imperfections, however, appear to offer potential gains for the more credit-worthy LDCs (for example, the NICs) in the sense that the flaws discussed earlier tend to expand the supply of credit at going market rates. That credit comes with few strings attached during the hypothesized normal conditions, allowing the borrower substantial room to carry out spending plans. Such plans may be sensible investment projects or may even involve a wise smoothing out of consumption (not all consumption loans are necessarily dead weight; see Eaton and Gersovitz 1981). Of course, the loans also may be used on arms consumption or foolish investments, in which case, repayment problems would be likely even under tranquil macro-economic conditions.

Leaving aside sensible consumption loans, a good test of any financial system is how successful it is in transferring resources toward capital formation that earns social rates of return sufficiently high to compensate lenders and leave a surplus for borrowers. Under these non-zero-sum circumstances, everyone benefits—or, at least, no one loses.

There is some evidence that, during the 1970s, much LDC borrowing went into capital formation and did not reduce domestic savings effort (see Sachs 1981, and Bacha and Diaz Alejandro 1982). The evidence, however, is soft for several reasons. Such aggregate data, particularly on domestic savings, are notoriously shaky. One wonders, to give an example, how the Argentine arms purchases made since 1976 are registered in the national accounts. Even if the evidence is accurate with regard to aggregate amounts, the data are silent on the quality of investment projects. Casual empiricism will turn up doubtful investment projects carried out by both public and private agents in many of the NICs that borrowed heavily during the 1970s. Note that a negative correlation between risk spreads charged to different countries and those countries' ratios of investment to gross domestic product (obtained by Sachs 1981, p. 245) may simply reflect that both variables are sensitive to a third one: shocks from commodity-price fluctuations or similar disturbances originating in the world economy or in nature. A frost, for example, may increase coffee prices, relaxing Brazilian balance-of-payments constraints. This both will allow higher investment rates in Brazil and could make the country appear more credit worthy, which would lead to a decline in risk spreads.

The safest generalization appears to be that whether NIC borrowing went mainly into what proved to be sound investment projects or into extravagant expenditures (of either a consumption, investment, or military nature) depended more on the borrowing country's policies than on its banker's selectivity. The moral-hazard flaws and expected subsidies described previously blurred (in bankers' eyes) the differences between Brazilian hydroelectric dams, Chilean shopping centers, and Argentine Mirages.

Who within LDCs benefitted from wise borrowing? Who bore the burden of extravagance? These are difficult questions, having as much to do with politics as with economics. Ironically, it seems that, in many cases, private international credit helped to strengthen public enterprises in LDCs. Even the 1982 nationalization of banks in Mexico was done (partly) to reassure international capital markets of the soundness of those institutions. The incidence of extravagance also can be disconcerting: those politicians responsible for excessive spending and borrowing in Mexico during 1981–82 may end up their tenure as heroes, while those who follow may have to face unpleasant economic choices. Behind the politicians, of course, a myriad of economic agents will benefit from successful investment programs or suffer from after-the-fall stabilization plans.

During the 1970s, many LDC borrowers, both public and private, bene-fitted from credit conditions that, until 1980, turned out to be quite attrac-tive, even when taking into account risk premia, fees, and commissions. The price of either extravagance or sensible capital formation was low. This, of course, has changed since 1980 because of the sharp rise in real interest rates. The major losers of the low real rates of interest in the 1970s appear to have been the oil-rich countries, whose financial investments at the time earned less than did oil they left underground. At least during the 1970s, those countries were not in dire financial circumstances.

Macroeconomic and Financial Collapse?

The dilemma that arises because confirming and strengthening moral-hazard considerations may risk chain-reaction financial bankruptcies becomes salient during recessions and depressions. During the early 1930s, the U.S. monetary authorities allowed massive bank failures, thereby aggra-vating the recessionary trends; during 1982, the authorities seemed to have (temporarily and wisely) decided to cast to the winds concerns about moral hazard and inflationary expectations. In the very short run, such action by lenders of last resort stems the urge, felt by smaller and weaker banks, to take the money and run, which, by drying up short-term credit and halting normal roll overs, can generate very large swings in net lending. The effec-tiveness of the international financial system during the 1980s, however, depends more fundamentally on the rapidity and vigor of the industrialized countries' recovery from the recession of the early 1980s and the contain-ment of the protectionist pressures observed in those countries.

If recession deepens and/or protectionism advances further in indus-trialized countries, defaults, reschedulings, and even repudiations will be unavoidable. Under such circumstances, rescheduling at market conditions is unlikely to be feasible, even if real interest rates are at long-term normal levels. A more complex and intriguing scenario for the 1980s would involve neither deepening recession nor vigorous recovery in the north and neither galloping protectionism nor a return to liberalizing trends in international trade. What would Brazil and South Korea do given this mediocre scenario, which could involve not only a slow growth in their exports but also low real interest rates? Would they continue to punctually service their debt even though net capital inflows might be meager and prospects for rapid export growth would be poor? Note that the default and repudiation option becomes less attractive to major debtors when the excess of gross capital inflows over debt-service payments is greater than expected, export prospects to major creditors improves, and frontier technological change in industrialized countries occurs faster than expected. Even if expected net inflows are low, Brazil would be reluctant to default and repudiate its debt for fear of having its links to suppliers of advanced machinery and technology cut off and its other trade links harassed. Besides the turmoil that would be created in the short run by the drying up of even trade credits, violently cutting off capital-account links while maintaining trading ones with major creditors does not seem to be an option in the foreseeable future.

Whatever happens, however, it is clear that no one is going to cart away debt-financed Brazilian hydroelectric dams and that there are limits to the austerity and policy measures that can be dictated from abroad to countries such as Argentina, Brazil, and Mexico. Complex and even dangerous bargaining games between large borrowers and those acting on behalf of lenders are already under way, covering not just balance-of-payments and macroeconomic policies but also home-country regulations on direct foreign investments and even foreign-policy stances. Some LDCs may be able to maintain a greater degree of policy autonomy than others under these circumstances, just as during the 1930s Brazil's room for policy maneuver enlarged while Argentina's shrank. The International Monetary Fund (IMF) could play an important role during the 1980s, but much depends on how it adapts to the times, a matter to which this chapter will return later.

International Monetary Arrangements and Domestic Financial Markets in Some LDCs

Exchange Rates of Key Currencies and LDC Optimal Pegs

LDCs expressed their unhappiness with floating rates among key currencies shortly after the adoption of the floating rates. Many observers regarded this reaction as yet another sign of the economic obtuseness of LDCs, although the reasons for it were fairly obvious, even if the wisdom of the LDCs' advocacy of fixed rates for major currencies was debatable (see Diaz Alejandro 1975). Today, the unhappiness with flexible exchange rates has become widespread, as foreign-exchange markets appear as turbulent as stock and other asset markets. Yet the alternatives to floating for key currencies, under present and likely circumstances, remain unappealing. LDCs, even those with tranquil domestic circumstances, have been forced to reconsider their exchange-rate policies. Traditional "peggers" have had to think about which key currency would be their optimal peg. External and domestic shocks, as well as changing priorities of domestic policies, also have led many LDCs to reconsider whether to crawl without preannounced rules, to preannounce schedules of minidevaluations, to have multiple rates, or even to float like the big boys.

Although faith in stable big brothers has eroded, considerations about the optimum currency area still lead most LDCs to peg: 90 out of the 114 LDCs whose exchange-rate policies were classified by the IMF as of June 1980 declared themselves to be pegging, generally to the U.S. dollar, the French franc, the Special Drawing Right (SDR), or another basket currency. Careful empirical work has established that, for the vast majority of countries maintaining a peg to another currency or basket, externally induced instability (for example, fluctuations among key currencies) in effective nominal and real exchange rates increased between 1966 and 1971 and between 1973 and 1979. Seeking greater stability, a growing number of LDCs have switched their pegs to foreign currency baskets (see Brodsky, Helleiner, and Sampson 1981, and Bacha 1981). The trend and gyrations of the U.S. dollar since 1979 have shown that the choice of a peg is far from a minor matter, as central-bank officials in Argentina, Chile, and Uruguay have belatedly found out.

A prima facie case has been made about how the increased instability of LDC effective exchange rates induced by key-currency fluctuations has had harmful effects on LDCs, increasing terms-of-trade instability and complicating the management of LDCs' international assets and liabilities. Quantification of these effects, however, has proven elusive. Thus, the magnitude of the welfare costs imposed on LDCs by the floating-rate regime is moot. Indeed, the costs could turn out to be minor, at least for those LDCs with relatively sophisticated policy tools at their disposal.

Basket pegging can, of course, offset some of the instability arising from key-currency gyrations. The 1970s witnessed a vast expansion of the literature on the optimal peg, mercifully surveyed by John Williamson (1982a). Williamson notes that one point on which there is (almost) complete agreement is that choice of the unit to act as peg should be made with the aim of stabilizing something, rather than with the object of optimizing anything. He argues that there are two distinct aspects to exchange-rate policy: the unit to which to peg, and the rules governing changes in the peg. He concludes that the choice of the unit to which a country will peg its currency should be guided principally by the pursuit of internal balance (rather than external balance, which is, on average, attained over the medium term) and that this requires pegging to a basket of currencies that reflects the direction and elasticity of total trade. Longer-term questions concerning, notably, neutralizing inflation differentials, promoting payments adjustment, and imposing an external discipline should be addressed by making changes in the value of the peg rather than by influencing the unit to which the currency is pegged. Finally, Williamson notes several attractive features, from a cosmopolitan viewpoint, of pegging to the SDR.

Some qualifications may be made to these conclusions. The distinction between stabilization and optimization is debatable: why stabilize unless some optimization justifies it? For many small and very open LDCs, the distinction between the choice of peg and the rules for changing the peg may remain academic: for optimum-currency reasons, their size, and the possible feebleness of their monetary institutions may rule out anything but fixed exchange rates. Having ruled out changes in the peg for the sake of preserving the moneyness of the local currency, longer-term considerations, such as a desire to minimize local inflation, could influence whether an LDC pegs to, say, the U.S. dollar, the pound sterling, or the French franc (a choice not so theoretical for small Caribbean islands, for example).

A second qualification to Williamson's conclusions involves the need for further work on how the capital account should influence the choice of the peg; with the exception of Stephen J. Turnovsky (1982), so far analysts have focused almost exclusively on the current account. Suppose a country trades mainly with Germany but borrows in New York: how should this affect its choice of peg? Given the high degree of capital mobility since the late 1960s, short-run swings in the capital account have become a major preoccupation of central banks in semiindustrialized LDCs. This topic, then, is worthy of some discussion.

Some Dilemmas and Experiments

The interaction of exchange-rate policy with local and international financial markets became a matter of serious concern during the 1970s and early 1980s, particularly in LDCs with a history of erratic inflation and macroeconomic turbulence. A permissive international monetary system has allowed room for experimentation; as with borrowing, the experimentation has resulted in some hits and some errors.

A central policy question is whether to attempt to loosen the links between domestic and international financial markets. Floating rates perform some of this delinking function in industrialized countries, although experience has shown that their success in this area has been far from satisfactory, and some observers have called for policies to widen the breach (Tobin 1978). Note that, among industrialized countries, with the major exceptions of Germany and the United States, there is a widespread recognition that short-term financial flows can pose problems for macroeconomic management. Most of those countries do, in fact, maintain restrictions of various sorts on short-term banking operations, restrictions that are accepted in the Organization for Economic Cooperation and Development

(OECD) *Code on Capital Movements* (Bertrand 1981) and, of course, by the IMF.

The most spectacular LDC experiments to reduce domestic inflation have involved the combination of liberalization of domestic financial markets, loosening of links between domestic and international capital markets, and the use of preannounced or fixed exchange rates. Beginning in 1978, Argentina, Chile, and Uruguay, among others, undertook such experimentation, which culminated in assorted catastrophes around 1981–82. The experimental policies did lead to a (temporary) reduction in inflation, massive capital inflows, and increases in foreign-exchange reserves. However, they also led to a trend toward real appreciations of the exchange rate and, eventually, to reversals of the capital flows, financial panics, crisis devaluations, and a renewal of inflationary pressures in the context of severe recessions. During the euphoric miracle phase, the external debt and reserves expanded with great speed; the busts also proceeded with remarkable momentum, reducing reserves but leaving behind serioud debt-servicing problems. Ex-post explanations for these melancholy results have included external shocks, failures to bring public-sector deficits under control, and excessive generosity to workers (full-wage indexing that made real wages rigid downward). Of greater importance were errors in assuming that domestic financial markets needed no more effective control than spot apple markets and faith in crude versions of the "Law of One Price" and in automatic mechanisms of adjustment for obtaining balance-of-payments equilibrium with full employment. It is remarkable that those advocating and implementing Southern Cone domestic financial liberalization overlooked or ignored the fact that, in the case of the paradigmatic experiment in successful domestic financial liberalization (that of South Korea during the 1960s), most of the financial institutions were owned or controlled by the government, facilitating the prudential supervision of both national and international financial transactions and giving the government a powerful influence over credit allocation (see Gurley, Patrick, and Shaw 1965, p. 45). Indeed, much of the literature advocating financial liberalization has compared LDCs' repressed markets with mythically perfect credit markets with full information, misleading policymakers into believing that, if only ceilings on interest rates were removed, a sound, competitive, and vigorous financial sector would spontaneously appear. Little attention was given (until the 1981–82 catastrophes) either to irreduceable informational imperfections or to the rich variety of financial systems and regulations that exist in the industrialized countries, most of which are hardly perfect credit markets with full information.

Tendencies toward the generation of oligopolistic financial groups and conglomerates, found in industrialized countries and checked in some of those countries by regulatory legislation, became virulent after LDC financial liberalizations, the analytical underpinnings of which went little beyond demand-and-supply schedules for credit (Foxley 1982). Related incorrect assumptions about small-country borrowing in international credit markets led to the belief in Southern Cone countries that the current-account consequences of increasingly overvalued exchange rates could be covered easily by tapping the infinitely elastic supply of external funds. The liberalization of domestic financial markets in the Southern Cone generated considerable short-term transactions, but no substantial and permanent increase in private fixed-capital formation. Real interest rates, measured in a number of plausible ways, remained inexplicably high. Beyond fairly predictable explanations, an interesting conjecture links those high interest rates to the moral-hazard imperfections emphasized in this chapter: financial intermediaries in trouble, shielded by portfolio secrecy and expecting to be bailed out, seek fresh deposits from the public by offering ever-higher interest rates (Baeza Valdes 1982).

The control and elimination of inflation has proven to be quite difficult and costly in both industrialized countries and LDCs. The experience of Southern Cone countries in particular has highlighted the dangers of dogmatic liberalizations in the midst of macroeconomic turbulence. It is now widely recognized that maintaining macroeconomic control during the transition toward more stable conditions is a difficult task that is likely to require some form of exchange controls over capital outflows and inflows (see McKinnon 1982). Given the frequently large differentials in domestic and foreign interest rates, taxes, rather than purely quantitative control, seem the proper instruments for reducing destabilizing short-term capital movements. Enormous rents could be captured by arbitrage between local and international capital markets; because of both macroeconomic and prudential considerations, it would not be desirable to eliminate those rents simply by allowing more private agents into the business. Taxes or controls no doubt will have many leaks and will introduce inefficiencies; the point is that, under some circumstances, they may avoid worse ones.

International Liquidity, the LDCs, and the
Great Gold Swindle

At least under some plausible definitions, during the 1970s, aggregate international reserves increased dramatically, while reserve composition also was drastically altered. Neither event was foreseen, much less planned, during the 1960s. The increase in the price of gold was the major cause for both events; by the late 1970s, gold had become de facto the major international reserve asset, although its price fluctuations limited its classical reserve function.

During the 1960s, the LDCs were encouraged, if not pressured, to hold reserve increases in the form of interest-earning key-currency-denominated assets. The dollar was said to be not just as good as gold; because it could earn interest, it was said to be better. Choosing gold was regarded as an unfriendly act, and LDCs were lectured on the irrationality of gold holding. Three-fourths of the world's reserve gold remained in the hands of the United States, the Federal Republic of Germany, France, Italy, Switzerland, the Netherlands, and Belgium, countries that registered massive (paper) profits as a result of gold-price increases. David Brodsky and Gary Sampson (1981) estimate those profits at more than $300 billion. Gains to LDCs from the gold-price increase, including those from the liquidation of IMF gold, are tiny next to that figure.

The instrument intended as the principal reserve asset of the international monetary system, the SDR, accounted for around 2 percent in the growth of international reserves during the 1970s, and the figure is unlikely to be much higher during the 1980s. Even without the link, LDCs would be better off today had the increse in international liquidity registered since the late 1960s taken the form of expanded SDR allocations. Ironically, the countries that benefited from the increase in gold prices during the 1970s now argue that further SDR allocations are not needed and would be inflationary. By the early 1980s, nongold international reserves had fallen sharply relative to trade; during 1982, some LDCs were reported to be selling some of their meager gold holdings. Today, IMF quotas have slipped way behind world trade and payments imbalances, reducing access to the low-conditionality facilities of the IMF.

Not surprisingly, nostalgia for the days of the gold standard, fashionable in the industrialized countries, has found few echoes in LDCs, most of which remember those days as involving subjugation to colonial powers or the imposition of substantial instability on their sovereign but weak economies (Triffin 1964).

International Financial Institutions

The International Monetary Fund and Other
Lenders of Last Resort.

Those who launched the IMF in 1944 expected a world with adjustable but mostly fixed rates and a low degree of international private capital mobility. Is the IMF really necessary in a world of floating rates, in which private finance seems plentiful? Before 1944, after all, there were some periods of tranquil international prosperity without an IMF.

It was noted earlier that many small countries (not all LDCs) prefer to maintain parities pegged to key currencies or baskets of them. Even authorities in charge of key currencies have not foresworn intervening in exchange markets. Exchange rates, in other words, will not bear the full burden of adjusting to shocks to the balance of payments in the foreseeable future. There will remain deficits and surpluses generating financial transactions. Also noted earlier were microeconomic and macroeconomic reasons that indicate that purely private financial markets may not be the optimal way to handle deficits and surpluses; informational and organizational flaws may lead to circumstances where the required finance will not be forthcoming at a reasonable cost when it is most needed. Countries could be pushed into emergency adjustment measures that have substantial externalities and that are less than optimal from both national and international viewpoints. This is why, except among those who advocate a return to the gold standard, immediate world revolution, or free banking, there is widespread agreement that a desirable international monetary and financial system should have at its center something like an IMF to act as a lender of last resort to national central banks, in a manner partly similar and partly different to how those central banks act toward their commercial banking and financial systems. This systemic consideration also explains why LDCs, which are harsh critics of the IMF, also advocate a large increase in IMF quotas. Events during the second half of 1982, when the U.S. administration used its muscle as international lender of last resort (ILLR) partly to undermine the foreign-policy independence of Brazil and Mexico, confirmed to LDCs the importance of multilateral financial institutions.

Neither at the national nor at the international level is there a robust theory of lender of last resort; instead, we have history and ad hoc judgments (see Solow 1981). Note the differences between the IMF and central banks: the latter have, in most countries, a good deal of power over their national financial institutions, even those located abroad, while the IMF generally must wait until central banks come to it before it can influence their policies. National central banks, however, have tighter limits on their ability to print internationally acceptable money than does the IMF. A plausible argument seems to be that whoever acts as international lender of last resort should have enough of those funds that are likely to be demanded during a crisis to make its reassurances credible. It should also be on speaking terms both with potential customers for funds and with those providing its financial muscle. It must be able to move very fast during emergencies. Since at least the first oil shock, there have been doubts, on all counts, as to whether the IMF is really up to an ILLR role. Its lending potential has not kept up with possible balance-of-payments deficits, and its authority has been eroded by proposals for ad hoc safety nets. Its long estrangement from many LDCs, including key ones such as Brazil, has not been overcome. Its rules call for time-consuming negotiations and procedures.

During 1979–80, the IMF seemed on the way toward enlarging its lending capacity and adopting more flexible lending conditions, with the trend culminating in a large loan to India. This trend was suddenly stopped during 1981 as a result of pressure from the new U.S. administration. Events that occurred during 1982 persuaded at least some skeptics of the wisdom of the 1979–80 initiatives, although it remains to be seen how forcefully those initiatives will be pursued this time. The crucial issues are still the need for a major increase in the financial resources of the IMF and the need for a substantial improvement in its lending practices.

Williamson (1982b) has given us another helpful survey of crucial points in this area. His discussion can be criticized because of its minimizing of past IMF inflexibility in dealing with LDCs, especially in the Western Hemisphere, and its exaggeration of the theoretical (in contrast with the practical) grounds for advocating the use of credit ceilings in stabilization plans. However, his estimates indicating the need to raise IMF resources to at least SDR 100 billion (from SDR 61 billion) and most of his suggestions about how to liberalize IMF lending practices are persuasive. Indeed, his characterization of the IMF theoretical position as eclectic and his conclusion that criticisms of the IMF are largely misplaced will be tested by, inter alia, how that institution reacts to his proposals over the next few years.

Few would deny that the IMF, or any ILLR, should attach some form of economic conditionality on its loans. (See Sidney Dell [1981] for a masterful review of the evolution of conditionality). Given the lack of consensus on macroeconomics, not just among academics but also among IMF patrons (consider the contrast between macroeconomic policy in France and that in the United States), the case for IMF conditionality focused narrowly on balance-of-payments targets is strengthened. It is true that observed performance in the balance of payments is the result both of domestic policies and factors beyond the country's control. Yet a number of indicators, such as stable prices and market shares, could be used to evaluate performance and to analyze failure to meet agreed targets. The compensatory facilities of the IMF have accumulated experience in this area.

It is the business of the IMF to insist on balance-of-payments targets consistent with the repayment of its loans, to monitor closely performance in this area, and to suspend its credit (either subsidized or cheap relative to alternatives) to countries that do not repay promptly without a good reason, such as unexpected exogenous shocks. It is not the business of the IMF to make loans conditional on policies whose connection to the balance of payments in the short or even medium run is tenuous, such as food subsidies, utility rates, controls over foreign corporations, or whether the banking system is public or private. It was a brilliant administrative stroke when the IMF staff developed the monetary approach to the balance of payments during the 1950s; this allowed the translation of balance-of-payments targets into those involving domestic credit. For many LDCs, however, the assumptions needed to validate such translation have become less and less convincing.

Focusing on balance-of-payments targets would keep the IMF away from the more political aspects of short run-macroeconomic policymaking. Countries could, of course, actively solicit IMF advice on those aspects and, under those circumstances, the IMF staff could give full expression to its views on inflation control, optimal trade regulations, food subsidies, and so forth.

Balance-of-payments flow targets are intertwined with estimates of the stock of a country's foreign debt; a country asking the IMF for a loan will have to discuss its other outstanding loans, if nothing else, to clarify priorities in debt servicing. Thus, IMF conditionality inevitably involves this institution in discussions about debt limits and servicing, including rescheduling exercises. All of this could, in principle, be handled so as to reduce uncertainty and informational flaws, so that both private lenders and borrowing countries, as well as innocent bystanders, could, on balance, gain relative to a scenario in which laissez-faire prevails. As noted earlier, lack of resources and overly intrusive notions of conditionality have kept the IMF from fully playing such a constructive role. Until there are clear indications that a new IMF has come into being, some countries may continue to handle their debt, and possible debt reschedulings, on their own. To make even a new IMF a kind of central committee of an international credit cartel would, under normal circumstances, be a remedy worse than the disease, at least from the viewpoint of many borrowing countries.

The difficulties surrounding the Mexican external debt during 1982 showed that not even the Reagan administration expected financial crises and potential bank failures to be handled by the magic of the market place. As the managing director of the IMF noted, in a commendable brief period, the central banks, the Bank for International Settlements (BIS), the U.S. Treasury, the commercial banks, and the IMF acted in full cooperation. Similarly, the government of the Federal Republic of Germany appears to have played a role in containing the impact Polish difficulties with punctual debt servicing had on German banks. While these two cases showed the efficacy of lenders of last resort, the melodramatic collapse of the Luxembourg subsidiary of the Banco Ambrosiano and the failure of the Bank of Italy to back any of its debts underline the ambiguities of the 1975 Basle concordat among key central banks, which laid down a division of responsibilities designed to prevent any element of an international bank from escaping supervision and, presumably, having access to some lender of last resort. So far, the quantitative and psychological impacts of the rescue operations for Poland and Mexico exceed by far those of the Ambrosiano affair—so much so that one detects among some concerned observers an eagerness to witness exemplary bankruptcies for banks and exemplary stabilization plans for countries in order to avoid validating much too obviously the subsidy expectations and moral-hazard features of international lending. The search must be on for victims too weak, unpopular, or small for their sacrifice to shake the financial system. Meanwhile, low quotations for their shares and difficulties in the interbank deposit market are expected to give the boldest banks a salutary fright.

The key lesson of the second half of 1982 may turn out to be that, under present political and economic conditions, the real ILLR is the U.S. government, whose treasury and Federal Reserve can mobilize, by the proverbial stroke of a pen, vast sums of dollars with more secrecy and speed than the IMF or even the BIS. The mechanisms available to the U.S. executive for these purposes are plentiful and free from ex ante congressional checks. In a crisis, big and politically centralized LDCs, such as Brazil and Mexico, will prefer to deal directly with the U.S. government. IMF blessings to bilateral deals may or may not come ex post facto. One may conjecture that big borrowers will trade off foreign-policy autonomy—less opposition to U.S. policies in Central America and in the General Agreement on Tariffs and Trade (GATT)—for more resources and somewhat more lenient economic conditions.

Over the longer term, an IMF with ample resources as well as the trust of most of its members could help not only to complement the lender-of-last-resort facilities of national central banks but also serve as a forum for effective coordination of national macroeconomic policies. During 1980–82, LDCs were severely hit by the side effects of antiinflationary policies in industrialized countries, particularly in the United States, without having the opportunity to have their case heard in potentially responsive forums. Extravagant interest rates directly increased the debt burden and indirectly led to low primary-product prices and a lower demand for LDC-manufactured exports. Recession in the North induced protectionist pressures, which, even when resisted, harmed the outlook for LDC exports and hence reduced their credit worthiness. A reinvigorated IMF, perhaps together with a new GATT, could act as a forum where the interconnections among macroeconomic, trade, and financial policies, North and South, could be discussed. It is conceivable that such an IMF could play a worldwide countercyclical role, as visualized by some of its founding fathers, using its power to issue SDRs and, by making a more vigorous use of its compensatory financing facility, becoming an important automatic stabilizer for the world economy.

Although a renewed IMF would entail substantial mutual gains for the North and the South, it also would involve zero-sum aspects, which makes the immediacy of this "second coming" doubtful. One cannot increase the voting weight of the South, for example, without reducing that of the North. A more technical and built-in approach to debt scheduling could reduce opportunities for some Northern groups to have their governments link credit roll overs to changes in host-country rules on direct foreign investment and in their energy and even foreign policies. Those in the Reagan administration, for example, who have successfully exploited the financial difficulties of Brazil and Mexico to advance U.S. political hegemony in the Western Hemisphere naturally would be reluctant to work for an expanded and autonomous IMF.

Other Multilateral Institutions as Financial Intermediaries

As with the IMF, one may question whether the 1944 justifications for creating a World Bank remain valid in the 1980s. In what follows, the role of the World Bank and the role of other multilateral lending agencies, such as the Inter-American and Asian development banks, as financial intermediaries will be separated from their roles as dispensers of concessional finance, or aid, as is the role of the International Development Association and other "soft" windows.

Why should the World Bank borrow in more or less open financial markets to lend to Brazil, which has direct access to those markets on its own? Why would Brazil want to use the World Bank as intermediary, anyway? Again, the answer must be sought in the informational imperfections of capital markets, which can be reduced by multilateral banks, whose solvency is backed by financially powerful countries. Multilateral banks also can exploit economies of scale in monitoring borrowers. Faced with rationing or steeply rising marginal borrowing costs, Brazil could welcome indirect borrowing channels that may expand credit availability and reduce costs. Borrowing from the World Bank would, in turn, increase Brazil's credit worthiness among private lenders. These considerations apply a fortiori to LDCs whose direct access to international private credit markets is less fluid than Brazil's. Although international capital markets revived since the 1960s beyond 1944 expectations, the World Bank still has the role assigned to it in Bretton Woods, that is, to substitute partly for private international markets for long-term bonds, which collapsed in the 1930s. Even in industrialized countries with fairly well-developed credit markets, there are public institutions that act as financial intermediaries or guarantors to channel resources toward borrowers overlooked or neglected by purely private markets; examples in the United States include the Small Business Administration and student loans.

In contrast with the role of the IMF, then, the role of multilateral banks is not to engage in short-term crisis lending but to finance those investment opportunities with high social rates of return that are not being banked by private sources. They have their own form of conditionality, which may range from a minimalist one, dealing with specific projects, to a maximalist one, involving all aspects of the development policies of borrowing countries. This is not the place to rehash the stale arguments of the 1960s on this form of conditionality nor the related debate on project versus program lending. See Diaz Alejandro (1971) and Albert O. Hirschman and Richard M. Bird (1968) for discussion of these issues. New circumstances that arose during the early 1980s warrant a few remarks, however.

Brazil may borrow from international markets both directly and via multilateral banks, and its option to do either reduces the leverage that multilateral banks have over that country and other borrowing NICs. At the same time, given the circumstances of the early 1980s, abrupt graduations of NICs from multilateral banks appear unwise. During the 1980s, multilateral banks could pioneer in experimenting with financial instruments and loans with flexible repayment schedules (for example, those contingent on commodity prices) and various forms of indexing. Cofinancing of loans with private lenders, as practiced by the International Finance Corporation, could play a useful but modest role in expanding the volume of finance, as long as this practice does not distort priorities in the rest of the World Bank system.

LDCs without direct access to international credit markets will have to rely both on the intermediating role of multilateral banks and on multilateral and bilateral aid if they want to invest beyond what they save, either temporarily or for a longer term. Among LDCs, the dependence of sub-Saharan Africa on multilateral institutions and on aid remains singularly acute and worthy of special emergency attention (Helleiner 1982). Willy-nilly, this type of LDC will continue to participate in a dialogue with multilateral lenders and donors about their investment plans and other development policies. Apparently correct conventional wisdom argues that such a dialogue is best handled multilaterally rather than bilaterally; it is therefore strange that the Reagan administration appears to favor both a tighter development conditionality and a weakening of multilateral institutions.

Memories, Dreams, Reflections

Throughout history, international monetary and financial arrangements have been the aspect of the world economy most obviously connected to political power. The Pax Romana, the Pax Britannica, and the Pax Americana had counterparts in coinage and credit. Between pax and pax, chances for panics and depressions grew (Kindleberger 1973). It may be argued that, although in the early 1980s the hegemonic power of the United States has been seriously eroded, a great deal of consensus among capitalist industrial powers remains regarding desirable international economic arrangements, so a repetition of past interpax catastrophes may be avoided (Ruggie 1982). Yet the diffusion of commercial, financial, and political power of the early 1980s remains historically unprecedented, generating large actual and potential frictions among major international actors, including those arising from attempts by the United States to reassert hegemony and discipline among its allies. This dangerous situation, however, also can be interpreted as a necessary precondition to building a more equitable and participatory international economic system.

Most LDCs that have economic development as their highest priority are passive spectators in this turmoil. They often are lectured about how they must adjust to the realities of the 1980s. If such adjustment is compatible with the maintenance of a minimum rate of development, they are likely to make the adjustment. Most, however, are not likely to put up with a pseudoadjustment involving long periods of stagnation. Rather, they will face possible new international realities by reorienting their development strategies. Quite sensibly, they will not adjust if adjustment involves having high rates of unemployment and excess capacity and wasting opportunities for capital formation. Some LDCs, of course, are in a better position to carry out such reorientation than are others, due to larger domestic markets and a greater availability and willingness to use policy instruments. As a participant at the September 1982 IMF/World Bank meeting in Toronto put it: "Brazil is too big to fall into the abyss."

A reorientation of LDC development policies would involve, as did reorientation during the 1930s, a greater emphasis on import substitution, this time perhaps involving more South-South cooperation. The new strategy also could involve import postponement and investments using non-traded goods (for example, housing) intensively; these elements are consistent with greater attention to the welfare needs of the population at the bottom of the income scale. If stagnation and protectionism in the North became chronic, hampering the reverse real transfer involved in debt servicing, financial arrangements would have to be reexamined and renegotiated. The IMF, the World Bank, and other multilateral lending agencies would have to exercise some imagination in order to serve as more than debt-collecting agencies.

This scenario, gloomier for the North than for some development-prone LDCs, still remains an unlikely one. Whatever happens, the combination of business cycles in major capitalist economies and contractually rigid loan agreements will continue to generate the periodic North-South financial frights that were almost forgotten during the 1950s and 1960s because of the relatively smooth, high growth and the miniscule debt with which LDCs emerged from World War II. It is doubtful that the smoothing of the Northern business cycle will be successful during the 1980s; therefore, instability in the prices of Southern export commodities (almost declared a nonproblem during the 1960s) is likely to remain high, also. Note that, among highly indebted LDCs, one finds both oil importers and oil exporters; a fall in oil prices may help some (for example, Brazil) while provoking a crisis in others (for example, Mexico). Instability in that price is likely to hurt both. One would imagine that, in a cyclical world, financial arrangements that include provisions to deal with contingencies such as sharp fluctuations in the prices of key exports of borrowing countries, rather than provisions that establish fixed repayment schedules, come hell or high water, would emerge. Historically, lenders have preferred to use ad hoc rescheduling rather than ex ante flexible conditions, probably because of moral-hazard considerations. Bank regulators in lending countries also have preferred, so far, to deal with the issues raised by more or less forced roll overs in an ad hoc fashion.

Both at the national and international levels, banks and other financial intermediaries have come under closer academic and public scrutiny during the 1970s and early 1980s. After early enthusiasm for ending financial repression and most regulations, sober second thoughts have appeared. Few would argue that financial intermediation is just one more competitive industry, with no more externalities than the apply industry. At the national level, financial reform could take sharply divergent paths, depending on macroeconomic strategies and on the confidence policymakers have in their own administrative capacities versus their faith in the public's capability to sift information and make wise decisions regarding risks and returns. France has ended up with nationalized banks, while the United States may reduce deposit insurance and force banks to reveal more information about their portfolios. Deregulation in the United States will involve some subtle rhetorical exercises. Henry Wallich, as a member of the Board of Governors of the Federal Reserve System, speaks of " . . . building a more flexible and more competitive banking system . . . " almost in the same breath that he urges banks " . . . to remember that their actions in troubled situations impinge on all other banks. Their interests will be best served if they stand together in defense of a common position." He also advises that " . . . in analyzing [LDC] creditworthiness, . . . banks should seek out and make available to each other the necessary information" (Wallich 1982, pp. 1, 2, and 3). Singular advice for the promotion of competition!

No country, developed or developing, can afford not to think through these dilemmas in the context of their own specific national circumstances; just copying the financial laws and practices of another will not do, nor will relying on old practices be enough in the 1980s. The LDCs, preferably acting as a group, also have a large stake in monitoring and influencing how changes in the financial practices of industrial countries affect international capital markets. Regardless of how each country handles its domestic financial system, what are the interests of LDCs, or of different types of LDCs, regarding international financial markets? Should they lobby for laissez-faire international banking or for greater controls, inevitably to be exercised mostly by parent industrialized countries?

For semiindustrialized and socialist countries, the late 1970s represented a golden era of borrowing, cheap both in economic and political terms, thanks to the uncontrolled segment of international banking. It may be argued that the early 1980s proved that such a golden era was a passing mirage, bound to end in collapse, as did the Southern Cone domestic financial liberalizations. The ease of borrowing tended to encourage domestic mismanagement and overspending by public and private agents in weak projects (as in the cases of Argentina and Mexico); however, the unexpected severity of macroeconomic circumstances during 1981–82 is largely responsible for others' payments difficulties (as in the Brazilian case). During 1982, many LDCs saw the dollar value of their exports fall sharply, even as the export quantum grew, provoking charges of dumping by industrialized countries. Yet, in other cases, such as Colombia, very prudent policies have kept the country out of the financial pages of international newspapers. During 1982, it has become clear that, although an international lender of last resort is at hand, it will extract its pound of flesh.

Indeed, there are hints that the 1982 crisis may be used by some industrialized countries, particularly by the United States, to reassert discipline, that is, to cartelize bank lending not just to socialist countries but also to LDCs. The cartelization could bring some paternalistic benefits: making the system less vulnerable to crises and eliminating some foolish loans. However, the dangers to self-reliant borrowers, confident of their own economic and political management, are obvious.

Somewhat paradoxically, both semiindustrialized and other LDCs would be wise to fight for the integrity of the IMF, even as they press for more rational IMF conditionality. The same posture could apply toward the World Bank, and other multilateral lending agencies (and, indeed, for the GATT). The imperial pretensions emanating from Washington during 1981–82 have underlined the potential benefits to many LDCs of both a lightly regulated international banking system and a set of supporting multilateral financial agencies, including an IMF that could act as a genuine ILLR. The multilateral financial agencies should play a particularly important role with regard to the poorest LDCs during the 1980s.

How much pressure can LDCs exercise in international financial bargaining? Can Southern debts be aggregated into one powerful bargaining chip? Mexico is unlikely to want its debt lumped with that of Bolivia or even Brazil for bargaining purposes. Yet demonstration effects among debtors could occur during a severe international crisis, leading them to sequentially suspend normal debt service, as was done during the early 1930s. This may be enough to give at least some semiindustrialized LDCs a bit of influence to press for a reexamination of rescheduling and ILLR arrangements. The ideas put forth at the United Nations Conference on Trade and Development (UNCTAD) Manila conference on rescheduling and on how to ameliorate the real consequences of the periodic financial scares that are inevitable in private financial markets are worth a fresh look. The sharing of costs between lenders and borrowers of loan decisions that eventually turn out to have been mistakes also needs reexamination, both to check moral hazard and on equity grounds; at present, the burden is born disproportionately by borrowers, with private banks often doing quite well in reschedulings.

In spite of the troubles in formal South-South integration schemes, intra-LDC trade grew vigorously during the 1970s. Such a trend could be encouraged and accelerated during the 1980s by bolder cooperation among LDC central banks. More generous reciprocal credit lines could be particularly important in encouraging trade in machinery and other capital goods. This type of relatively modest step in financial cooperation, say, among the central banks of Brazil and Mexico, may be quite useful given the environment of the 1980s and, indeed, may pave the way toward joint bargaining with third parties.

References

Bacha, Edmar. 1981. "The impact of the float on LDCs: Latin American experience in the 1970s." In *Exchange rate rules: The theory, performance and prospects of the crawling peg,* ed. John Williamson. London: The MacMillan Press Ltd.

Bacha, Edmar L., and Carlos R. Diaz Alejandro. 1982. *International financial intermediation: A long and tropical view.* Princeton Essays in International Finance no. 147. Princeton N.J.: Princeton University, International Finance Section, May.

Baeza Valdes, Sergio. 1982. "El costo de desvincular la rentabilidad del riesgo." *Economia y Sociedad* (Santiago de Chile) (October):13–17.

Bertrand, Raymond. 1981. "The liberalization of capital movements—an insight." *The Three Banks Review,* no. 132, (December):3–22.

Brodsky, David A., and Gary P. Sampson. 1981. "Implications of the effective revaluation of reserve asset gold: The case for a gold account for development." *World Development* 9, no. 7.

Brodsky, David; Gerald Helleiner; and Gary Sampson. 1981. "The impact of the current exchange rate system on developing countries." *Trade and Development: An UNCTAD Review,* no. 3 (Winter):31–52.

Colchester, Nicholas. 1981. "A doomsayer on doom avoidance." *The Financial Times,* July 7:18.

Cooper, Richard N., and Edwin M. Truman. 1971. "An analysis of the role of international capital markets in providing funds to developing countries." *Weltwirtschaftliches Archiv,* no. 2 (June):153–183.

Dell, Sidney. 1981. *On being grandmotherly: The evolution of IMF conditionality.* Princeton Essays in International Finance no. 144. Princeton, N.J.: Princeton University, International Finance Section, October.

Diaz Alejandro, Carlos F. 1975. *Less developed countries and the post-1971 international financial system.* Princeton Essays in International Finance no. 108. Princeton, N.J.: Princeton University, International Finance Section, April.

Diaz Alejandro, Carlos F. 1971. "Some aspects of the Brazilian experience with foreign aid." Chapter 20 in *Trade, balance of payments and growth,* ed. Jagdish N. Bhagwati et al. Amsterdam: North-Holland Publishing.

Diaz Alejandro, Carlos F. 1981. "Stories of the 1930s for the 1980s," National Bureau of Economic Research Conference Paper no. 130, November.

Dornbusch, Rudiger. 1982. "Flexible exchange rates and interdependence." Mimeographed, Massachusetts Institute of Technology, October.

Eaton, Jonathan, and Mark Gersovitz. 1982. *Poor country borrowing in private financial markets and the repudiation issue.* Princeton Studies in International Finance no. 47. Princeton, N.J.: Princeton University International Finance Section, June.

Foxley, Alejandro. 1982. "Towards a free market economy: Chile 1974–1979." *Journal of Development Economics* 10:3–29.

Frieden, Jeff. 1981. "International finance and the nation state in advanced capitalist and LDCs." Mimeographed, Columbia University, September.

Fritsch, Winston. 1979. *ANPEC VII Encontro Nacional de Economia* 2 (Atibara, Sao Paulo) (December):673–732.

Gurley, John G.; Hugh T. Patrick; and E.S. Shaw. 1965. *The financial structure of Korea.* Reprinted by Research Department, The Bank of Korea.

Helleiner, Gerald K. 1982. "The IMF and Africa in the 1980s." Mimeographed, University of Toronto, November.

Hirschman, Albert O., and Richard M. Bird. 1968. *Foreign aid. A critique and a proposal.* Princeton Essays in International Finance no. 69. Princeton, N.J.: Princeton University, International Finance Section, July.

Kindleberger, Charles P. 1978. *Manias, panics and crashes: A history of financial crisis.* New York: Basic Books.

Kindleberger, Charles P. 1973. *The world in depression, 1929-1939.* Berkeley: University of California Press.

McKinnon, Ronald I. 1982. "The order of economic liberalization: Lessons from Chile and Argentina." In vol. 17 of Carnegie-Rochester Conference Series on Public Policy, *Economic policy in a world of change,* ed. K. Brunner and A. Meltzer. Amsterdam: North-Holland Publishing.

Ohlin, Goran. 1976. "Debts, development and default." In *A world divided: The less developed countries in the international economy,* ed. Gerald K. Helleiner. Cambridge: Cambridge University Press.

Ruggie, John R. 1982. "International regimes, transactions, and change: Embedded liberalism in the postwar economic order." *International Organization* 36, no. 2, (Spring):379-415.

Sachs, Jeffrey, and Daniel Cohen. 1982. "LDC borrowing with default risk." National Bureau of Economic Research Working Paper no. 925, Cambridge Mass.

Sachs, Jeffrey. 1981. "The current account and macroeconomic adjustment in the 1970s." *Brookings Papers on Economic Activity,* no. 1.

Solow, Robert M. 1981. "On the lender of last resort." In *Financial crises: Theory, history and policy,* ed. Charles P. Kindleberger and Jean-Pierre Laffargue. Cambridge: Cambridge University Press, 237-248.

Tobin, James. 1978. "A proposal for international monetary reform," *Eastern Economic Journal* 4, nos. 3-4 (July-October).

Triffin, Robert. 1964. *The evolution of the international monetary system: Historical reappraisal and future perspectives.* Princeton Studies in International Finance Section. Princeton, N.J.: Princeton University.

Turnovsky, Stephen J. 1982. "A determination of the optimal currency basket: A macroeconomic analysis." *Journal of International Economics* 12:333-354.

Wallich, Henry C. 1943. "The future of Latin American dollar bonds." *The American Economic Review* 33:321-335.

Wallich, Henry C. 1982. "Notes on the banking scene." Washington, D.C.: Board of Governors of the Federal Reserve System. Mimeographed, October.

Williamson, John. 1982a. "A survey of the literature on the optimal peg." *Journal of Development Economics* 11:39-61.

Williamson, John. 1982b. *The lending policies of the International Monetary Fund.* Policy Analyses in International Economics no. 1. Washington, D.C.: Institute for International Economics, August.

Comment

José D. Epstein

Over the last decade, there has been an enormous expansion of international private-bank lending to LDCs. This has resulted in unprecedented levels of both the total debt and the debt-servicing obligations contracted by LDCs, particularly in the case of the newly industrializing countries (NICs). Financial markets today confront a mixture of recession, inflation, excessive exchange-rate fluctuations, and high interest rates. Thus, many LDCs, and especially NICs, face a difficult and complicated situation, highlighted by, but certainly not limited to, Mexico's current debt crisis. Although formal defaults are being avoided by roll overs, the impact of postponements on the banks' cash flow may bring about loan losses that will affect their bond ratings.

How did the international financial markets reach this point? Was it because of imperfections and flaws existing in those markets or because of deficiencies on the borrowing side? Carlos Diaz Alejandro discusses what he calls informational asymmetries and moral-hazard imperfections. Despite what he suggests in the chapter, commercial lenders are seldom project oriented; therefore, they rarely establish the soundness of specific projects as a basis for deciding whether to approve a loan to an LDC. They are, rather, concerned with the borrower's balance of payments and macro-economic situations, that is, the quality of the guarantee. Beyond the lending nation's symbolic gunboats, the attitude of both borrowers and lenders is influenced heavily by the issue of continuing lending. Moreover, the amount and terms of a prospective loan, as well as the degree of mutual confidence, is often determined by a long-term bank-borrower relationship or by whether the transaction is of a one-shot type. To a great extent, this relationship is a function of the nature of the lender, that is, whether it is a money center or a regional bank.

As to prudential regulations covering financial intermediaries, the chapter acknowledges that controls over domestic lending are greater than those over international lending from offshore centers. Recent events show that, despite supervision, both U.S. and Italian regulators failed to prevent the collapse of Penn Square and Banco Ambrosiano. The situation of these two banks has affected the financial system in two different ways. Penn

The opinions expressed in this comment are those of the author and do not necessarily reflect the points of view of the Inter-American Development Bank.

146

Square demonstrated to depositors that their money could be at risk at a time when banks are confronting disintermediation by money-market instruments. On the other hand, the apparent reluctance of the Bank of Italy to rescue the overseas subsidiary of Banco Ambrosiano has surprised the Euromarket, which may have expected that domestic and foreign operations would be treated equally. This leads to the issue of lender of last resort. The assumption by the banking community that there is such a lender, the central bank at a country level and the International Monetary Fund (IMF) at an international level, may have resulted in the banks' running excessive risks. As Diaz Alejandro wisely quotes, "the lender of last resort should exist, but his presence should be doubted."[1]

The lack of regulation of the Euromarket, compounded by its high liquidity after the 1974 oil crisis, resulted in large amounts lent, or rather pushed out, at times after somewhat perfunctory analysis. The availability of resources may have been a great incentive for LDCs to borrow more than they might have done otherwise.

From the standpoint of the LDCs, besides organizational or informational flaws and the issues just discussed, exchange-rate and incentive considerations also may have induced their borrowing beyond prudent limits for purposes other than capital formation. The rates of return were presumed high enough to compensate both lenders and borrowers, but, in many instances, that did not prove to be the case. I have to take exception with Diaz Alejandro, however, on the issue of the responsibility of public agents in signing a loan. Current events in at least some NICs demonstrate that such officials may indeed be held responsible in the future for what takes place during their tenure. Additionally, there often has been a lack of consistency in economic management as a result of the high rotation of managing teams in many LDCs. In any case, as the chapter acknowledges, "During the 1970s, many LDC borrowers . . . benefitted from credit conditions. . . . " Since 1980, however, the credit conditions have resulted in increased (and forced) LDC reliance on short-term financing, which, coupled with high floating interest rates, has raised debt-service costs to dangerous proportions. This trend is occurring in conjunction with deteriorating terms of trade and weak demand for LDCs' exports in the North and within a framework of increased protectionist pressures. Nevertheless, one should assume that "the remarkable feats of maturity transformation," whereby long-term investments have been financed with short-term bank debt, imply a tacit understanding between borrowers and lenders that there were to be roll overs under whatever name (for example, rescheduling) one would wish to use.

Indeed, reschedulings and renegotiations simply will have to take place for defaults to be avoided. Either formally or informally, indebted LDCs have had to establish debt-servicing priorities when liquidity constraints have not permitted their honoring all commitments in a timely fashion. Lowest priority has been assigned to commercial nonguaranteed debt, which requires private banks to be flexible when dealing with rescheduling requests. Even though higher spreads over interest rates may be called for, LDCs need to continue borrowing both to finance imports and to service debt. It is important to stress that this is not just a problem for the South; it is global in nature. Recession in the North will deepen if demand from the South for its exports continues to decrease—and there will be other economic, financial, and political consequences if there is an organic breakdown in the financial system.

A decade after the collapse of Bretton Woods, an alternative system has yet to emerge. It would seem that the introduction of generalized floating in August 1971 began a domino effect of financial profits and losses on appreciations and depreciations of substitute reserve currencies, which rendered the foreign-exchange markets unstable and volatile. The boom of the Euromarket, coupled with countries' greater access to private credit, encouraged experimentation at the end of the last decade, particularly, as noted by Diaz Alejandro, in the Latin American Southern Cone.

With regard to the International Monetary Fund, the chapter stresses the need for "something like an IMF" as a lender of last resort to national central banks. The role of lender of last resort requires that it have available enough resources to back it up, and the IMF's lending potential has not kept up with the evolution of balance-of-payments deficits. Any consideration of the IMF's role in the restoration of a condition that would lead to sustainable noninflationary growth must touch upon the issues of conditionality and surveillance. Historically, the subject of conditionality has been sensitive politically, reflecting wide divergence between LDCs and industrial countries. Diaz Alejandro argues for "IMF conditionality focused narrowly on balance-of-payments targets," and he decries the "intrusive" nature of those components of conditionality that transcend the South's position that the IMF places too much emphasis on domestic demand management and thereby puts a heavy burden on the population. Nonetheless, the implementation of sound fiscal and monetary policy as well as the improvement of economic efficiency and the strengthening of the productive system are important components of a IMF-supported adjustment program.

This is a continuing battle; it is difficult to concentrate exclusively on balance-of-payments targets, and economic adjustment may not be achievable without a comprehensive program. In addition, it is imperative that, if sacrifice is imposed on the LDCs via adjustment programs, control, or surveillance, of macroeconomic policies in the developed world be undertaken to promote convergence in seeking reduced inflation, greater rates of growth, and exchange-rate stability (as was recently discussed at the Versailles summit). A more stable economic environment translates into lower interest rates, thereby reducing the burden of the indebted LDCs and providing relief to their adjustment processes. A three-percentage-point decline in world interest rates, sustained over three years, would save Mexico's balance of payments the entire $4.5 billion it expects to receive from the IMF.

The role of the multilateral development banks (MDBs) has sparked controversy in recent months. Diaz Alejandro elaborates on this topic, correctly arguing that the MDBs reduce the informational imperfections of capital markets by borrowing in the open market and lending to LDCs, acting, in effect, as bridges in those markets. He explains convincingly why Brazil, and a fortiori other LDCs with limited access to private capital markets, seek financing from MDBs. Moreover, it is a fact that, in addition to issues to be discussed later, their more favorable lending terms, lower interest rates, and longer maturities have resulted in a long-term continuing relationship. Within this context, when liquidity constraints arise, LDCs' debt-servicing priorities reflect the overall relative importance of the role of MDBs. Indeed, NICs' repayment priorities illustrate this well: first, MDBs; second, government-issued bonds; third, publicly guaranteed loans to state enterprises; fourth, syndicated loans.

Even though multilateral banks do indeed fill a gap, there is a basic difference between their philosophy and that of the rest of the financial community. The multilateral banks are concerned with the long-term development impact of their lending operations. The World Bank and the regional banks (Inter-American, Asian, and African development banks) emphasize the efficient use of productive resources, attempting to ensure that resources are allocated to those sectors and activities with the highest social rates of return. Such banks examine the countries' growth prospects over the long run and the soundness of their investment programs given the framework of their resource endowments and constraints. The recipient countries benefit, not only from the transfer of resources and from the fact that those resources are devoted to sound investment projects, but also from the technical assistance and economic advice that accompanies the loan. Diaz Alejandro raises the point, which I strongly support, that the economic dialogue with the LDCs is best handled multilaterally. This approach ensures the impartiality of such a dialogue, as well as its freedom from political interference.

Regarding joint activities with private banks, cofinancing activities provide, and will continue to provide, a promising (but limited) way to stimulate additional capital flows to LDCs for investment purposes. They also benefit the private banks by reducing their perceived risk. However, results from cofinancing should not be overestimated. The boards of the International Bank for Reconstruction and Development (IBRD) and the Inter-American Development Bank (IDB) are presently discussing initiatives, but any activity will have to contend with borrowers' lack of enthusiasm for a variable interest rate in the context of development lending. Experiences with that type of rate structure involving adjustments based on the London interbank offer rate (LIBOR) have, so far, been circumscribed to commercial borrowing, although pressures for adopting variable interest rates are mounting.

An important point raised by Diaz Alejandro should be stressed: MDBs are both aid channels and external financing intermediaries. Their role as aid channels is smaller than ever, however. The International Development Association probably will soon amount to not more than 25 percent of IBRD lending. In the IDB's case, this year the concessional window will not go beyond 15 percent, with the remainder being lent with market-raised resources (for example, bond issues floated in markets such as Germany, Japan, Switzerland, and the United States) and at close to market rates. This downward trend in concessional financing has to be reversed. Otherwise, MDBs will not be able to provide their least-developed member countries with much-needed resources for development processes without burdening their already strained repayment capacities.

There are difficult times ahead. New financial arrangements and innovations in the rescheduling process may be required, and both North and South will need to follow appropriate and convergent policies, taking into account the mutual impact of such policies.

Note

1. Charles P. Kindleberger, *Manias, Panics and Crashes: A History of Financial Crises,* New York: Basic Books, 1978, p. 12.

Comment

Donald R. Lessard

Carlos Diaz Alejandro has provided a comprehensive and very clear summary of a complex subject in an entertaining and witty way. This comment will not review his entire analysis; instead, it will focus on and extend a few of his key conclusions regarding the weaknesses of the existing system and then will take issue with the analytical framework employed in the chapter. This discussion is meant as a criticism, not of the chapter in particular, but of the general frame of reference employed by most economists addressing this issue.

Indictments of the Current System

Diaz Alejandro draws two key indictments of the current system of North-South finance:

1. The system is subject to collapse due to the Keynesian "beauty-contest" nature of country risk analysis and lending choices.
2. The system is likely to misallocate credit due to distortions.

Both indictments are of the behavior of lenders within the system, not of the structure of the system itself. Both result from critical information issues—ex ante information assymmetry and ex post difficulties in enforcement resulting from the difficulty of distinguishing state (bad luck) from strategy (bad faith or bad management). I would like to add to the list of indictments, stressing structural rather than behavioral elements:

3. Scheduled debt service varies substantially with the nominal interest rate (LIBOR), a variable that bears, if anything, a negative relationship to less-developed countries' (LDCs') export revenues.
4. The claims of LDCs are concentrated in commercial banks rather than spread throughout financial markets.
5. The claims on LDCs are money fixed in external currencies and, hence, bear no relation to outcomes on specific projects or strategies.

Each of these structural characteristics have implications for the performance of the system that may dominate the (mis)behaviors identified by Diaz Alejandro. The variability of scheduled repayment would not be an issue if all claims were automatically rolled over. In a world with perfect information and complete enforceability, claims would be rolled over unless the present value of a borrowing country's future net exports fell short of the present value of outstanding claims. In other words, illiquidity would never be an issue and the only risk would be of insolvency.[1] However, given limited information and enforceability, rolling over is not a sure thing, and the arbitrary shortening of maturities via increases in LIBOR can create problems for borrowers as well as for the system as a whole.[2]

The fact that claims against LDCs are concentrated in commercial banks may lead to a magnification of the impact of nonperformance on the system and on the continued availability of finance for LDCs. Although the aggregate volume of LDC claims is a small fraction of total world financial claims, it is large relative to the capitalization of the key banks. A major default could force banks to limit additional credit or even to cease rolling over existing credits. Furthermore, the exposure of banks to such events brings lender-country authorities (with their varying political agendas) into North-South debt negotiations, perhaps further distorting the incentives facing industrial private lenders. Such distortions are likely to be exacerbated by the banks' practice of not marking to market loans to LDCs (or to anyone else for that matter), which provides potential nonperformers with additional bargaining power in case difficulties that require rescheduling do arise.

The nonspecific nature of bank credit has two effects. First, it trivializes the role of private banks and public institutions in project evaluation or the overseeing of national economic strategies because, given the fungibility of claims, a loan to a good project is no better than a loan used to acquire arms or maintain consumption during a reverse in the terms of trade. Second, and probably much more important, it means that, within the present system, risks inherent in projects or strategies are shifted only through nonperformance. This must be a costly and inefficient mechanism, resulting in limited risk spreading. In fact, the repeated assertions of bankers that few if any defaults are imminent is clear evidence that the system provides little risk shifting, especially given the radical fluctuations in terms of trade and other project- or strategy-specific risks incurred by LDCs.

The first two structural issues are widely recognized and frequently discussed. The third, however, receives little attention. This may be because it is a nonissue, but I believe it is because the issue does not arise within the frame of reference employed by most economists who are evaluating North-South finance.

Limitations of the Conventional Analytical Framework

In virtually all of the literature on this subject, finance is viewed as a transfer of resources over time—a country benefits if the rate of return on domestic assets exceeds the interest; a country is insolvent if national income grows at a lower rate than the interest rate. The critical role of financial transactions in spreading risks to minimize their negative effect on welfare is almost totally ignored.

The new literature on the subject stresses the strategic nature of risks of nonperformance, but it downplays the extent to which the system succeeds in "passing through" exogenous risks faced by borrowers to representative investors with a comparative advantage in bearing such risks due to the greater diversification of their holdings.[3] Thus, the reduction of risks in the system is seen largely as the search for mechanisms to enhance the enforceability of claims. Given their nonspecific nature, this would effectively preclude the shifting of any exogenous risks. A perspective on international finance that incorporates both time bridging and risk sharing would, in contrast, lead to the search for vehicles that reduce the dead-weight costs associated with nonenforceability while increasing the shifting of exogenous risks.

The myopia of the existing frame of reference also shows up in statements such as Diaz Alejandro's that, with bank financing, "the price of either extravagance or sensible capital formation was low." It is true that real interest rates were low in the 1970s. However, it is also true that, when they traded off increased current consumption or investment against future debt-service obligations, borrowers should have taken into account the noncontingent nature of these obligations.

This trade off would have been characterized in money space by discounting the certainty equivalent of future benefits at the real interest rate on foreign borrowing. This certainty equivalent, though, would have been less than the expected value of these benefits if they had covaried positively with national income. Such discounting for the single-period case can be expressed as:

$$PV = \frac{E(NB)}{1 + r} - \lambda \text{ covariance } (NB, Y)$$

where PV is the present value of the project, r is the real interest rate, NB is the uncertain future net benefit, Y is national income, and λ is a parameter reflecting the price of risk, which, in turn, will depend on both a nation's preferences and its risk endowment.[4] With such a calculation, while real interest rates might have been low, the certainty equivalents of future project returns, especially for investments representing a deepening of exposure to a set of key risky variables affecting national income (for instance, Organisation for Economic Cooperation and Development [OECD] income-dependent manufactures for Brazil, oil for Mexico), should have been significantly lower than their expected values to reflect their national systemic risk.

Alternatively, the trade off could have been made in utility space by pricing specific state-contingent receipts and obligations according to their impact on the utility of consumption.[5] For example, potential oil revenues for Mexico would have been priced down to reflect their coincidence with overall economic conditions in Mexico, while nonspecific credit claims would have been priced up to reflect the fact that they must be met under all states, even by countries whose national income and, hence, consumption are extremely depressed. In such trade offs, debt with LIBOR-linked payments is likely to appear even worse than riskless debt because LIBOR appears to vary slightly negatively with the export revenues of many LDC borrowers.

Interactions between the Conventional Analytical Framework and the Structure of the System

Whether the increasing dependence of LDCs on commercial bank financing represents a rational trade off by all parties between the potential spanning of time and risk by finance and the minimization of dead-weight costs resulting from limits to contract enforceability or whether it results in part from the myopia (outlined in the previous section) on the part of borrowers or lenders, it has several important implications for both borrowers and lenders. As noted by Diaz Alejandro, because of ex ante and ex post uncertainty, credit is likely to be misallocated, the existence of free riders will represent a tax on other users of the systems, and, most important, the whole system could collapse because of a single, potentially diversifiable default or even an event in Northern credit markets unrelated to LDC fortunes. A further critical implication of the increasing dependence is that the system's primary exposure is to the overall economic (mis)management of particular borrowing countries rather than to the outcomes of specific projects or strategies. This is consistent with the demonstrated desire of most LDCs for economic sovereignty, but it also has the effect of increasing the extent to which international finance resembles a gaming situation among a small number of players rather than an insurance market covering a wide range of outcomes with limited elements of moral hazard. Clearly, the position of the institutional structure along this continuum has important implications for the economists' choice of an appropriate analytical framework for analyzing the behavior of the system. However, I also believe that the employment of conventional analytical frameworks in the analysis of North-South finance has had a significant impact on the evolution of the system. As participant observers we should examine this issue with great care.

Notes

1. Aliber (1980) draws the distinction between illiquidity and insolvency crises.

2. See, for example, Kincaid (1981).

3. Contributors to the new literature include Eaton and Gersovitz (1981) and Sachs (1982).

4. See, for example, Leland (1982) in his comment on Wilson (1982). Also, see Arrow (1982), in the same volume, who admits to the possibility of a social-risk premium in contrast with his earlier work.

5. Blanchard (1982) develops the concept of disutility of foreign debt.

References

Aliber, Robert. 1980. "A conceptual approach to the analysis of external debt of developing countries." World Bank Staff Working Paper no. 421, Washington, D.C.

Arrow, Kenneth. 1982. "The rate of discount on public investments with imperfect capital markets." In *Discounting for time and risk in energy policy,* ed. R. Lind. Resources for the Future.

Blanchard, Olivier. 1982. "Debt and the current account deficit in Brazil." Harvard Institute for Economic Research, Discussion Paper no. 882. Cambridge, Mass.: Harvard University, February.

Eaton, Jonathan, and Mark Gersovitz. 1981. "Poor country borrowing in private financial markets and the repudiation issue." *Studies in International Finance* no. 47. Princeton, N.J.: Princeton University International Financial Section, June.

Kincaid, C. Russell. 1981. "Inflation and the external debt of developing countries." *Finance and Development* (December):45–48.

Leland, Hayne. 1982. "Comment" on R. Wilson. In *Discounting for time and risk,* ed. R. Lind.

Lessard, Donald. 1983. "Appropriate non-concessional financing for developing countries." Working paper, Sloan School, M.I.T., March.

McDonald, Donogh. 1982. "Debt capacity and developing country borrowing: A survey of the literature." *IMF Staff Papers* (December):603–46.

Sachs, Jeffrey. 1982. "LDC debt in the 1980s: Risks and reforms." National Bureau of Economic Research Working Paper, no. 861, Cambridge, Mass., February.

Wilson, R. 1982. "Risk measurement of public projects." In *Discounting for time and risk,* ed. R. Lind.

7 The Japanese Financial System in Transition

Eisuke Sakakibara

As the 1980s unfold, the Japanese financial markets seem to be undergoing a significant transformation. The trend that started in the early seventies and had become quite explicit by the end of that decade is proceeding at an ever-accelerating pace in the eighties.

On the one hand, the changes associated with this trend have caused severe problems because they have required that the traditional domestic financial system be readjusted. The postwar Japanese system was built around the banks, as was most of continental Europe's system (in opposition to the Anglo-Saxon system, which was and still is characterized by the central role of open markets). During the thirty-some years following World War II this system functioned quite efficiently and contributed substantially to the successful performance of the Japanese economy as a whole.

On the other hand, many of the changes, such as the liberalization of foreign-exchange controls, rapid internationalization of the activities of Japanese banks and nonbanks, and increased access of foreigners to Japanese money and capital markets have already made Japan quite an important international market with considerable potential for further development.

The ramifications pose difficult policy questions for the authorities. If the pace of deregulation and liberalization is accelerated, Tokyo would quickly emerge as a major world financial center, a situation that, in itself, would be quite desirable. It would not only enlarge the international activities of Japanese banks and nonbanks but also benefit foreign institutions in their use of yen and in their activities in the Asia-Pacific area. However, such acceleration in the pace of deregulation, or even a hands-off policy, might create serious confusion and chaos, given the effects of the ongoing changes. Aspects of the traditional Japanese system, such as long-term credit banking, the separation of banks from securities companies, the post office, and corporate-savings system, and the principle of securing debts through collateral would have to be changed quickly. However, the smooth transition to a U.S.-style system seems very difficult, if not impossible,

The views expressed in this chapter are the author's and do not represent those of the Japanese government.

157

because these traditional aspects are deeply ingrained in Japanese culture and everyday life.

In this chapter, facts about these current changes are documented carefully, and their ramifications for the future of the Japanese financial system are analyzed. In the first section, the postwar Japanese financial system is outlined very briefly. In the second section, the current markets are described. The third section analyzes the implications of the ongoing changes for banks and nonbanks. The fourth section investigates policy issues and proposes a possible strategy to resolve the dilemma. Specifically, the creation of an offshore market in Tokyo is presented as the next major step authorities could undertake. In the last section, a brief summary and conclusions are presented.

The Postwar Japanese Financial System

It is extremely difficult to summarize any financial system in one section, but a brief sketch of the postwar Japanese financial system is presented here. For a more detailed description, the reader is referred to another publication.[1]

In comparing the Japanese experience with that of the United States and in analyzing the interaction of the real and financial sectors in Japan, four major characteristics peculiar to the Japanese system can be identified. We will consider them in turn.

Continuous Deepening of Debts

One distinctive development of the Japanese financial markets since World War II has been the rapid, continuing rise in the ratio of the financial liabilities of the nonfinancial sectors to total gross national product (GNP).

Table 7-1 shows this liability ratio, both as an aggregate figure and broken down by major sectors or categories of borrowers (central government, local government, incorporated business, and individuals).

The rapid rise in the liability/income ratio in the early postwar years can be explained, at least partially, as a restoration of the earlier liability/income levels. However, the ratio continued to rise well into the 1970s. Thus, today the Japanese nonfinancial sector is more deeply in debt than is its U.S. counterpart. It is not clear from the data whether liability deepening has stopped, but, because of the recent deceleration, no substantial further rise in the ratio is in sight.

Table 7-1
Financial Liabilities as a Share of Total GNP

Period	Total		Central Government		Local Authorities		Corporations		Individuals[a]	
	Japan	United States	Japan	United States	Japan	United States	Japan	United States	Japan	United States
1953–1955	0.779	1.374	0.085	0.605	0.076	0.108	0.547	0.288	0.091	0.372
1956–1960	0.995	1.411	0.072	0.500	0.101	0.130	0.682	0.352	0.138	0.454
1961–1965	1.211	1.480	0.043	0.422	0.128	0.149	0.851	0.360	0.189	0.548
1966–1970	1.387	1.442	0.084	0.323	0.175	0.148	0.890	0.396	0.238	0.574
1971–1975	1.598	1.476	0.108	0.279	0.214	0.151	0.965	0.444	0.307	0.601
1976–1978	1.761	1.503	0.222	0.300	0.273	0.137	0.897	0.452	0.364	0.614

Source: Data are adapted from the flow-of-funds accounts of the Federal Reserve System and those of the Bank of Japan. Flow-of-funds data for Japan used in the SNA accounts were not included because they do not go back far enough in history and because of the incompleteness of that set of data.

Note: Figures in the table represent the geometric averages of ratios for the years listed.

[a]This includes unincorporated businesses in both countries.

The High Degree of Financial Intermediation

The basic activity of financial intermediaries is holding various assets with the aim of transforming them into a single liability, usually deposits. This activity is important to an economy because it not only reduces the costs of asset holding to depositors but also transforms the nature of risk. For example, one result of this activity is maturity transformation; that is, financial intermediaries collect deposits of short maturity and make investments or loans of long maturity. The extent of the mismatch of asset-side and liability-side maturities cannot be too large because financial intermediaries must have sufficient liquidity for unforeseen withdrawals of deposits. The risk of a liquidity crisis is reduced, however, by interbank markets, money-market instruments, and central-bank financing.

Table 7-2 shows one measure of the importance of financial intermediation—the ratio of total liabilities of financial intermediaries to GNP. Because of the systematic, intertemporal, and compositional differences between intermediaries' liabilities in the United States and their liabilities in Japan, the ratios in table 7-2 are not directly comparable. They do, however, indicate several facts. Between 1953 and 1978, the degree of financial intermediation rose in both countries, but much less in the United States than in Japan. In the United States, "the continuation and even acceleration of the trend toward intermediate markets" was accompanied by a "simultaneous rise in the economy's reliance on privately issued debt."[2] That is, despite the small rise in the overall ratio in the United States, the amount of risk increased. As table 7-1 shows, this is because, during that time period, the composition of liabilities shifted substantially from public to private. Because private debt is more risky than public, overall risk rose. This increase in the aggregate liability-side risk in the United States encouraged advances in financial intermediation to blunt the effect on individuals' asset-side risk.

Table 7-2
Financial-System Liabilities as a Proportion of GNP

Period	Japan	United States
1953–1955	0.919	1.106
1956–1960	1.238	1.166
1961–1965	1.566	1.313
1966–1970	1.729	1.371
1971–1975	1.961	1.427
1976–1978	2.044	1.486

Source: Calculated from flow-of-funds accounts of the Federal Reserve System and the Bank of Japan.

In Japan, between 1953 and 1978, the rise in financial intermediation was extremely rapid and closely associated with the overall deepening of debts. Moreover, although the share of public debt in total financial debt rose after 1960, implying less risk, the rapid surge in the overall ratio of liabilities to GNP more than offset this change in composition. In Japan, the increase in intermediation was encouraged not by the shift in debt composition by by the overall deepening of debt.

Table 7-3 shows the composition of financial assets of the nonfinancial sectors in both countries between 1953 and 1978. Holdings of equities and bonds were much larger in the United States, although M2 was much more important in Japan. This figure clearly indicates that, during this period, intermediation in Japan was dominated by banks and post offices. Moreover, the proportion of financing through trade credit was much larger in Japan than in the United States, reflecting the fact that Japanese nonfinancial corporations engaged in substantial financial intermediation for their customers and subsidiaries. Hence, the degree of overall intermediation was even larger than the ratio of liabilities of financial intermediaries to GNP implies. All in all, postwar Japan saw a tremendous rise in financial intermediation, to a level of greater than that in the United States.

Low Public Debt and High Public Financial Intermediation

Another striking contrast between the United States and Japan is the evolution of public debt. In the United States, the ratio of outstanding public debt to total nonfinancial-sector liabilities was 71 percent in 1946. For Japan, the ratio was only 10 percent in 1953. Gradual and steady decline in the United States and rapid increase in Japan after 1971 brought the ratios to 19 percent and 14 percent, respectively, by the end of 1978.

The initial low value for Japan was the result of the rampant inflation of the late 1940s. This initial low value, together with the balanced budgets of the central government, made possible extremely low stocks of public debt. The central-government deficit started to bulge after 1971 and grew very rapidly throughout the 1970s. Despite this bulge, it would not be wrong to characterize the years between 1953 and 1973 as a period when the share of public debt remained low in Japan.

A natural counterpart to the low liability share of the government was the high share taken by the private sector in Japan. In particular, the share of financial liabilities of corporations remained extremely high throughout the period. By 1978, their share had fallen to "only" 47 percent, compared to a share of 30 percent for U.S. corporations. Before the first oil shock, however, the share had never gone below 60 percent and had stayed near 70

Table 7-3
Wealth Composition of Nonfinancial Sector: Assets
(percent of total)

Period	M1		M2		Long-Term Savings[a]		Equities	
	Japan	United States	Japan	United States	Japan	United States	Japan	United States
1953–1955	0.249	0.153	0.526	0.298	0.047	0.136	0.124	0.272
1956–1960	0.189	0.122	0.491	0.272	0.065	0.140	0.147	0.320
1961–1965	0.159	0.096	0.438	0.273	0.072	0.145	0.137	0.344
1966–1970	0.154	0.085	0.446	0.279	0.087	0.149	0.110	0.333
1971–1975	0.161	0.084	0.467	0.336	0.091	0.160	0.102	0.245
1976–1978	0.149	0.078	0.487	0.367	0.104	0.167	0.088	0.204

Period	Financial Investments[b]		Loans		Trade Credit	
	Japan	United States	Japan	United States	Japan	United States
1953–1955	0.025	0.201	0.010	0.023	0.263	0.065
1956–1960	0.028	0.180	0.006	0.019	0.260	0.068
1961–1965	0.047	0.151	0.002	0.019	0.303	0.067
1966–1970	0.038	0.139	0.001	0.021	0.318	0.078
1971–1975	0.045	0.142	0.000	0.021	0.293	0.087
1976–1978	0.060	0.154	0.000	0.023	0.261	0.084

Source: Calculated from flow-of-funds accounts of Federal Reserve System and the Bank of Japan.
[a]Includes trusts and insurance.
[b]Includes securities other than equities.

percent most of the time. This high liability share of the corporations was no doubt an underlying factor for high investment and high GNP growth. The low public share of debt contributed to growth by not causing significant crowding out and by encouraging financial intermediaries to take more risk on private debts. Although the direction of causality is ambiguous, it could be argued that the paucity of riskless government securities induced the economy to devise more ways to bear more risk, the chief method being more intermediation.

The Japanese government itself played a very significant role in raising the degree of financial intermediation. Table 7–4 gives two indicators of this for the period from 1953 to 1978: the share of government financial institutions in loans granted, and the share of government intermediaries in total liabilities of all intermediaries. The shares for Japan were significantly higher than those for the United States throughout the period. Moreover, the significance of this intermediation was much greater than the numbers suggest. On the liability side, the postal-savings system, administered through post offices, created an atmosphere of intense competition in the collection of deposits. On the asset side, lending by governmental financial institutions (for example, the Japan Development Bank) not only injected extra funds into the system but also gave de facto government guarantees to projects in which they participated.

Low Levels of Consumer Credit

Another distinctive feature of Japanese financial markets is the low level of liabilities of individuals. The category of individuals includes unincorpo-

Table 7–4
Government Financial Intermediation: Government Financial-Institution Shares in Financial-Sector Loans and Total Liabilities

	Loans (Assets)			Total Liabilities	
	Japan				
Period	Gross	Net [a]	United States	Japan	United States
1953–1955	0.221	0.191	0.043	0.191	0.010
1956–1960	0.228	0.179	0.045	0.192	0.015
1961–1965	0.206	0.156	0.065	0.171	0.020
1966–1970	0.215	0.156	0.066	0.184	0.027
1971–1975	0.220	0.156	0.073	0.202	0.046
1976–1978	0.283	0.210	0.086	0.232	0.063

Source: Calculated from flow-of-funds accounts of the Federal Reserve System and the Bank of Japan.
[a]The net column excludes loans among government institutions.

rated business in the Japanese flow-of-funds statistics, and U.S. statistics are adjusted accordingly. Hence, the numbers given in table 7-1 include, among other things, bank loans to unincorporated business. Although consumer and mortgage credit in Japan expanded quite rapidly in the seventies, they were still only 17.5 percent of GNP in 1978 (in the United States, they were 68.1 percent of GNP). It is fair to characterize the postwar Japanese financial markets as closed to consumers.

When liquidity constraints are binding, the life-cycle pattern of income affects the life-cycle pattern of consumption. In Japan, the pattern of income has been biased toward old age because of the seniority-based wage system. Due to borrowing constraints, the young have had to save to build houses instead of borrowing to do so. The old, on the other hand, have been allowed to save whatever remained after consumption. Thus, the combination of the seniority-based wage structure and poor consumer financing has generated higher overall savings.

Comparison of flow-of-funds data of the United States and of Japan during the postwar period yields four distinct features of Japanese financial evolution: (1) a continuous deepening of financial debts; (2) a high degree of financial intermediation; (3) high government financial intermediation and investment in contrast to low government consumption; and (4) low consumer financing. These financial features seem to provide some suggestions as to why the savings rate and perhaps the real growth rate accelerated during that period.

The ability to deepen debts made it possible for corporations to borrow heavily, raise the level of investment, and reduce the real cost of financing. The small amount of government debt along with the de facto closing of markets to consumers until the 1970s meant that most funds could go only to corporations and for investment purposes. These developments were encouraged by the rapid advancement of financial intermediation, which raised savings by lowering the average risk per yen of assets.

Behind these functional characteristics of the Japanese financial system lay structural idiosyncrasies that were molded into the standard institutional mode of operations. Although it is impossible to describe the entire spectrum of such interactions, it is useful to mention some key features.

As table 7-3 indicates, in the postwar era the composition of wealth of the Japanese nonfinancial sector was very biased toward bank liabilities. Excluding trade credit, the Japanese nonfinancial sector held 66 percent of wealth in M2 in 1976-78, while its U.S. counterpart invested only 40 percent in M2 during that time. On the other hand, during the same period, investments in equities and other securities were only 20 percent of the total (excluding trade credits) in Japan as opposed to 39 percent of the total in the United States. These figures clearly indicate the relative importance of commercial banks and thrift institutions compared to security companies (or investment banks) in Japan.

A comparison of the Japanese and U.S. financial systems before the Monetary Control Act of 1980 shows that Japanese regulations on commercial banks and thrift institutions were less stringent than U.S. regulations. Commercial banks were allowed to branch nationwide, to hold equities of up to 5 percent of a company's total shares, and even to take part in the underwriting function for the latter through the mechanism known as the commissioned bank system. Partly because of these less stringent regulations, nonprice competition among commercial banks and thrift institutions at the retail level was very keen.[3] This competitive environment was quite conducive to increased savings in small denominations at the household level. The competitive structure of retail banking is indicated by table 7–5: the shares of the five largest commercial banks showed a consistent decline relative to the shares of post offices.

In contrast to the retail market, the wholesale money markets were regulated fairly stringently until the late 1970s, when call (federal funds) and bill rates were liberalized (in April 1979 and October 1979, respectively) and a certificates-of-deposit (CD) market was created (in May 1979). These regulations prevailed until very recently and were closely related to the regulations in the capital markets.

Unlike in the United States, in Japan the majority of long-term funds were raised through banks or post offices, as table 7–6 shows. When borrowing was large and relatively risky, syndication often was used to diversify risk. However, syndication and diversification of only long-term loans were not sufficient to reduce the asset-side risk of Japanese commercial banks to levels suitable to the liability-side risk. The long-term credit-bank system was quite important in supplementing the function of commercial banks, both quantitatively and qualitatively.

There is a significant difference between long-term credit banks and regular commercial banks. On the asset side, the credit banks are restricted mostly to long-term instruments, both loans and bonds. On the liability side, they are permitted to issue debentures and are allowed deposits only from the government and from borrowers. In practice, most funds come from debentures. With much less volatility on the liability side, the long-term credit banks could easily devote almost all their resources to long-term assets and function as the key institution in many loan syndications.

Long-term credit banks also perform a critical role in the Japanese bond market. The market has a unique feature called commissioned underwriting, in which banks act as commissioned companies, advising on amount, timing, the terms of flotation; coordinating negotiations; preparing contracts; receiving proceeds; and delivering certificates. Securities companies only underwrite in the strict sense, that is, to ensure that the issuer obtains the funds it requires in the event of undersubscription. Thus, the functions that are solely performed by investment banks in the United States are undertaken jointly by banks and securities companies in Japan.

Table 7-5
Shares of Various Financial Institutions to Total Deposits and Bank Debentures
(percent)

	1910	1920	1930	1940	1950	1960	1970	1979
Commercial and savings banks[a]	72.8	70.3	47.4	46.4	57.4	49.9	41.9	35.0
Big five[b]	12.7	14.4	14.7	15.5	38.3	32.8	26.2	20.5
Local banks[c]	60.1	55.9	32.7	30.8	19.1	17.1	15.6	14.5
Long-term credit banks[d]	14.4	14.9	13.0	10.4	8.9	5.7	6.0	5.7
Trust banks			7.6	8.1	2.7	10.1	9.6	11.7
Thrift institutions, including cooperatives[e]	0.3	2.2	7.1	13.5	17.4	19.5	25.5	25.1
Life insurance companies	3.8	4.4	6.6	5.6	2.0	4.1	6.0	5.7
Post offices	8.6	8.2	18.3	16.0	11.6	10.7	11.0	16.8
Total deposits and bank debentures (in yen)[f]	Y2,010	Y10,916	Y21,680	Y62,816	Y1,617	Y17,020	Y92,658	Y377,994

Source: Prewar figures are derived from "Evolution of the Japanese Financial System During the Interwar Period," In *Analysis of the Japanese Economy During Interwar Period*, ed., I. Nakamura, February 1981. Postwar figures are derived from *Economic Statistic Annual*, Bank of Japan, various issues.

[a]Figures are sums of commercial and savings banks before the war. There were no savings banks after the war.

[b]Figures represent Daiichi, Sumitomo, Yasuda, Mitsui, and Mitsubishi for prewar period. Postwar figures given are the share of city banks.

[c]Figures in 1940 include the share of Sanwa Bank, created in 1933 by mergers.

[d]Prewar figures are for specialized banks.

[e]Including Shokochukin Bank and Norinchukin Bank.

[f]Prewar figures are in millions of yen, while postwar figures are in billions of yen.

The participation of long-term credit banks in bond markets is consistent with the standard procedure of securing bonds with collateral because such practice is normal in long-term bank lendings.

Some analysts have argued that bank dominance in long-term lending was due to controls on the bond market, but they have the causality the wrong way around. Given the structure of the market, existing restrictions were not inefficient, at least until very recently, because the bond market performed only a marginal function in the raising of long-term funds for corporations.

Moreover, a stable market in corporate bonds would have required that a developed market in risk-free government securities exist to act as reference against which to determine appropriate corporate bond yields. The low quantities of government bonds outstanding in Japan before 1975 would have prevented the existence of such a developed government bond market, even if controls imposed on members of the government-bond syndicate with regard to resale had been nonexistent. Hence, with no frame of reference within which to set corporate bond rates, the development of a major market in long-term corporate bonds would have been difficult.

**Transformation of the Japanese Financial System—
The Facts**

One of the fundamental premises of the postwar Japanese financial system disappeared in the late seventies. The outstanding amount of government bonds totaled 82.3 trillion yen at the end of 1981, equivalent to 33 percent of GNP. If the obligations of local government and public corporations were included, the percentage would be as high as 54.6, far surpassing the percentage in the United States. This amount is the result of large government deficits, which stood at 5.5 percent of GNP in fiscal 1981.

Until the mid-sixties, fiscal deficits were unheard of in Japan. However, with the flotation of government bonds to cover postwar deficits in 1966 and the bulge in deficits in 1971, this happy state of affairs came to an end. Although the amount of annual flotation of central-government debt averaged only 550 billion yen in the late sixties, the level doubled by the early 1970s, jumped quickly to nearly 5 trillion yen in the recession year of 1975, and soared progressively over the next five years to a total of 14.4 trillion yen in 1980. Although the 1981 deficit declined somewhat (to 13.8 trillion yen), by 1993 new issues of national bonds are expected to amount to 20 trillion yen, assuming that there are no major cuts in expenditure or tax increases, both of which are very difficult to do politically.

As a reflection of these developments, the size of the Japanese capital markets expanded very quickly. As table 7-7 shows, the outstanding

Table 7–6
Supply of New Funds for Plant and Equipment
(billions of yen/[percentage of total]; fiscal years)

	1952–1955		1956–1960	
	Total Industry	Four Major Industries[a]	Total Industry	Four Major Industries
Securities	217.3(11.9)	55.0 (6.5)	1,410.1(21.6)	578.8(24.9)
Equities	182.4(10.0)	40.7 (4.8)	996.5(15.3)	379.0(16.3)
Bonds	34.9 (1.9)	14.3 (1.7)	413.6 (6.3)	199.8 (8.6)
Private financial intermediation	1,096.6(59.8)	473.2(51.3)	3,968.0(60.7)	1,250.1(53.8)
Banks	711.7(38.8)	392.5(46.7)	2,230.6(34.2)	835.9(36.0)
Others	384.9(21.7)	80.7 (9.6)	1,727.4(26.5)	414.2(17.8)
Public financial intermediation	519.6(28.3)	312.6(32.7)	1,150.2(17.7)	494.9(21.3)
Japan Development Bank	244.1(13.3)	202.6(24.1)	299.9 (4.6)	241.5(10.4)
Others	275.5(15.0)	110.0(13.1)	850.3(13.1)	253.4(10.9)
Total	1,833.5(100.0)	840.8(100.0)	6,518.3(100.0)	2,323.8(100.0)

Source: Source: I. Ishikawa and T. Gyoten, eds., *Fiscal Investments and Loans* (in Japanese) (Kinya Zaisei Jijo Kenkyukai, 1977).

[a]Electricity, shipping, coal and steel.

amounts of Japanese bonds mushroomed from 8.2 trillion yen in 1965 to 173.3 trillion yen in 1981. Transactions in the Japanese bond market reached 301.4 trillion yen in 1981, approximately thirty times that recorded ten years earlier. Consequently, Tokyo has become the second largest capital market in the world as far as the outstanding amount of securities and their transactions is concerned. During this process of rapid expansion, various measures were implemented to liberalize the markets. The first major step, taken in 1977, was the partial relaxation of restrictions on bond sales imposed on financial institutions. Until 1977, financial institutions had been, in effect, barred from selling bonds to the markets. Instead, the Bank of Japan (BOJ) had absorbed the bonds held for a year or two through outright purchases when adding liquidity to the system. As the amount of bond issues ballooned however, such absorption became impossible. Initially, relaxation was meant to apply only to bonds held in banks' portfolios for a year or longer. Gradually, however, the time restriction for holding bonds was reduced to one hundred days.

These developments in the capital markets had a significant impact on the short-term money markets. The repurchase (repo) market grew as a natural outcome of the expansion in the bond markets in the late seventies and soon became the major money market. At the end of 1981, total pur-

Table 7–6 continued

1961–1965		1966–1970	1971–1975	1979
Total Industry	Four Major Industries	Total Industry	Total Industry	Total Industry
2,872.5(17.8)	810.5(25.1)	3,904.6(11.2)	9,434.8(12.2)	2,601.5(12.0)
2,094.5(13.0)	486.0(15.0)	2,055.0 (5.9)	3,599.1 (4.6)	798.7 (3.7)
778.0 (4.8)	324.5(10.0)	1,849.6 (5.3)	5,835.7 (7.5)	1,802.8 (8.3)
10,681.7(66.4)	1,707.8(52.8)	25,783.8(73.7)	57,564.1(74.2)	14,936.4(69.3)
4,971.0(30.9)	944.2(29.2)	16,965.3(48.5)	39,144.4(50.4)	9,388.4(43.5)
5,710.7(35.5)	763.6(23.6)	8,818.5(25.2)	18,419.7(23.7)	5,575.0(25.8)
2,540.4(15.8)	715.6(22.1)	5,282.1(15.1)	10,597.8(13.7)	4,026.1(18.6)
672.6 (4.2)	391.6(12.1)	1,362.9 (3.9)	2,825.8 (3.6)	948.9 (4.4)
1,867.6(11.6)	324.0(10.0)	3,919.2(11.2)	7,772.0(10.0)	3.077.2(14.2)
16,094.4(100.0)	3,233.9(100.0)	34,971.5(100.0)	77,597.6(100.0)	21,591.2(100.0)

chase balances in the repo market stood at 4.5 trillion yen, compared to 4.2 trillion yen and 3.9 trillion yen in the call money (federal funds) and bill markets, respectively. Although the call and bill markets are still partially guided by the BOJ through brokers, the repo market is completely free of any controls and administrative guidance. In May 1979, an open market in CDs was created, and its size quickly grew to 3.3 trillion yen by the end of 1981. Because repos in CDs are not subject to the security-transaction tax to which repos involving securities are subject, the number of short-term repo transactions in CDs skyrocketed. Although the Japanese money markets are not yet comparable to those of the United States in that their scope for open transactions is limited, there is every indication of their quickly becoming so, as table 7–8 and table 7–9 indicate.

Traditionally, almost all treasury bills (TBs) had been held by the BOJ and not marketed. In May 1981, however, the BOJ sold 1.5 trillion yen of TBs to the market. Such sales have been made periodically since then. Although these sales do not amount to the creation of a TB market, they, along with the expected appearance of huge amounts of short-maturity bonds in a few years, are believed to be paving the way for the development of such a market. Moreover, sales of foreign-issued CDs and commercial paper (CPs) in Japan are expected to be initiated shortly, because all legal

Table 7–7
Outstanding Amounts of Japanese Bonds
(trillions of yen)

Year	Total	National Bonds	Private Bonds	Financial Debentures	Repurchase Market
1965	8.2	0.2	1.7	3.0	0.1
1966	10.7	0.9	1.9	3.6	0.1
1967	13.3	1.6	2.1	4.2	0.2
1968	15.7	2.1	2.4	4.8	0.3
1969	17.7	2.5	2.6	5.5	0.4
1970	20.3	2.8	3.0	6.3	0.6
1971	25.3	4.0	3.6	7.9	0.9
1972	31.3	5.8	4.1	9.7	1.2
1973	37.7	7.6	4.8	11.4	1.7
1974	45.4	9.7	5.4	13.3	1.5
1975	58.2	15.0	6.6	15.9	1.6
1976	72.8	22.1	7.2	18.4	1.9
1977	90.8	31.9	7.9	20.7	3.1
1978	109.7	42.6	8.5	22.9	4.2
1979	131.2	56.3	9.5	24.1	4.0
1980	152.7	70.5	9.9	26.2	4.5
1981	173.3	82.3	11.1	28.6	4.5

Source: Data from Ministry of Finance, internal documents.

Table 7–8
Comparison of Major Bond Markets
(billions of dollars)

	Japan	United States	Germany	United Kingdom
Issues (1980)	90.5	158.3	83.8	39.8
Outstandings	732.3 (1980)	1,515.8 (1980)	345.8 (1980)	124.1 (1979)
Transactions	725.0 (1981)	3,700.0 (1981)	228.0 (1981)	322.0 (1981)

Source: Data from Organisation for Economic Cooperation and Development, *OECD Financial Statistics,* various issues.

obstacles to such sales were eliminated as of April 1982. These sales not only would increase the number of open-market instruments but also are expected, in some quarters at least, to lead to the creation of a full-fledged CP market.

The other important factor that contributed to the extremely rapid growth of markets in Japan was successive efforts to ease controls over foreign-exchange transactions. As of September 1982, all exchange controls

Table 7-9
Comparison of Major Stock Markets, 1980
(billions of dollars)

	Tokyo	New York	London	Frankfurt	Paris
Numbers of firms listed	1,417	1,570	3,141	370	752
Numbers of stocks listed	1,424	2,228	2,679	406	975
Market value	379.7	1,242.8	204.5	63.5	53.1
Total transaction	179.8	382.4	36.7	5.6	12.6

Source: Data from Organisation for Economic Cooperation and Development, *OECD Financial Statistics,* various issues.

on investments by foreigners had been removed. Accordingly, foreign nonresidents' holdings of yen-denominated assets have been skyrocketing, especially by the Organization of Petroleum Exporting Countries (OPEC). As table 7-10 shows, investment by nonresidents surged from $507 million (acquisition) in 1972 to $24 billion in 1981. Foreign banks' and nonresidents' access to the Japanese money markets have also improved dramatically (see table 7-11).

Thus, the yen's transformation into a reserve currency is occurring at an extremely rapid pace, although official holdings of yen assets as calculated by the International Monetary Fund (IMF) remain below 4 percent.[4]

In addition, yen transactions by nonresidents outside Japan are estimated to be three times domestic-transaction volume, and the stock of yen-denominated assets held by nonresidents, including the amounts held abroad, is believed to be worth just under $100 billion as of year-end 1981.

In summary, then, Japan has come to have the second largest capital market in the world, and the scope of open-market transactions in short-maturity bonds also is expanding very quickly. Internationalization of the Japanese markets accelerated after the revision of the Foreign Exchange Control Act of December 1980, and it seems only a matter of time before Tokyo thrives as a major world financial center. The pace of such liberalization and internationalization has been extremely rapid and seems to be gaining increasing momentum in the eighties.

The major problem of the rapid development of an open-market system is that it is not necessarily consistent with some of the standard modes of operations established in the past. Although there is no doubt that Japan is becoming more and more like the United States, whether Japanese institutions should be "Americanized" is a question that involves values and culture. This issue is analyzed in detail in the following sections.

Table 7-10
Portfolio Investment by Nonresidents
(millions of dollars)

Year	Acquisition	Disposal	Net
1972	507	250	257
1973	222	241	19
1974	423	185	238
1975	2,437	1,513	924
1976	2,986	1,274	1,712
1977	4,853	2,760	2,094
1978	10,742	8,278	2,464
1979	10,366	8,635	1,731
1980	15,353	10,043	5,310
1981	24,305	18,531	5,774

Source: Data from Ministry of Finance, internal documents.

Transformation of the Japanese Financial System—Implications

The transformations that were described briefly in the previous section have far-reaching implications for the future of the Japanese financial system. The traditional Japanese system was founded on the basic premise that the size of open markets should remain relatively small and that the extent of the participation of corporations and individuals in these markets should be limited. Rapid expansion of an international open-market system implies that the traditional system has to be modified in one way or the other. The question is not whether the system be modified; the question is when and how fast it can be modified. It must be added, however, that this required modification does not necessarily point to the inefficiency of the traditional Japanese system. On the contrary, the system was very efficient in providing a stable supply of long-term funds for rapid economic growth and industrialization. As the Japanese economy matures and internationalizes however, the criteria of efficiency and internal stability may be traded off for the criteria of equity and external compatibility.

This section will briefly analyze the impact of the changes mentioned earlier on five basic aspects of the Japanese financial system: (1) conventional practices in the capital market, such as the commissioned bank system; (2) separation of the securities and banking businesses; (3) separation of commerical banks and long-term credit banks; (4) regulation of interest rates; and (5) Japanese style of monetary policy.

Although the list is by no means exhaustive, these five elements are important parts of the postwar Japanese financial system. If very rough gener-

Table 7-11
Access of Foreign Banks and Nonresidents to Japanese Markets
(billions of yen and percent)

	End of 1979			End of 1981		
	Total Borrowing Balance	*Foreign-Bank Borrowing*	*Ratio (%)*	*Total Borrowing Balance*	*Foreign-Bank Borrowing*	*Ratio (%)*
Call-money market	3,408.6	111.1	3.3	4,206.3	475.2	11.3
Bill market	6,120.4	565.3	9.2	3,876.1	713.9	18.4
CD market	1,819.9	254.7	14.0	3,290.9	413.7	12.6
Total	11,348.9	931.1	8.2	11,373.3	1,602.8	14.1
	Total Purchase Balance	*Foreign-Bank Borrowing*	*Ratio (%)*	*Total Purchase Balance*	*Foreign-Bank Borrowing*	*Ratio (%)*
Repurchase market	3,960.4	73.9	1.9	4,481.0	811.7	18.1

Source: Data from Ministry of Finance, internal documents.
Note: Nonresident yen deposits at year end were (in billions of yen): 351.7 for 1975, 743.7 for 1979; 1,569.3 for 1980, and 1,869.9 for 1981.

alization is allowed, one can characterize the postwar system as one wherein a stable supply of long-term funds was provided by a banking system that centered around city banks and long-term credit banks. Close cooperation between these banks and securities companies in the capital market along with a well-established division of labor between securities companies, long-term credit banks, and commercial banks were key elements in the system. The underwriting securities companies and commission banks formed a group called the *Kisai-kai* (Committee for Security Issues) to coordinate the issue of securities (issues of convertible bonds and Samurai bonds labeled "spot" items were excluded from this scheme). In this commissioned-underwriting system, banks act as commissioned companies and securities companies act as underwriters. A commission company serves as (1) financial adviser to the issuer on methods of flotation, amount, timing, and terms of the issue; (2) coordinator for any negotiations on these matters; and (3) agent for the execution of such necessary procedures as the preparation of related contracts and forms, the receipt and delivery of any proceeds, and the delivery of certificates. The role of securities companies is confined to underwriting in the strict sense of the word, that is, ensuring that the issuer obtains the amount of funds it requires in the event of undersubscription.

Thus, functions that are performed by investment banks in the United States are undertaken jointly by banks and securities companies in Japan. Before World War II, these investment-banking functions were performed mainly by the banks. However, because the Securities and Exchange Law of 1948 prohibited banks from underwriting corporate bonds, this system of commissioned companies evolved. In other words, even after the prohibition of bank underwriting, banks continued to perform investment-banking functions except for underwriting in the very strict sense of the word.

Some proponents of direct financing, particularly those who advocate a more important role for securities companies in the bond markets, believe that bank participation in underwriting symbolizes the backwardness of the Japanese financial structure. Given the similarity in function of banks in Japan in making long-term loans and of investment banks in the United States in issuing corporate bonds, however, Japanese banks are natural candidates for originating bond issues. They have the knowledge and experience to appraise the long-term credit worthiness of companies. The experience and know-how of the commercial and long-term banks in making long-term loans are what make them the dominant players in the bond market. Arguments to the effect that bank dominance in the bond markets is due to governmental controls do not seem to be supported by the evidence. Given this dominance of large commercial banks and long-term credit banks in the bond market, it is only natural that the principle of securing bonds by collateral, like long-term bank loans, be institutionalized.

However, the recent internationalization of the markets has induced substantial modifications in the system. When Sears, Roebuck & Company wished to float an uncollateralized Samurai bond in 1978, it was decided that the long-established custom of collateralizing would be abandoned in favor of promoting internationalization of the market. At that time, rating standards for uncollateralized bonds were established to integrate these bonds with the collateralized bonds in the market, opening the road for foreign corporations to issue uncollateralized bonds in Japan.

Furthermore, when Dow Chemical issued bonds in January 1982, extremely flexible rating standards were applied. National Cash Register followed with an issue in April, and more foreign private flotations are expected in the near future. Also, as these rating standards were being formulated, a limited number of highly regarded Japanese companies, such as Matsushita and Hitachi, were allowed to float bonds without collateral.

Although the rating standards of the *Kisai-kai* are said, in some quarters, to be stricter than those of U.S. rating agencies, there is no doubt that the market is moving rapidly toward the adoption of more international procedures.[5] As the volume of securities transactions skyrocketed and as the market began to deregulate, internationalize, and, hence, alter structurally, the traditional demarcation between various financial institutions blurred as well.

Beginning in 1968, when the Bank of Tokyo established an investment-banking subsidiary in London, Japanese banks have progressively expanded their investment-banking activities in Europe. Since the first overseas subsidiary of a securities company was established in 1978, banks have gained more experience in international securities transactions. Although there are some restrictions imposed on the investment-banking activities of Japanese banks abroad (Article 65 of the Securities and Exchange Act of 1948, which separated securities and banking activities), overlapping, along with the internationalization of the banks, has increased considerably. This overlapping is becoming a major source of friction between the two types of financial institutions. This dispute could not be confined to the realm of international operations. The question of bank "window sales" and dealing in national bonds has become a hotly debated domestic issue. The issue involves the interpretation of Article 5 of the Banking Act and Article 65 of the Securities and Exchange Act. A compromise was reached in March 1982, allowing banks to sell national bonds to the public on a limited scale as of April 1983. The issue of bank dealings in national notes was left pending, to be decided sometime in the near future. Another new area where the activities of banks and securities companies overlap is the sale of foreign CDs and CPs. Because all legal obstacles have been eliminated, and given the Ministry of Finance's announcement of operational rules on March 31, 1982, sales on a limited scale may commence at almost any time.

Although outright revision of Article 65 of the Securities and Exchange Act—counterpart of the Glass Steagal Act—is not likely in the near future, de facto crossing of categorical delineations is expected to increase, whether it be through international transactions or through financial innovation, which would further blur the demarcation.

Traditionally, there has been a functional differentiation between long-term credit banks and commercial banks. On the asset side, the credit banks are restricted largely to long-term lending. They are allowed to make short-term loans (for no more than six months) only if the amount of loans does not exceed the amount of deposits. On the liability side, long-term credit banks are permitted to issue financial debentures but are not allowed to receive deposits from the public. Although they can accept deposits from government and borrowers, close to 70 percent of their funds are from debentures. Their debentures are of two types: five-year notes paying interest semiannually and one-year discount notes. A substantial proportion of these five-year notes are held by commercial banks, serving to deepen financial intermediation and liquidity transformation.

These bank debentures constitute almost 16.5 percent of total bonds outstanding in Japan and as much as 2.6 times the total amount of corporate bonds outstanding. In other words, a large share of the bond market consists of funds intermediated by the long-term credit banks. The market for financial debentures developed as a result of the vacuum left by the nonexistence of public and private notes of comparable maturities and contributed considerably to the stable provision of long-term funds to growing Japanese industries. As the supply of public securities has mushroomed, however, the government has felt an increasing need to issue securities in a broader spectrum of maturities. As a result, since 1977 five-year discount notes and two- to four-year interest-paying notes have been issued in limited amounts, creating the possibility that financial debentures will be crowded out. Because the government deficit has not shown any signs of decreasing, government issues that compete here are expected to increase in the future.

A CD market was created in May 1979 and quickly grew to 3.3 trillion yen by the end of 1981. This proliferation of CDs squeezes the market for financial debentures from the shorter end. Because long-term credit banks are still prohibited from collecting deposits from the public and the number of branches they maintain is small compared to the number maintained by commercial banks, the squeeze from both the longer and shorter ends of the market for financial debentures has put long-term credit banks in a difficult position. Their outlet seems to be in medium- to long-term international syndicated loans and active participation in overseas securities transactions, the latter being pursued with an eye toward eventual expansion into the domestic market. Because the activities of Japanese long-term credit banks closely resemble those of U.S. investment banks and U.K. merchant banks, the activities just mentioned constitute a natural course of development for long-term credit banks and tend to blur the distinction between financial institutions even further.

All of the developments described so far—rapid expansion of an open market, both on the long and short ends, increasing internationalization, and the blurring of the demarcation between the different types of financial institutions—lead to increasing competition and the freeing of formal and informal controls on interest rates.

Japanese interest rates have long been closely regulated by the authorities. Although such controls, formal and informal, may have interfered with market efficiency, they were an inherent part of the strategy of ensuring a sufficient and low-cost supply of funds to priority corporate borrowers in a generally funds-short postwar Japan. With its strong influence over interbank rates, the Bank of Japan made possible the channeling of funds from highly liquid regional banks and other depository institutions—agricultural and fishery cooperatives, mutual savings banks, credit banks, and credit associations—to the city banks that provided funds to large industrial corporations. The banks often circumvented interest-rate controls to some degree by requiring substantial compensating balances of anywhere from 20 to 40 percent of a loan.

Another major reason for the control of interest rates was to contain the costs of government borrowings. The share of government bonds issued to the members of a syndicate of financial institutions usually is determined in accordance with the size of the respective financial institutions. Since 1976, city banks, for example, absorbed 42.2 percent of these issues, whereas regional banks accepted 17.8 percent. In such a captive market, the authorities would be inclined to lower the issue rates of government securities as much as possible through some form of interest-rate control. Deposit rates, on the other hand, are regulated by the Temporary Interest Control Act of 1947, a law similar to Regulation Q in the United States. Thus, Japanese interest rates are determined by the controlled deposit rates and bond-issue rates. The discount rate; short-term prime rate; deposit rates; rates on financial debentures; issue rates on national, regional, and private bonds; and long-term prime rate and mortgage rate all fluctuate in a narrow band so that their relationships with one another are consistent.

Because of the appearance of many new open-market rates (for example, repo and CD rates and secondary market rates on bonds and notes), the structure of regulated rates has to be adjusted quite frequently these days.

In addition to the cited market rates, rates on loans and deposits denominated in foreign currencies were liberalized in December 1980, when the Foreign Exchange Control Act was revised. Although a total deregulation of interest rates, particularly those on deposits, does not seem imminent, interest rates on wholesale market instruments are likely to be liberalized soon because the present state of partial liberalization will not be sustainable for long. Such liberalization, in turn, is expected to have an impact on the prime rates on bank loans and on the issue rates of bonds, leading to the establishment of a much wider spectrum of market-determined interest rates.

The liberalization of all prices in the market has been deemed desirable by a majority of economists, and an acceleration of interest-rate liberalization in Japan may be looked at from this perspective. The increase in market efficiency through such liberalization, however, is not without costs. In Japan, not one financial institution went bankrupt during the past thirty-some years. Severe competition and bankruptcies resulting from liberalization may cause serious social disruption. Moreover, reorganization of the financial structure by market forces alone may be very difficult to achieve in a country where acquisitions through take-over bids or other capitalistic means are deemed inappropriate. Mergers through persuasion and government involvement have been the normal mode of reorganization in Japan. In such an environment, interest-rate liberalization may have to be accompanied by administrative measures to promote mergers by persuasion.

Unlike in the United States, where open-market operations are the key instrument of monetary policy, the Bank of Japan has used the interbank markets—the call and bill markets—as the major channel through which monetary policies are implemented. In the earlier days, BOJ lending to the city banks was used as the key instrument. The provision of funds through these interbank markets has been common, however, since outstanding lending by the BOJ hit its peak level. Because brokers in the interbank markets are directly under the control of the Bank of Japan, rates and the allocation of funds can be monitored relatively easily by the BOJ. Although interest rates are adjusted daily to other markets rates, they are said not to necessarily reflect demand-supply conditions. Accordingly, some rationing of funds is said to exist and to be used as leverage to implement the BOJ's qualitative controls, such as "window guidance."

These measures, along with the policy of setting a discount rate below market rates, have been central to the management of monetary policies in Japan. Although this type of strategy could be criticized as non-market-oriented, a closer look reveals quite a different picture. As Modigliani persuasively argued in his comment on chapter 3, Japanese and Continental European financial regimes can be described in a credit paradigm, in contrast to the United States and the United Kingdom, where they can be described in a money paradigm. Control on bank loans in a credit paradigm is logically equivalent to control of money supply in a money paradigm. To argue that credit controls are illegitimate in Japan is tantamount to arguing that money-supply controls are illegitimate in the United States. Thus, the attitude that the traditional Japanese system is a control regime, while the U.S. system is a free regime, is unfounded. The question is not one of control versus markets, but rather of different types of control in different institutional settings.[6]

With the rapid expansion of open markets and the resulting liberalization of interest rates, the traditional mode of Japanese monetary policy is bound to change, and the Bank of Japan has moved gradually toward such a change by emphasizing money-supply and interest-rate liberalization. In July 1978, the BOJ began to publish its forecasts on the growth of money supply. Restrictions on the call and bill markets have been lifted gradually. Although these and other moves do not necessarily imply that traditional credit policies have been completely abandoned in favor of the type of money-supply policies employed in the United States, there seems to be some apparent convergence between the two types of policies.

Policy Issues

The rapid transformation of the traditional Japanese financial system poses various complex policy issues for that country's authorities. The most difficult and perhaps logically unanswerable question is what system is most compatible with both international standards and Japanese values and cultural heritage. The policy-adjustment process could converge to some acceptable middle point only after much trial and error, and any a priori judgment in favor of one or the other system would have to be modified as events unfold. Accordingly, it is perhaps wise to avoid the issue of value judgments here and to accept the result that some convergence of Japanese and U.S. systems should emerge after experimentation.

More realistic and imminent issues are: (1) how the authorities should cope with the inequities of the partial liberalization of regulations for the various financial and nonfinancial institutions, and (2) at what speed the authorities should relax existing regulations.

As has often been pointed out, the existing state of affairs in the financial markets is such that regulations on financial institutions are stronger than those on nonfinancial companies, which has resulted in giving the nonfinancial institutions a competitive edge. Liberalization under the Foreign Exchange Control Act of December 1980 is said to have accelerated this phenomenon. The logical solution to this problem is either to tighten regulations on nonfinancial corporations or to relax the controls on financial intermediaries. Because tightening regulations on the former seems somewhat difficult under the current political environment, the only feasible solution is relaxing them for the latter.

The question, then, is how fast these regulations should be relaxed. Without directly answering this question, Japanese authorities have adopted the strategy of the so-called "soft-landing" which implies a transition to a new state without causing major frictions. The recent liberalization of domestic and foreign-exchange controls and the recent relaxation of administrative guidance are reflections of this soft-landing policy. Whether the implementation of these measures has been too rapid or too slow depends on one's perspective.

Value judgments apart, recent changes in the Japanese financial markets have been very dramatic, and the authorities have not discouraged these trends, even though they may not have acted as fast as some have wanted them to. The revision of the Foreign Exchange Control Act in December 1980, along with various other foreign-exchange liberalization measures taken prior to this revision, was certainly consistent with the trend of the market. Complete liberalization of residents' foreign-currency-denominated deposits with and loans from resident banks, for example, was a major step forward toward interest-rate liberalization, although its importance is often overlooked because the liberalization applied only to foreign currencies.

By using the forward-exchange market, however, foreign-currency deposits and loans having market interest rates are immediately convertible into yen and, in fact, 95 percent of foreign-currency loans have been so converted. During the one-year period after liberalization (December 1980 to December 1981), city banks' foreign-currency-denominated loans at market rates of interest and without compensating balances (which are customary in the case of yen loans) increased by as much as 16.3 trillion yen, more than 20 percent of the total increase in loans. Although yen loans at either of the prime rates still account for close to 80 percent of the total, this rapid increase in market-oriented transactions is quite remarkable.

Among the measures that are now being implemented or contemplated by the authorities, sales of foreign CDs and CPs and the creation of the Tokyo offshore market may be worth mentioning.

With the implementation of the new Banking Act in April 1982, legal groundwork was completed for the sale of foreign CDs and CPs by both banks and securities companies. Although overseas subsidiaries of Japanese corporations are prohibited from issuing CDs and CPs for the time being, sales of other overseas CDs and CPs can be conducted as soon as the Ministry of Finance gives the green light. The measure is seen by many observers as a major step toward the liberalization of the Japanese money markets. Japanese banks are very much opposed to the issuance of CPs in the domestic market on the grounds that issues of unsecured securities are not consistent with the long-established Japanese tradition of securing loans and securities with collateral. However, permission to sell foreign CDs and CPs may be seen as a step in the direction of domestic-market issuance, particularly if sales of the CDs and CPs of Japanese subsidiaries are sanctioned.

As these liberalizations proceed, the need for the creation of an institutional infrastructure has increased drastically. First, if the principle of collateral is partially abandoned, some authoritative rating agencies must be established and accepted by the market. Although one private company has recently commenced such a business, it is still far from establishing the prestige and reputation of Moody's or Standard and Poors'. Moreover, some competition in rating is absolutely necessary for impartiality to be secured. Second, disclosures of corporate financial conditions have to be expanded so that investors, in the absence of security provided so far by government regulations, can collect enough information to make their own judgments. Also, forms of financial covenants, such as negative pledges, restrictions on sales and lease back, and so forth, have to be standardized and firmly established.

The creation of a Tokyo offshore market has been advocated by a recent blue-ribbon commission. Tokyo already has many of the essential prerequisities for being an international financial center, both for yen and for dollars. It has a highly efficient communication and transportation network, interconnected with all the major financial and industrial centers of the world. As described in the previous section, its capital market is the second largest in the world, and the size and scope of its short-term money markets are quickly expanding. Tokyo's foreign community has grown rapidly in recent years and, as of the end of July 1982, a total of seventy-one foreign banks and six foreign securities companies are operating either in branch or representative-office form. Moreover, Tokyo has the distinct merit of being in a different time zone than New York and London and of having different sovereign risk.

Internationalization of Japanese banks has reached the stage where further expansion requires the increasing use of yen and the Tokyo market. Foreign-currency assets of the major Japanese banks have already exceeded $300 billion, financed mostly in London. From the point of view of managing risk, however, further dependence on London is not desirable. In terms of net profit, international operations made up approximately 15 percent of city banks' net profit in the second half of 1981, as compared to their less than 10 percent contribution two years earlier.

As any currency becomes internationalized, one effect is for the offshore market in that currency to develop. Although the size of the Euroyen market is still relatively small (estimated at around $28 billion at the end of 1981), it is triple the level it was at the end of 1980. One reason for its growth is that interest rates on nonresidents' yen deposits in Japan (except for those of foreign monetary authorities) are still regulated and subject to a 10 percent withholding tax. As long as such disincentives exist, the Euroyen market is expected to thrive and expand. The rapid growth of yen transactions outside the jurisdiction of the Japanese authorities is a possible destabilizing factor in the conduct of Japanese monetary and foreign-exchange policies.

Given this background and given the fact that there is a limit to accelerating liberalization of the domestic market, creation of an offshore market is seen as an ideal intermediate step to accommodate the need for internationalizing the Tokyo market. The Ministry of Finance is now conducting an intensive study to evaluate the desirability and feasibility of such a market, and Japanese financial institutions have started to prepare themselves for such an event.

Despite difficulties with timing, the creation of a Tokyo offshore market may be an appropriate measure, especially if disruptions of foreign and domestic markets can be avoided.

Summary and Conclusions

To summarize, this chapter has analyzed the changing state of the Japanese financial system, from its traditional postwar regime to a more international one.

The traditional system, however, is in no way viewed as underdeveloped or inefficient. On the contrary, when the country had a balanced budget and a minimal amount of public debt, the system was very efficient and conducive to a high rate of economic growth.

The basic prerequisite of the traditional system, however, disappeared in the 1970s, when public debts skyrocketed to a level exceeding that of the United States. Increasing internationalization, on the other hand, induced the conversion of the Japanese system to a more open Anglo-Saxon-type model.

Consequently, Japanese financial markets have undergone a very rapid transformation since the late seventies, and the trend seems to be accelerating in the eighties. Both the Ministry of Finance and the Bank of Japan have accommodated these changes through various liberalization measures. The revision of the Foreign Exchange Control Act of December 1980 was one such major step.

The basic policy of the Japanese authorities is to "soft land" on the new system, that is, to monitor the metamorphosis of the regime without causing major disruptions. Given Japanese values and culture, which consider take-over bids and similar capitalistic measures aimed at drastic changes inappropriate, careful coordination of changes is required, both by market participants and by authorities.

Among the various policies being contemplated is the creation of a Tokyo offshore market. This can be seen as one measure that will allow the system to soft land. In other words, it can be considered as the liberalization measure that is both feasible and effective at this point in time.

Notes

1. E. Sakakibara et al., "The Japanese Financial System in Comparative Perspective" (Study prepared for the use of the Joint Economic Committee, U.S. Congress, March 12, 1982).

2. Benjamin Friedman, "Postwar Changes in the American Financial Market," in *The American Economy in Transition,* ed. M. Feldstein (Chicago: University of Chicago Press, 1981), 9–79.

3. With regard to the nonprice competition among banks, deposit rates are regulated, as in the United States; the relevant law is the Temporary Interest Regulation Act of 1947. As is explained later in the chapter, wholesale open markets had not developed until the 1970s and are still partially regulated.

4. The figure does not include, for example, holdings of long-term securities by OPEC monetary authorities and is expected to approximately triple if these holdings are included.

5. In addition to these rating standards, some financial restrictions are imposed on the issuer. Regulatory items relating to corporate financial conditions include items on negative pledges, sale and lease back, additional debt-burden restrictions, and dividend restrictions. Among these, the restrictions on negative pledges and on sale and lease back are extremely common in all major international capital markets. Additional debt restrictions and dividend restrictions exist in some but not all western countries. These regulations are deemed necessary as substitute protection for investors, because the private yen-denominated bonds have no collateral. The system was adopted by market participants as a means of accommodating demands of foreign private corporations in a market where collateral is customary.

6. Franco Modigliani, "Monetary Mechanism Revisited and Its Relations with the Financial Structure," Mimeographed, Massachusetts Institute of Technology, November 1980.

References

Eguchi, H. "Comments on Effectiveness of the Window Guidance." *Japanese Economic Studies* (Winter 1977–78).

Friedman, B. "Postwar Changes in the American Financial Markets," In *The American Economy in Transition,* edited by M. Feldstein. Chicago: University of Chicago Press, February 1981.

Fukui, H. "Studies in Policy Making: A Review of the Literature." In *Policymaking in Contemporary Japan,* edited by T.J. Pemper, Ithaca, N.Y.: Cornell University Press, 1977.

Hamada, K.; Y. Ishiyama; and K. Iwata, "Structure of Japanese Loan Market—Loan Rates of City and Local Banks." (in Japanese). *Keizai Bunseki* Economic Planning Agency (March 1976).

Hasegawa, K. "Can Foreign Banks Compete with Japanese Management?" (in Japanese). *Shokun* (March 1981).

Hayden, E. "Internationalizing Japan's Financial System." An occasional paper of the Northeast Asia-United States Forum on International Policy, Stanford University, December 1980.

Horiuchi, A. "Effectiveness of 'Lending Window Operation' as a Restrictive Monetary Policy Measure." *Japanese Economic Studies* (Winter 1977–78).

Ishikawa I.; and T. Gyoten, ed. *Fiscal Investments and Loans* (in Japanese). Kinyu Zaisei Jijo Kenkyukai, 1977.

Japan Economic Journal. *Gendai no Koshasai Shijo 1: Koshasai Ryutsu Shijo* (Contemporary securities Markets 1: Secondary Markets in Securities). April 1982.

Japan Economic Journal. *Gendai no Koshasai Shijo 4: Kokkyo ga Nakunary Kinyu Shihon Shijo* (Contemporary securities markets 4: Internationalization of money and capital markets). July 1982.

Komiya, R. "Effectiveness of Japanese Monetary Policy." in *Analysis of Contemporary Japanese Economy* (in Japanese), edited by R. Komiya. Tokyo: Tokyo University Press, 1975.

Komiya, R. "The Supply of Personal Savings." In *Postwar Economic Growth in Japan,* edited by R. Komiya. University of California Press. 1968.

Kuroda, I. "On the Determination of Japanese Loan Rate—Re-examination of the Conventional View and a New Perspective" (in Japanese). *Kinyu Kenkyu Shiryo 2* (Bank of Japan, 1979).

Kuroda, I., and Y. Oritanic. "Re-examination of 'Peculiarities' of Japanese Financial Structure—Comparison of Balance Sheets of U.S. versus Japanese Corporations" (in Japanese). *Kinyu Kenkyu Shiryo 2* (Bank of Japan, April 1979).

Kure, B. *Monetary Policy* (in Japanese). Tokyo: Toyo-Keizai Shimpo-Sha, 1973.

Kure, B. "Window Guidance of the Bank of Japan." *Japanese Economic Studies* (Winter, 1977–78).

Lincoln, E. "Keiretsu." *Council Report,* no. 61. U.S.-Japan Trade Council, October 30, 1980.

Lincoln, E. "Monetary Mechanism Revisited and Its Relations with the Financial Structure." Mimeographed, November 1980.

Lincoln, E. "The Role of Monetary Policy in Demand Management, the Experience of Six Major Countries." 1975.

Patrick, H. "Evolution of the Japanese Financial System During Interwar Period" (in Japanese). *Analysis of the Japanese Economy During the Interwar Period.* edicted by T. Nakamura. February 1981.

Sakakibara, E., and R. Feldman. "The Japanese Financial System in Comparative Perspective." *Journal of Comparative Economics* (forthcoming).

Sakakibara, E. et al. *The Japanese Financial System in Comparative Perspective.* Study prepared for the use of the Joint Economic Committee, U.S. Congress, March 12, 1982.

Shimura, K. Analysis of the Japanese Capital Market (in Japanese). Tokyo: Tokyo University Press, 1969.

Suzuki, Y. *Money and Banking in Contemporary Japan.* New Haven, Conn.: Yale University Press, 1980.

Wallich, H., and M. Wallich. "Banking and Finance." In *Asia's New Giant: How the Japanese Economy Works,* edited by H. Patrick and H. Kosousky. Brookings Institution, 1976.

Yoshino, T. *Japanese Financial Institutions and Policies* (in Japanese). Shisei-do, 1954.

Comment

Hugh Patrick

The purpose of Eisuke Sakakibara's chapter is to introduce Asia more explicitly into this book's considerations of the international monetary system, although Ronald McKinnon brought in Japan in chapter 4. It is appropriate to view the Asian experience in a broader financial market as well as in the context of the monetary system, as has been stressed in earlier chapters.

Japan, China, and the Pacific Basin provide quite disparate cases of the interrelationships of components of the international financial system. Sakakibara has correctly chosen the most important case, namely, that of Japan. Moreover, this chapter focuses mainly on the evolution of domestic financial markets in Japan, with a somewhat more tangential discussion on how they relate to Japan's international financial transactions. This emphasis is appropriate because, first, Japan is now a huge, very important participant in the world economy and its financial markets and, second, the nature of the relationships between Japan's domestic and foreign transactions are determined to a large extent within Japan itself, in terms of both underlying economic and political forces.

First, let me note briefly some other components of the Asian experience, even though they are less central to the effective operation of the international monetary system. Certainly, in terms of that system, China is not yet important; it is merely a gleam in the eyes of bankers. Its main financial importance is as a major new competitor for concessional International Development Association (IDA) World Bank loans now going to India and other established needy borrowers. The debt-servicing problems of the Asian newly industrialized countries (NICs) are important; such North-South problems are covered in the chapter by Carlos Diaz Alejandro.

One interesting institutional contribution of Asia to the international monetary system lies in the rise of the Asian dollar markets in Hong Kong and Singapore. Their main functions are basically quite simple: they help solve the time-zone problem for foreign-exchange traders who view eight hours as the long run, and they are useful regional centers for Asian participants in the international short-term money-market system that has developed in Europe. However, these regional centers are derivative as well as supportive of the international monetary system. They help make markets more efficient, but they do not fundamentally alter the operations of international financial markets.

186

In terms both of financial and monetary flows and of impact on shaping the rules of the game, clearly the major Asian participant in the international monetary and financial systems is Japan. Indeed, one of my relatively few quibbles with Sakakibara's chapter is that it does not discuss in sufficient detail the extent to which Japan, very quietly and not particularly willingly, has already become an important center and entrepôt in international finance, on approximately the same order of magnitude as West Germany. A few facts are suggestive of this importance. First, the yen is beginning to be used as a reserve currency. Although the amounts are still small, only 4 percent or so of international monetary reserves, it is startling that the yen now has surpassed the British pound as a reserve currency. Second, nonresident holdings of yen assets amount to about $100 billion. Of this, about $28 billion is held in Euroyen assets outside Japan, holdings over which the Japanese monetary authorities have no control. Third, Japan has become a financial entrepôt, borrowing short and lending long. Between 1973 and 1981, the cumulative net long-term capital outflow amounted to about $37.5 billion, approximately one-third of the comparable outflow from the United States over the same period. The Japanese long-term capital outflow was not financed by current-account surpluses, which amounted to only about $900 million over the period. Rather, it was due to short-term borrowing and to some shifting from official reserves to private long-term capital outflows. Of course, the gross inflows and outflows were far larger. Fourth, in 1981 the number of yen-denominated foreign bond issues in Japan was about equal to that of deutsche-mark-denominated bonds issued in West Germany, and the total capital outflow from Japan ($22.8 billion) was almost double that from West Germany.

Several important patterns have emerged in Japan's financial transactions with the rest of the world over the past decade. First, there has been an underlying trend of extremely rapid growth in foreign financial transactions, although from a low base. Second, there have been very large cyclical swings in gross and especially net flows, reflecting the wild swings in Japan's current account as a consequence of the two oil crises and the Japanese adjustment to them. Third, as Sakakibara stresses, there has been substantially increased liberalization of what was initially a highly restrictive regime for foreign financial transactions by Japanese and for yen transactions by foreigners. Fourth, a number of large Japanese financial institutions, notably a half-dozen or so very large banks and several securities companies, have developed considerable international financial capability—in foreign-exchange trading, borrowing and lending in foreign currencies, placement of foreign-currency-denominated securities or yen securities abroad, and the like.

Sakakaibara's chapter exemplifies Richard Cooper's opening comment in chapter 2, namely, that history is not irrelevant. Sakakibara examines the transition of the Japanese financial system from what he terms a Continental European regime to an increasingly Anglo-American one. I want to complement (as well as compliment) his discussion of the specific characteristics of the evolution of the Japanese financial system.

The turning point from the earlier postwar regime occurred in 1973–75, when, because of the oil crisis and other factors, Japan moved from superfast (10 percent) supply-dominated growth in the gross national product (GNP) to moderate (5 percent) Keynesian-dominated growth.

Until the early 1970s, the postwar period was characterized by very high private-saving rates, which were exceeded by even higher ex ante private-investment demand, and a small government with balanced budgets and little government debt. The financial system was highly regulated. When Sakakibara refers to "small open financial markets," he really means controlled markets in which interest rates were pegged and inflexible, various markets were segmented, credit rationing was widespread, and foreign capital flows both inward and outward were severely restricted. There were few alternative financial assets in the regime, especially for ordinary individual savers, who had little choice except among savings deposits of various maturities and fixed interest rates. The structure of interest rates was low in both nominal and real terms, and the nominal rates seldom changed. These rates applied not only to savings deposits and short-term loans but also to long-term government, financial institution, and corporate bond issues as well as long-term loans. The limited amounts of bonds issued under the system were flogged off to financial institutions, where they were viewed as a way of sharing the benefits of cheap savings deposits with large, preferred long-term borrowers and other financial intermediaries.

Sakakibara judges that this system worked well for Japan. After all, the economy did grow very fast due to the very large amount of productive business investment.

My view is somewhat different. Financial intermediation worked despite financial policy, not because of it, and at some cost in terms of the equity of the system. Whether the resultant investment allocation among firms was efficient or not is an open question.

The Japanese financial system did allocate resources to productive business investment and away from housing and consumer purchases. This allocation reflected basic social choice and social policy. Certainly, the contrast between Japanese and U.S. policies during this time period is instructive. Within business, the Japanese financial policy gave priority to large-scale enterprises in virtually all sectors, as well as to some priority industries—at the expense of small business. As part of the adjustment process to these financial allocations, large firms became, in effect, financial intermediaries, extending immense amounts of trade credit to each other on a gross basis and to small business on a net basis. The general trading companies played a particularly important role.

In essence, Japanese small savers subsidized the owners of financial institutions and of large businesses through the pattern of low interest rates that prevailed. It can be argued that individual savers were bought off by the rapid increases in GNP and in their own disposable income, which were generated by the productive investment that this system of finance accommodated and, to some extent, engendered.

I disagree with Sakakibara's argument that the basic reasons for the limited development of the corporate bond market were the efficiency of long-term lending by commercial banks and credit banks and the lack of a broad and deep government bond market as a reference point. Certainly, term lending was an important (Continental-European-style) alternative to bond issues. However, the fact is that the monetary authorities, by administrative fiat, severely restricted entry into bond-market issues and set unattractively low issue yields.

The past decade has seen a gradual but profound breakdown of this system. The transition to a much more free market-oriented system of financial flows (the Anglo-American model) has accelerated in recent years. This has not come about as the direct consequence of exogenously determined policy by the Japanese authorities. Rather, it has been a consequence of important changes in the underlying structure of the economy and of consequent financial flows.

The most important feature of the past decade has been the decline (to only moderately high levels) in business-investment demand while private-saving rates have continued to be very high. Thus, since 1974, the economy of Japan has been a Keynesian one of seriously deficient private domestic demand. As Sakakibara documents excellently, the government of Japan has responded to the decline in business-investment demand with huge amounts of deficit financing, far greater than that in the United States, so that now the amount of Japanese central plus local government debt as a percentage of GNP is substantially above that in the United States. This was done without generating inflation once the 1973–74 inflationary crisis was brought under control. Thus, private savings have continued to flow through the intermediation of the banking system, but they have been allocated mainly to the government sector rather than to business. Not only were the Japanese the first successful practicing Keynesians, as evidenced by the policies of Finance Minister Takahashi in the early 1930s, but today they seem to be the only successful Keynesians, in contrast to the current European experience.

As a consequence, the ability of the monetary authorities to continue their rather cozy system of controlled financial markets has eroded seriously. The major domestic players in the financial systems—the various categories of large and smaller financial institutions and various large business enterprises—have found that their basic interest have changed substantially. Large businesses have wanted to find productive ways in which to hold their burgeoning financial assets. Some financial institutions, having seen their market share decline, have sought new opportunities by advocating changes in the rules; those who benefited from protected markets in the previous regime have, of course, resisted rule changes. While Japan has been emerging forcefully on the world economic scene, foreign pressures for the liberalization of financial transactions have been intensifying. Naturally, these pressures were consonant with the interests of those large Japanese financial institutions that wanted to internationalize their activities.

As a result, as Sakakibara shows, over the past decade there has been very substantial liberalization of the Japanese financial system in both domestic and foreign transactions. This liberalization has had three major dimensions. First, the free-market principle by which markets clear through changes in interest rates has occurred in an increasing number of Japanese financial markets, both short-run and long-run. Second, a wider range of financial instruments has been made available, although mainly in the large-scale or wholesale market rather than in retail markets. Third, Japanese financial institutions have been allowed to take on a wider range of activities, thereby reducing market segmentation.

When this liberalization process began, there existed severe restrictions. Although there has been great movement, substantial restrictions remain. In the domestic market, there are two major areas of restriction, often referred to as reflecting Japan's structure of low interest rates.

First, the issue market for government debt is still greatly restricted, with government debt issue forced onto buyers through nonmarket allocation devices. This is the case for both short-term and long-term debt. There is no effective treasury bill market; the amount of issue is very small, and essentially all issue is purchased by the Bank of Japan. Although the amount of issue of long-term government bonds has been immense in recent years, thus far the authorities have been able to issue this debt at yields below those in the secondary market. Not surprisingly, buyers have become very resistant. I agree with Sakakibara that it is inevitable that, in the next few years, as the large amounts of debt outstanding approach maturity, both long-term and short-term government debt markets will become price determined.

Second, the low and inflexible nominal interest rates on savings deposits, which also have been very low in real terms, have helped to keep interest rates low throughout the system. Because so much of individual wealth is held in the form of savings deposits, their interest rate has constituted a floor to the structure of interest rates in Japan. The Ministry of Finance has not allowed the development of alternative retail instruments, such as money-market funds. Savings-deposit holders have, in effect, been bought off because they have been allowed to evade income taxes on the interest on their deposits. Incidentally, this has been a major reason for the growth of the postal-savings system in recent years: tax evasion has been easier through multiple accounts. Japanese savers apparently think they have a good deal in these arrangements; they do not press hard for alternative financial assets that would generate higher pretax yields in a competitive market place. Recently, this has been an important political issue in Japan: when the Ministry of Finance attempted to collect interest on savings deposits by imposing an individual tax-payer identification-number system analogous to that in the United States, popular resentment was sufficiently strong that the Liberal Democratic Party indefinitely postponed the inauguration of the system.

Also remaining are certain major restrictions on transactions with foreigners. There is little restriction on foreign short-term or long-term portfolio investment in yen financial assets; they simply are not very attractive given the low nominal interest rates in Japan. However, foreigners cannot easily borrow yen and convert it into foreign currencies for use abroad; the amounts are limited by Ministry of Finance restrictions. Similarly, Japanese financial institutions cannot hold as much in net foreign assets as they might choose.

On net balance, the short-run effect of the elimination of these restrictions on domestic and foreign financial markets probably would result in net capital outflows from Japan and a further depreciation of the yen. The long-run effects in a general equilibrium setting are much less clear-cut. Sakakibara raises the very important question as to what is the best paradigm for Japan's effective participation in the international financial system. This is a broad issue underlying all the chapters in this book. Sakakibara notes certain institutional differences between Japanese and U.S. financial practices, such as the major role of long-term lending by banks in Japan, collateral requirements for bonds issued in Japan, and the separation (at least nominally) of banking and underwriting activities. He argues that differences in national cultures, traditions, and institutions must be taken into account as the international financial system is crafted.

There is real merit to his line of thinking, although it is something of a red herring in this particular context. In terms of the Japanese financial system, the tradition to which Sakakibara refers is that of a set of institutions and arrangements that developed during World War II and were carried over into the postwar period. It is noteworthy that, in prewar Japan, financial markets and interest rates were free and competitive, the bond market flourished, and financial intermediation was well developed. The tradition to which he refers is that endorsed by the Ministry of Finance, which naturally wants to retain its instruments of control as much as possible. Moreover, in practice, regardless of theory, Japan has been moving much closer to the Anglo-American model of free markets, nonrestricted capital flows, and efforts to make markets ever more perfect.

Is this the ideal system? This book, and recent U.S. experience, suggest that Japanese skepticism may not be unwarranted. Certainly, it is true that many Japanese do not seem convinced that high and variable nominal interest rates in a completely free market, where many alternative financial instruments exist, is the best system. They worry about problems of stability, encouragement of real fixed investment, and the like.

Although he raises the issue, Sakakibara does not provide any concrete answer as to what would constitute the optimal system. I surmise that this issue has not been thought through any more in Japan than elsewhere. Japan, after all, is still following the leadership of the United States in the determination of the rules of the game of the international monetary system. After initial panic, Japan has come to live with, even to love, a floating exchange-rate system. In terms of its increasing interaction with the international financial system, Japan seems much more pushed by circumstances—by market forces at home and abroad—than pulled by autonomous domestic-policy initiatives.

This may simply reflect a Japanese approach to policy. It can be argued that, in the Japanese view, the future is uncertain but is bound to have some unpleasant, unanticipated shocks. Therefore, it is better to be pragmatic, flexible, and experimental—and let others spend their energies arguing about principle. This perspective fits well into the cautionary statements made earlier in this book about how carefully monetary reforms must be undertaken because, with so few opportunities for major experimentation, if they do not work then the system is in real trouble. It would seem that Japanese prefer not to take the risks of making true innovations, in finance at least, but rather emulate the successful innovations of others. They argue, as does Richard Cooper in chapter 2, that, in practice, institutions and even systems evolve over time in response to the historical context. And that is an important reality we should all appreciate.

The process and pace of Japanese international financial liberalization has some policy implications for the U.S. policymakers who are negotiating with Japan over current bilateral economic difficulties. Recently, the arena of those discussions has moved to the financial sphere. It has been argued that the United States should use its negotiating chips to force Japan to remove remaining domestic- and foreign-transaction deviations from free competitive markets.

I offer three pieces of advice to U.S. negotiators. First, keep these issues alive but do so through low-key, steady pressure that is not highly visible. Second, do not bet many U.S. negotiating chips on these issues.

Financial change is a high-stakes domestic political game in Japan. The U.S. impact on that game is likely to be marginal, although the cost to the United States for playing the game could be very high. Japan is bound to continue to change, but it will do so primarily on its own terms. The United States cannot do much to affect the broad contours of the outcomes or even the pace at which they are reached. Third, negotiators should not let the United States become the scapegoat for the changes that will occur in the Japanese financial system. They should not let themselves become caught up in Japanese bureaucratic and vested-interest politics, which in the past have so skillfully utilized U.S. "pressure" as a way of trying to resolve the dilemmas of deep conflicts within Japan—at the expense of the United States.

The United States has made such mistakes in mishandling its trade negotiations with Japan. Fortunately, it appears that U.S. financial negotiators, and, indeed, U.S. financial interests, have been well aware of these problems and, accordingly, have been much more effective in pursuing a steady, quiet approach that has, on the whole, worked very well.

8

Some Aspects of the Adjustment Problem in an Interdependent World

Matthew Canzoneri and
Jo Anna Gray

In a world characterized by short-term wage or price rigidities, unanticipated supply-side disturbances such as an oil-price increase may cause temporary deviations of output from the full-employment level. Although corrective monetary or fiscal policies may effectively neutralize the effects of such shocks on output and employment, they also may incur a higher price level and increased inflationary expectations. These short-run macroeconomic costs constitute an important part of the adjustment burden that is shouldered by the world's economies following global disturbances such as the oil-price increases of the 1970s. The purpose of this chapter is to identify some of the ways in which the interdependence of the world's economies affects adjustment to an oil-price shock.

Our analysis focuses on the spill-over effects of monetary policy—that is, the way in which one country's monetary policy affects output and employment in other countries. These spill-over effects depend on the structural and institutional features of the individual countries involved and may be positive or negative for any given country. They create a situation in which policymakers in one country may be expected to condition their actions on the policies pursued in other countries; policy has unavoidable game aspects.[1] In studying this global policy game, we find that the overall size of the adjustment burden is unambiguously increased by the absence of cooperation among policymakers. Furthermore, the output losses associated with an oil-price shock do not, in general, provide an adequate measure of the reduction in social welfare caused by such disturbances.

The chapter begins by constructing a three-country model with one oil-producing "country" (the Organization of Petroleum Exporting Countries, or OPEC) and two oil-importing "countries" (the United States and the rest of the world, or ROW). This framework is used to develop the con-

We would like to thank Robert Cumby, Dale Henderson, Robert Hodrick, Preston Miller, and Jeffrey Sachs for helpful discussions. The views expressed in this chapter are the authors' alone. They do not represent official views of the Federal Reserve System, its Board of Governors, or any other members of its staff.

straints for the game played by policymakers in the two oil-importing countries. As already indicated, an important element of these constraints is the spill-over effects of monetary policy. These spill-over effects, in turn, depend on the channels through which a country's monetary policy is transmitted abroad. A number of possible channels may be indentified.[2] The chapter focuses on four. The first was introduced formally by Robert Mundell in the early 1960s (see Mundell 1963). This channel, which depends critically on capital mobility, operates through the real interest rate. The second channel also is well known. This channel, which depends on the existence of two or more goods in the model, operates directly through the demand for goods. The other two channels were selected because of their increasing relevance for a number of countries over the past decade. One stems from the now-common practice of contractually linking nominal wage rates to an index that includes the prices of imported goods as well as domestically produced goods. The other arises from the nature of OPEC's oil-pricing policy; the price of oil is denominated in dollars but is not always adjusted quickly in response to changes in the purchasing power of the dollar.

The first channel described produces negative spill over, a beggar-thy-neighbor effect. In the absence of fully indexed input prices, an expansionary monetary policy in one country raises that country's output and lowers its real interest rate. The real-interest-rate movement is transmitted abroad, where its net impact is deflationary. (The lower real interest rate produces a fall in the foreign nominal rate and this, in turn, increases foreign money demand.) Thus, the spill-over effects that are channeled through the real interest rate are negative and symmetric across countries. By comparison, the channels that operate through goods demand and wage indexation generate spill-over effects that are positive and symmetric. An expansion in one country raises output and expenditure in that country. Some, but not all, of the increased expenditure falls on each country's good, generating an excess supply of the expanding country's good and an excess demand for an other country's good. As a result, both the relative price and the output of the second country's good rise. Thus, an expansion in either country increases output in the other by generating increased-demand for the other country's good. The third channel of transmission, wage indexation, depends on the terms of trade change generated by an increased demand for a good. Again, an expansion in one country results in a rise in the relative price of the good produced by the other country. If nominal wages are linked to a consumer price index, the second country's real product wage falls and its output increases. The channel associated with the fixed dollar price of oil is, in contrast to the other three channels, an asymmetric one. An expansionary U.S. policy lowers the real price of oil, for both U.S. and ROW producers, and this can lead to an increase in output in the ROW. An expansionary ROW policy, on the other hand, has an effect on real oil prices that is ambiguous in sign. Accordingly, the spill-over effects produced by this channel are positive for U.S. policy but are ambiguous in sign for ROW policy.

The nature of the game that is actually played by policymakers depends on the relative importance of the four channels of transmission just described. It can be argued that, as the institutional structures of the world's larger economies have changed, so has the relative importance of these channels. This perspective may be particularly useful in attempting to understand apparent inconsistencies in policy prescriptions over time and across countries.

The second section of the chapter shows that, regardless of the specific nature of the game played by world policymakers, the noncooperative solution to that game is destructive in the sense that, generally, there exist coordinated policies that would make all players better off. In a symmetric game in which spill-over effects are negative, the noncooperative solution is inflationary; both countries would be better off if they could both somehow manage to inflate less. The converse is true for a symmetric game in which spill-over effects are positive. Welfare in both countries would be raised by more expansionary policies. In the asymmetric game in which the dollar price of oil is fixed, all would be better off if the United States inflated more while other countries inflated less. Clearly, then, the overall size of the adjustment burden following an oil-price shock is increased by the absence of cooperative behavior on the part of policymakers.

The games discussed in the third section are treated in more detail in "Monetary Policy Games and the Consequences of Non-Cooperative Behavior" (Canzoneri and Gray 1982b). That paper also discusses Stackelberg and fixed exchange-rate solutions; only a sample of those results are presented here. The fourth section concludes the chapter with a brief discussion of the difficulties involved in selecting an observable measure of the adjustment burden born by an individual country or by the world economy as a whole following an oil-price shock. Output losses are shown to be a generally inadequate measure of this burden.

A Three-Country Model

This section develops an analytical framework that is used to study the effects of both an oil-price shock and the monetary policy responses to that shock. Of particular interest are the spill-over effects of monetary policy. These effects produce the policy games analyzed in the next section of this chapter.

The one-period, discrete time model of this section is an extension of the framework developed in "Oil Price Changes and Monetary Policy in a Three Country Framework" (Canzoneri and Gray 1982a).[3] There are three countries, one oil-producing country called OPEC and two oil-importing countries called the United States and the rest of the world (ROW). Oil is an intermediate good that is used by the United States and ROW to produce two consumption goods that are consumed in all three countries. Each oil-importing country specializes in the production of one of these consumption goods. Labor is the only other variable input employed in the production of each consumption good; it is used in fixed proportions with oil. OPEC sets the price of oil in terms of U.S. dollars, but this price may be partially or fully linked to a consumer price index. The nominal wage in each oil-importing country is contractually fixed in terms of the local currency, but also may be partially or fully linked to an index of consumption good prices. The absence of completely flexible wage rates introduces the possibility of short-run deviations of output from the full-employment level. There are three assets in the system: U.S. money, which is held only by U.S. residents; ROW money, which is held only by ROW residents; and a real bond that is held by the residents of all three countries. The model includes three exogenous policy variables: the price of oil and the rates of growth of the U.S. and ROW money supplies. Shocks to the model take the form of unexpected once-and-for-all changes in these policy variables.

The model is summarized in the following subsections.

Notation

Note: With the exception of interest rates, lowercase letters denote the log value of a variable and uppercase letters denote the variable itself in the following equations. An asterisk refers to the ROW, while a superscript *o* refers to OPEC.

x is real output.

h is the composite input, consisting of equal numbers of units of labor and oil.

l is labor employed in production of x.

o is oil employed in production of x.

w is nominal wage rate.

p is domestic currency price of x.

pi is consumer price index.

q is dollar price of oil.

e is the exchange rate (units of ROW currency per dollar).

γ is the degree of wage indexation.

γ^o is degree of oil-price indexation.

c is real expenditure.

y is real income.

t is terms of trade (relative price of U.S. output).

b is OPEC's net holdings of real bonds issued by U.S. residents.

b^* is OPEC's net holdings of real bonds issued by ROW residents.

r is the real interest rate.

i is the nominal interest rate.

m is the nominal money stock.

g is the rate of growth of the money stock.

$\delta(\cdot)$ denotes the deviation of the current value of a variable from its full-equilibrium no-shock value. Thus, for example, δx represents the deviation of the log value of output from the log value of its full-employment level. For small changes, $\delta(\cdot)$ approximates the percentage deviation of a variable from its full-equilibrium no-shock value.

The Model

Note: The model has been log linearized around its no-shock equilibrium and written in log-deviation form. For real variables, the model's no-shock equilibrium is identical to its preshock equilibrium. A bar over a variable indicates its no-shock (or, equivalently, its preshock) equilibrium value. The two oil-importing countries are assumed to be identical in all respects in the preshock equilibrium. The superscripts d and s denote demand and supply, respectively. Subscripts refer to time. Unless otherwise indicated, Greek letters represent parameters.

$$\delta x = (1 - \alpha)\delta h$$

$$\delta x^* = (1 - \alpha)\delta h^* \tag{8.1}$$

where $(1 - \alpha) = [(\overline{W/P}) + (\overline{Q/P})]\overline{H}/\overline{X}$

$$\delta h = \delta l = \delta o = -(1/\alpha)[\beta(\delta w - \delta p) + (1 - \beta)$$
$$(\delta q - \delta p)]$$

$$\delta h^* = \delta l^* = \delta o^* = -(1/\alpha)[\beta(\delta w^* - \delta p^*)$$
$$+ (1 - \beta)(\delta q - \delta e - \delta p^*)] \tag{8.2}$$

where $\beta = (\overline{W/P})\bar{L}/[(\overline{W/P})\bar{L} + (\overline{Q/P})\bar{O}]$

$$\delta w = \gamma \delta pi$$
$$\delta w^* = \gamma^* \delta pi^*$$
$$\delta q = \delta \bar{q} + \gamma^o \delta pi \tag{8.3}$$

$$\delta pi = 0.5(\delta p + \delta p^* + \delta e)$$
$$\delta pi^* = 0.5(\delta p^* + \delta p - \delta e) \tag{8.4}$$

$$\delta c = \delta y - \sigma \delta r$$
$$\delta c^* = \delta y^* - \sigma \delta r \tag{8.5}$$

$$\delta c^o = 0 \tag{8.6}$$

$$\delta y = (\overline{X/Y})(\delta x + 0.5\delta t) - (\overline{Q/PI})(\overline{O/Y})$$
$$(\delta q - \delta pi + \delta o) - (\overline{rB/Y})\delta b - (\overline{B/Y})\delta r$$

$$\delta y^* = (\overline{X/Y})(\delta x^* - 0.5\delta t) - (\overline{Q/PI})(\overline{O/Y})$$
$$(\delta q - \delta pi + \delta o^*) - (\overline{rB/Y})\delta b^* - (\overline{B/Y})\delta r \tag{8.7}$$

$$\delta t = \delta p - \delta p^* - \delta e \tag{8.8}$$

$$\delta b = (\overline{Y/B})(\delta c - \delta y)$$
$$\delta b^* = (\overline{Y/B})(\delta c^* - \delta y^*) \tag{8.9}$$

$$\delta x = 0.5(\overline{C/X})[\delta c + \delta c^* - (1 + 2\psi)\delta t]$$
$$\delta x^* = 0.5(\overline{C/X})[\delta c + \delta c^* + (1 + 2\psi)\delta t] \tag{8.10}$$

$$\delta m^s = \delta p + \delta x - \lambda \delta i$$
$$\delta m^{*s} = \delta p^* - \lambda \delta i^* \tag{8.11}$$

$$\delta i = \delta r + \delta pi_{+1} - \delta pi$$
$$\delta i^* = \delta r + \delta pi^*_{+1} - \delta pi^* \tag{8.12}$$

$$m^s = m^s_{-1} + g$$

$$m^{*s} = m^{*s}_{-1} + g^* \qquad\qquad (8.13)$$

Equation 8.1 gives the production technologies of the two oil-importing countries. Output of each consumption good is proportional to the amount of the composite input employed in its production. One unit of the composite input consists of one unit of labor and one unit of oil, which are used in fixed proportions.

The conditions for profit maximization yield equation 8.2, which gives the derived demands for the composite input, as well as the derived demands for labor and oil in each oil-importing country. These demands depend on the real product price of the composite good—that is, on its price in terms of the domestically produced consumption good. This, in turn, is equal to the sum of the real product wage and the real product price of oil. Accordingly, equation 8.2 shows that derived demands in each country depend negatively on the domestic currency prices of labor and oil and positively on the price of domestic output.

Nominal wage rates and the dollar price of oil are determined by equation 8.3. As in Gray's "Wage Indexation: A Macroeconomic Approach" (1976), nominal wages are set at the beginning of each period (before any oil-price or monetary-policy shocks are realized) at a level that is expected to clear the labor market. In addition, each country's nominal wage is linked to its price level by an indexing parameter, γ (or γ^*), which generally is assumed to lie between zero and one, inclusive. The price of oil is set in dollars and is linked to the U.S. price level by the indexing parameter γ^o. The term $\delta\bar{q}$ represents unanticipated disturbances to the dollar price of oil, or oil price shocks.[4]

Equation 8.4 defines each country's price level as a weighted average of the domestic currency prices of the two consumption goods. Because the two countries are identical in all respects in the preshock equilibrium, the two goods are assigned equal weights of 0.5 (one-half).

In equation 8.5, total spending in each of the two oil-importing countries is shown to be an increasing function of domestic net income and a decreasing function of the real rate of interest. Both spending and income are measured in terms of the same consumption basket used to define the price levels of the two countries.

A critical feature of the model is the assumption that OPEC is unable to adjust immediately its level of consumption to changes in the level of its income. Specifically, OPEC's short-run marginal propensity to save is assumed to be one. This assumption is captured by equation 8.6.

Real income in the two oil-importing countries is given by equation 8.7.[5] Real income in each country is an increasing function of the level of its output and the relative price of its output. It is a decreasing function of its real oil bill, OPEC's net holdings of its bond, and the real interest rate paid on those bonds. The relative price of U.S. output is defined in equation 8.8 as the terms of trade.

Equation 8.9 states that OPEC's net accumulation of each oil-importing country's bond is equal to that country's excess of spending over income. Thus, OPEC's total saving—or, equivalently, its current account surplus—is equal to the sum of U.S. and ROW dissaving.

Equation 8.10 is the log-deviation form of the goods-market equilibrium conditions.[6] The demand for each good must equal its supply. Demand for each good is an increasing function of total expenditure in the two oil-importing countries and a decreasing function of its relative price.

Equation 8.11 gives the equilibrium conditions for the U.S. and ROW money markets. For simplicity, the income elasticity of money demand has been set equal to unity.[7] The interest rate semi-elasticity of money demand is given by λ. Nominal interest rates are defined in equation 8.12, and the evolution of the U.S. and ROW money stocks is described by equation 8.13. Monetary policy in each country takes the form of setting a constant rate of growth, g (or g^*), of the domestic money stock. Any change in monetary policies—that is, any change in g or g^*—is assumed to be unexpected and, once it occurs, permanent.

The model outlined in equations 8.1 through 8.13 involves expectations of future prices and policy variables. To complete the model, the manner in which agents form their expectations must be specified. It is assumed that agents' expectations are "rational" given their assumptions about U.S. and ROW monetary policies and OPEC's oil-pricing policy. If their views about these policies are correct, then their price predictions will be realized.

The remainder of this section discusses the model's solutions for the levels of U.S. and ROW output. Of particular interest are the effects of the monetary policy adopted in one of the two oil-importing countries on the output of the other country. For simplicity, attention is limited to two special cases of the general model outlined in equation 8.1 through 8.13, which are presented in the following subsections. First, the special case in which the degree of wage indexation in the two oil-importing countries is variable, but the price of oil is fully indexed, is treated. This case produces the macroeconomic constraints necessary to yield the two symmetric games studied in the next full section of the chapter. Second, attention is turned to the special case in which both nominal wage rates and the dollar price of oil are fixed. This case produces the one asymmetric game studied in the next section.

A Fixed Real Price of Oil

The following equations, 8.14 and 8.15, give the solutions for U.S. and ROW output for the special case in which the price of oil is fully indexed (δ^o

= 1) but the degree of wage indexation may lie anywhere between zero and one, inclusive ($0 \leq \gamma = \gamma^* \leq 1$).[8] Each country's output is a linear function of the unanticipated changes in the model's three policy variables—the rates of growth of U.S. and ROW money and the price of oil.

$$\delta x = \rho_1 \delta g + \rho_2 \delta g^* - \rho_3 \delta \bar{q} \qquad (8.14)$$

$$\delta x^* = \rho_1 \delta g^* + \rho_2 \delta g - \rho_3 \delta \bar{q} \qquad (8.15)$$

where

$$\rho_1 = (1/D_1 D_2)(1 + \lambda)^2(1 - \gamma)\,\theta\,\{\xi\Delta[\theta(\lambda + \gamma)$$
$$+ (1 + \lambda)(\phi + 2\tau) + 2\tau\theta(1 - \gamma)]$$
$$+ \tau\lambda\theta(1 - \gamma)\} > 0$$

$$\rho_2 = (1/D_1 D_2)(1 + \lambda)^2(1 - \gamma)\theta\{\xi\Delta[\theta(\lambda + \gamma)$$
$$+ (1 + \lambda)\phi] - \tau\lambda\theta(1 - \gamma)\}\text{ (unsigned)}$$

$$\rho_3 = (1/D_1 D_2)2D_1\xi[(1 + \lambda)\Delta\phi + \nu\lambda\theta(1 - \gamma)] > 0$$

and

$$\tau = (\overline{Y/X})(1 + 4\psi) > 0$$
$$\Delta = (\overline{Y/X})[(1 - \bar{r})\sigma + (\overline{B/Y})] > 0$$
$$\xi = 1/(1 - \beta) > 0$$
$$\nu = (1 - \alpha)(1 - \beta) > 0$$
$$\theta = (1 - \alpha)\beta/\alpha > 0$$
$$\phi = (1 - \alpha)(1 - \beta)/\alpha > 0$$
$$D_1 = \lambda(\theta + \phi + \tau) + \tau + \tau\theta(1 - \gamma) + \theta\gamma$$
$$+ \phi > 0$$
$$D_2 = 2\xi\Delta(1 + \lambda) + 2\theta(1 - \gamma)(\xi\Delta + \lambda) > 0$$

As expected, each country's output responds positively to an increase in the rate of growth of its own money stock as long as wages are not fully extended. Monetary policy "works" because of the absence of completely flexible wages in the short run. An unexpected increase in the rate of growth of U.S. money, for example, produces an incipient excess supply of money that is offset, in part, by a rise in the U.S. price level. Provided U.S. wages are not fully indexed, this "price surprise" lowers the U.S. real wage product and induces an increase in U.S. output and employment.

A rise in the real price of oil lowers output in both oil-importing countries. It does so by increasing the price firms must pay for the composite input. This reduces the amount of the compositive input employed in production and, therefore, the level of output.

As equations 8.14 and 8.15 show, the spill-over effects of monetary policy are symmetrical but ambiguous in sign. With a sufficiently high degree of wage indexation, these effects are positive. That is, an expansionary monetary policy in one country raises output in the other. If the degree of wage indexations is less than one, spill over can be negative; an expansion monetary policy in one country may produce a contraction in the other. The larger is τ—that is, the higher the responsiveness of relative goods demand to relative price—the more likely is this outcome. Some intuition into these results can be gained by considering three competing channels through which one country's monetary policy may be transmitted to other countries. The first of the three channels produces negative spill over while the other two produce positive spill over. The actual spill-over effects of monetary policy depend, then, on the relative importance of these three channels.

The first of three transmission channels was introduced formally by Mundell in the early 1960s. This channel, which depends critically on capital mobility, operates through the real interest rate. With this channel in operation, an increase in the rate of growth of the U.S. money supply leads to a lower real interest rate. This occurs, in our model, because an expansionary monetary policy raises U.S. output and, simultaneously, U.S. oil imports. This, in turn, leads to a rise in OPEC's income. Because OPEC's short-run marginal propensity to save is assumed to be one, the increase in OPEC's income generates an equal increase in its desired saving. At an unchanged real interest rate, this produces an incipient world excess supply of goods. A fall in the real interest rate is required in order to equilibrate the goods markets.

The fall in the real interest that accompanies an expansionary U.S. monetary policy has, in and of itself, a contractionary impact on the ROW. This can be seen most easily by considering the ROW money market. At unchanged ROW prices and output, a fall in the real interest rate induces a fall in the ROW nominal rate and an excess demand for ROW money. At unchanged terms of trade, this excess demand can be eliminated by either a fall in the ROW price level, a fall in ROW output, or both. If terms of trade are held constant, a fall in the ROW price level means a fall in the price of domestic output. In the absence of full indexed wage rates, this produces a rise in the ROW real product wage and, accordingly, a fall in ROW output. Thus, at unchanged terms of trade, an excess demand for ROW money will result in a fall in both ROW prices and output. The spill-over effects of monetary policy that operate through the real-interest-rate channel alone, then, are negative.

The second of the transmission channels, which depends on the existence of two or more goods in the model, operates directly through the demand for goods. In and of itself (abstracting from the real-interest-rate channel), this channel produces positive spill over. For example, consider once again the effects of an increase in the rate of growth of the U.S. money supply. The resulting increase in U.S. output leads, at an unchanged real interest rate, to an equal increase in U.S. expenditure. At unchanged terms of trade, this expenditure increase falls equally on the U.S. good and the ROW good, generating an incipient excess supply of the U.S. good and an excess demand for the ROW good. This induces, in turn, an equilibrating rise in ROW output and fall in the terms of trade.[9]

Of course, increased production of the ROW good will occur only if the ROW real product wage falls. This fall could happen because the increased demand for the ROW good causes a rise in its relative price – a fall in the terms of trade. A rise in the relative price of ROW output can produce a rise in its absolute (domestic-currency) price even if the overall ROW price level falls.[10] This rise, in turn, lowers the ROW real product wage and induces increased production of ROW output. It follows, then, that the output response to the increased demand for the ROW good will be larger if the terms-of-trade change it produces is larger. Furthermore, if the induced terms-of-trade effect is sufficiently strong, the positive spill over channeled through goods demand will dominate the negative spill over channeled through the real interest rate. The change in the terms of trade will be larger if the responsiveness of relative demands to relative price is lower, or if τ (which is positively related to the elasticity of relative goods demand with respect to relative price) is lower. Thus, we see from equations 8.14 and 8.15 that a sufficiently small τ always will produce positive spill over, or a positive ρ_2.

The third transmission channel, for which the terms-of-trade change just discussed is a prerequisite, is wage indexation. It is a channel that has become increasingly relevant for a number of countries over the past two decades. Like the goods-demand channel, it produces positive spill over. To demonstrate this effect, consider once more the effects of an expansionary U.S. monetary policy. As already noted, such an expansion is accompanied by a rise in the relative price of ROW output. Even if the absolute (domestic-currency) price of ROW output remains unchanged, this relative price change will produce an increase in ROW output as long as ROW wages are indexed to some extent. This increase occurs because ROW wages are indexed to a weighted average of the prices of ROW and U.S. output, not to the price of ROW output alone. If the absolute price of ROW output remains unchanged, a rise in its relative price will be associated with a fall in the overall price level. Provided wages are indexed to some extent, this will result in a fall in the ROW nominal wage rate and, accordingly, a fall in the real product wage (the nominal wage rate deflated by the price of domestic output). This, in turn, will lead to a rise in ROW output. Examination of the terms entering ρ_2 reveals that, for a sufficiently high degree of wage in-dexation (a sufficiently large γ), the positive spill-over effects associated with this channel always will dominate the negative spill-over effects chan-neled through the real interest rate.

The three channels of transmission, and the spill-over effects they generate, are symmetrical for the two oil-importing countries. The effects of a U.S. expansion on ROW output are identical to the effects of an ROW expansion on U.S. output. A sufficiently high degree of wage indexation produces the positive symmetric game described in the next full section, while the absence of full indexation and a sufficiently high elasticity of relative goods demand with respect to relative price produces the negative symmetric game described in the next section. A version of our model that produces a transmission channel that does not operate symmetrically for the U.S. and ROW is considered in the following subsection. The essential feature of this version is that the price of oil is set in dollars and is not indexed to any price or basket of prices during the adjustment period.

A Fixed Dollar Price of Oil

Equations 8.16 and 8.17 give the solutions for U.S. and ROW output for the special case in which wage rates in both oil-importing countries and the price of oil are fixed in nominal terms ($\gamma = \gamma^* = \gamma^o = 0$).

$$\delta x = \rho_4 \delta g + \rho_5 \delta g^* - \rho_6 \delta \bar{q} \tag{8.16}$$

$$\delta x^* = \rho_4^* \delta g^* + \delta_5^* \delta g - \rho_6 \delta \bar{q} \tag{8.17}$$

where

$$\rho_4 = (1/D_1 D_2)(1 + \lambda)^2(\theta + \phi)$$
$$\{\xi \Delta [2\tau(1 + \lambda + \theta) + \lambda(\theta + 2\phi) + 2\phi]$$
$$+ \lambda\theta(\xi\nu + \tau)\} > 0$$

$$\rho_5 = (1/D_1 D_2)(1 + \lambda)^2(\theta + \phi)\lambda\theta(\xi\Delta - \tau - \xi\nu)$$
$$\text{(unsigned)}$$

$$\rho_6 = (1/D_1 D_2) 2 D_1 \xi [(1 + \lambda)\Delta\phi + \nu\lambda\theta] > 0$$

$$\rho_4^{\cdot} = (1/D_1 D_2)(1 + \lambda)^2 \{\lambda\theta(\xi\Delta - \tau - \xi\nu)$$
$$+ 2\xi\theta\tau[\lambda\nu(\theta + \phi) + \Delta(1 + \lambda + \theta + \phi)]\}$$

(unsigned)

$$\rho_5^{\cdot} = (1/D_1 D_2)(1 + \lambda)^2 \{\xi\Delta(\theta + \phi)[\lambda(\theta + \phi) + \phi(2 + \lambda)]$$
$$+ 2\xi\Delta\phi\tau(1 + \lambda) + \lambda\theta(\theta + \phi)$$

$$[\tau + \xi\nu(1 - 2\tau)]\} \text{ (unsigned)}$$

and

$$D_1 = \lambda(\theta + \phi + \tau) + \tau + \tau\theta + \phi > 0$$

$$D_2 = 2\xi\Delta(1 + \lambda + \theta) + 2\lambda\theta > 0$$

As before, with a fixed real price of oil, an increase in the price of oil reduces output in both the United States and the ROW, and it does so by the same amount in the two countries. An increase in the rate of growth of U.S. money has the same qualitative effect on U.S. output that it had in the previous case. However, with the same degree of wage indexation, this effect is stronger in the present case because the rise in the price of U.S. output associated with the monetary expansion lowers the real product price of oil as well as the real product wage.

The effect of an expansionary ROW monetary policy on ROW output may, in this case, be either positive or negative, whereas in the previous case it was unambiguously positive. The reasons for this anomalous result are as follows. As before, the spill-over effects of ROW monetary policy may be either positive or negative. If they are negative, the price of U.S. output declines, which can raise the real product price of oil for both the U.S. and the ROW. If the rise in the ROW real product price of oil is sufficiently large, it can dominate the positive effects normally associated with a monetary expansion and produce a decline in ROW output.

As equations 8.16 and 8.17 show, in this case, the spill-over effects of monetary policy are not only ambiguous in sign, they also are asymmetrical. For both countries, the real-interest-rate and goods-demand channels of the previous case still exist.[11] As before, the real-interest-rate channel produces negative spill over, the goods-demand channel produces positive spill over, and the spill-over effects generated through these channels are symmetrical for the two countries. For simplicity, the degree of wage indexation has been set equal to zero for both countries. Accordingly, the wage-indexation channel is not present in this version of our model.

The asymmetry of spill-over effects in this case stems from the fact that the price of oil is set in dollars and is not adjusted in the short run for movements in the prices of U.S. or ROW output. The fourth channel of transmission considered in this chapter, then, is the one associated with a less-than-fully-indexed dollar price of oil. In making production decisions, U.S. firms are concerned with the real price of oil in terms of U.S. output, and ROW firms are concerned with the real price of oil in terms of ROW output. To demonstrate the asymmetry of the spill-over effects that are transmitted through this fourth channel, the following examines, in turn, the impact of an expansionary U.S. monetary policy on the ROW real product wage and the impact of an expansionary ROW monetary policy in the U.S. real product wage.

An expansionary U.S. monetary policy lowers the real produce price of oil for the ROW. To understand this result, note that the expansion lowers the U.S. real product price of oil. This effect is due to the fact that the expansion generates a rise in the price of U.S. output. Given a fixed dollar price of oil, the real price of oil in terms of U.S. output necessarily falls. The effect on the price of oil in terms of ROW output is even stronger. The change in the ROW real product price of oil is equal to the change in the U.S. real product price less any change in the relative price of ROW output. Because the U.S. expansion results in a rise in the relative price of ROW output, any reduction in the price of oil in terms of U.S. output means an even greater reduction in terms of ROW output.

By contrast, an expansionary ROW monetary policy has an ambiguous effect on the U.S. real product price of oil. This result is due to the fact that the fixed dollar price of oil does not provide a direct channel of transmission from ROW monetary policy to the U.S. real product price of oil and, therefore, U.S. output. An ROW expansion effects the U.S. real product price of oil indirectly through its impact on the price of U.S. output. The ROW expansion is transmitted to the price of U.S. output through the real-interest-rate and goods-demand channels already discussed. The overall sign of the spill-over effects transmitted through these two channels may be positive or negative – that is, the price of U.S. output as well as the level of U.S. output may either rise or fall. Accordingly, the real price of oil in terms of U.S. output may either rise or fall.

The one asymmetrical game examined in the next section of this chapter involves the special case in which the spill-over effects of U.S. monetary policy are positive, while the spill-over effects of ROW monetary policy are negative. In the version of our model considered here, this special case will occur for sufficiently large values of τ and sufficiently small values of α.

Policy Games

Some of the game-theoretic aspects of monetary policy in an interdependent world are discussed in this section. The formal analysis underlying this discussion was developed in an earlier work (see Canzoneri and Gray 1982b). Only a subset of the results of that analysis is presented here.

Three policy games are examined in this section. Each game corresponds to one of the three types of policy spill over described in the preceding section: negative symmetric, positive symmetric, and asymmetric. Both the noncooperative and the cooperative solutions to these games are presented. The implications of our results for measuring the size and distribution of the adjustment burden following an oil-price shock are then discussed.

The section begins by describing the social-welfare function of the policymakers in each of the two oil-importing countries. Policymakers use the one tool at their disposal – monetary policy – to maximize this objective function, which is subject to the macroeconomic constraints developed in the last section. Consideration of OPEC's maximization problem is, by contrast, altogether omitted from this analysis; the price of oil is assumed to be exogenous.

The monetary authority in each oil-importing country is assumed to be concerned only with domestic employment and long-run expectations of the domestic rate of inflation. Specifically, the policymakers' utility functions take the following form:

$$U = -(\delta x)^2 - \mu \bar{\pi}^2, \qquad U^* = -(\delta x^*)^2 - \mu^* \bar{\pi}^{*2} \qquad (8.18)$$

Here δx and δx^* represent deviations of output from their full-employment values in the United States and the ROW, and $\bar{\pi}$ and $\bar{\pi}^*$ are long-run inflationary expectations.

By assumption, all games are initiated by an unanticipated increase in the price of oil that will, in the absence of corrective policy, cause output to deviate from its full-employment level. Such deviations are temporary; they persist for only one period, which is referred to as the adjustment period. At the end of the adjustment period, labor contracts are renegotiated with the new price of oil in mind and, absent further unanticipated shocks, output returns to its full-employment level.

Monetary policy can be used to offset some or all of the output effects of an oil-price shock, but only at the cost of changing the inflation rate expected to prevail in periods subsequent to the adjustment period. This is because it is assumed that private agents expect the money-growth rates established during the adjustment period to be permanent. This assumption is intended to capture, in a very simple way, the notion that policymakers are subject to a credibility constraint. The important implicit assumption is that the monetary authority cannot convince the private sector of a change in policy simply by announcing it. Agents expect past policy to continue until confronted with an actual policy change. Once a new policy has been in place for a period, it is then believed to be permanent.[12]

Thus, the trade off faced by policymakers following a shock such as an oil-price increase is this: they can increase the rates of growth of their money supplies and increase employment during the period of adjustment to the oil-price shock, but only at the price of higher expected rates of inflation in the period that follows. Policymakers have two choices in dealing with these expectations in the postshock period. They can accommodate them, thereby achieving full-employment output; or they can lower them by lowering the rates of growth of their money supplies, thereby forcing their economies through a second adjustment period. The terms $\bar{\pi}$ and $\bar{\pi}^*$ enter the utility functions (equation 8.18) because each of these choices has undesirable consequences in subsequent periods—higher steady-state inflation in the first case and additional periods of adjustment and unemployment in the second.

Under the assumptions just discussed, the long-run expected rates of inflation in the United States and the ROW are simply:[13]

$$\bar{\pi} = g, \qquad \bar{\pi}^* = g^* \qquad (8.19)$$

where g and g^* are the respective rates of growth of U.S. and ROW money supplies during the adjustment period. Note that:

$$\bar{\pi} = \pi_0 + \delta g, \qquad \bar{\pi}^* = \pi_0^* + \delta g^* \qquad (8.20)$$

where π_0 and π_0^* are the rates of inflation in the full-information equilibrium that is assumed to have preceded the adjustment period. These are the inherited rates of inflation with which each country enters the adjustment period. For most of the analysis, assume that the inherited rates in both countries are zero. Using equation 8.20, the utility functions (equation 8.18) may be rewritten as:

$$U = -(\delta x)^2 - \mu(\pi_0 + \delta g)^2, \qquad U^* = -(\delta x^*)^2 - \mu^*(\pi_0^* + \delta g^*)^2 \qquad (8.21)$$

The dependence of output levels in the United States and the ROW on the two policy instruments, g and g^*, is somewhat more complicated. As the analysis of the last section demonstrated, a variety of specifications is possible; we have selected three. In all three specifications, the effects of a country's monetary policy are assumed to be positive in that country; an unanticipated increase in the rate of growth of a country's money supply raises that country's output. The cross-effects of monetary policy are what distinguish the three specifications and produce the three different game situations studied in this section. In the symmetric-negative specification, an expansionary policy in either country exports unemployment to the other. In the symmetric-positive case, an expansionary policy in either country increases employment in the other. In the asymmetric game, a U.S. expansion increases employment both at home and abroad, but a ROW expansion causes unemployment in the U.S.

At the beginning of the adjustment period, the U.S. and ROW monetary authorities, in response to the exogenous oil-price shock, set the rates of growth of their money supplies to maximize the utility functions (equation 8.21) subject to the relevant set of macroeconomic constraints. The games corresponding to each of the three output specifications described are now considered in turn.

The Symmetric-Negative Game

With the symmetric-negative constraints, the spill-over effects of monetary policy are negative; an expansion in one country causes a contraction in the other. Reliance upon such beggar-thy-neighbor policies can, in a noncooperative setting, result in an excessively inflationary outcome.

If π_0 and π_0^* are both zero, then both policymakers will want to adopt expansionary policies. The oil-price shock would cause unemployment if they did nothing, and, if π_0 and π_0^* are both zero, the marginal utility of avoiding some of this unemployment outweighs the marginal disutility of the inflationary expectations engendered.[14] When each policymaker realizes that the other is going to expand, he will want to adopt an even more expansionary stance to make up for the negative spill over of the other's policy.

The noncooperative, or Nash, solution is the policy configuration from which neither player can move unilaterally to improve his position. If both π_0 and π_0^* are zero, both players will adopt expansionary policies in the Nash solution.[15]

The interesting point to note is that the negative spill-over effects of monetary policy give the Nash solution an inflationary bias. Each policymaker knows that the other will expand, and therefore each must run an even more inflationary policy to make up for the negative spill over of the other's policy. In fact, it turns out that there is a certain amount of needless competitive inflation (or devaluation) going on in the Nash solution. The Nash solution is always dominated by a range of cooperative solutions that are less inflationary and that improve both policymakers' positions.

The reason for the inflationary result is fairly straightforward. With the Nash solution, each country has pushed its money-growth rate to the point where its effect on domestic utility is zero at the margin. Yet, a decrease in either country's money-growth rate will increase output—and, therefore, utility—in the other country.[16] Clearly, both policymakers would be better off if they could agree to inflate less.

The problem with cooperative solutions is that they require coopera-tion. In any cooperative solution, there is always an incentive to cheat. Sup-pose that the U.S. and ROW policymakers agree to a less inflationary, Pareto optimal solution.[17] In any such cooperative solution, at least one of the two countries can increase its welfare by increasing its money-growth rate, provided the other country does not respond by altering its own money-growth rate. Thus, with any cooperative solution, unemployment will seem high, and the risk of inflation low, to a public that does not fully understand the nature of the solution and the possibility of foreign repur-cussions. The political pressure to cheat on cooperative solutions could well be great.

More generally, it is difficult to see how two very independent policy-makers would come to agree upon a cooperative solution in the first place. There is a continuum of cooperative solutions defined by a contract curve; some are more favorable to the United States, while others are more favorable to the ROW.[18]

An outcome closer to the Nash solution, with each country attempting to induce the other to run a less expansionary policy, seems more likely to occur. With the Nash solution, the ROW, for example, would have every incentive to maneuver the United States into running a less inflationary policy. If the United States acquiesced, ROW employment would be stimu-lated, but at the expense of U.S. employment. As a result, the ROW would find it desirable to reduce its own money-growth rate, moving back along its own reaction curve in the direction of cooperative solutions more favorable to the ROW.

In general, the opportunities for such manipulation appear to be limited. Outright political pressure and the engineering of public opinion, whatever else they achieve, appear not to be very effective means of altering the policies pursued in other countries. An alternative strategy is for one country to commit itself to a lower inflation rate in return for a similar com-mitment by the other country. Unfortunately, such movements toward a Pareto optimal solution require an effective means of precommitment. This requirement is extremely difficult to meet in a world composed of politically sovereign players. Any policymaker attempting to strike such a bargain con-fronts the problem that his promises, as well as the promises of other policy-makers, are, in the jargon of game theory, incredible.

The Symmetric-Positive Game

With the symmetric-positive constraints, the spill-over effects of monetary policy are positive; an expansion in one country causes an expansion in the other. The locomotive aspects of policy produce, in a noncooperative setting, a solution that is not sufficiently inflationary.

Each policymaker knows that the other is going to inflate and, therefore, that he does not have to inflate as much to get a given employment effect. The interesting point here is that the Nash solution does not sufficiently exploit the positive externalities embodied in the spill-over effects of monetary policy. The basic arguments are the same as in the symmetric-negative game, only the signs of the spill-over effects are reversed, as are the conclusions. At the margin, a more expansive U.S. policy would increase ROW employment without significantly affecting the U.S. policymaker's utility, and vice versa. Both would be better off if they could agree to inflate more.

As in the preceding case, it is not clear how a cooperative solution would be achieved in a world of decentralized policymaking. There are many cooperative solutions, and policymakers will not be indifferent to them. Furthermore, in the absence of binding contractual arrangements, all cooperative solutions are subject to credibility problems. As with the first case, we might expect a solution close to the Nash solution, with each country attempting to influence the other's monetary policy. In this case, however, the pressure would be in the direction of more, rather than less, inflationary policies.

The Asymmetric Game

With the asymmetric constraints, the spill-over effects of U.S. policy are positive, while the spill-over effects of ROW policy are negative. This means that U.S. policy has a comparative advantage over ROW policy in combating the unemployment caused by an unanticipated rise in the price of oil. The Nash and cooperative solutions for this game are quite different from those for the two symmetric games already discussed.

If inherited inflation rates are zero, each policymaker knows that the other is going to inflate. However, in this case, the two policymakers do not react to that fact in the same way. The United States will inflate more to compensate for the negative spill-over effects of ROW policy, while the ROW will inflate less because of the positive spill-over effects of U.S. policy. Thus, the Nash solution exploits the comparative advantage of U.S. monetary policy in this asymmetric game.

The interesting point, however, is that the Nash solution does not exploit the comparative advantage of U.S. policy enough. Both policymakers would be better off if the United States inflated more and the ROW inflated less. The argument should be familiar by now. With the Nash solution, neither policymaker incurs cost when making a marginal change in the rate of growth of his money supply. However, the ROW benefits from a more expansionary U.S. policy and the United States benefits from a less expansionary ROW policy.

Once again, it is not clear how a cooperative solution would be achieved in a world of decentralized policymaking. A solution close to the Nash might be expected, with each country attempting to influence the other's monetary policy. In this case, however, the ROW will attempt to induce the United States to inflate more, while the United States will attempt to induce the ROW to inflate less. Thus, although the pressures exerted by the two countries as they strive for a better outcome might be interpreted as reflecting differing objectives, in fact, the objective functions of the two countries are identical.

Measuring the Adjustment Burden

The analysis of the last section has one major implication for the size of the adjustment burden following an oil-price shock. The absence of cooperation between policymakers unambiguously increases the size of the adjustment burden for all players when the adjustment burden is measured by the reduction in policymakers' utility functions.[19] Perhaps equally important and interesting, however, are the lessons to be derived from the present section, which concerns the appropriate measurement of the size and distribution of the adjustment burden.

The appropriate measure of a country's adjustment burden following an oil-price shock is, presumably, the reduction in social welfare experienced by that country following the shock. In the game framework of this chapter, that reduction is measured by the utility loss suffered by policymakers. This loss is a weighted average of the changes in output and inflationary expectations that follow the shock, and it cannot be directly observed. Clearly, an observable proxy for the actual adjustment burden—a measure that is perfectly correlated with social welfare—would be useful.

One possible proxy for the adjustment burden borne by any individual country following an oil-price increase is the fall in its level of output. A casual reading of the popular literature suggests that this proxy is in wide use already. It appears to be common practice to gauge (1) the overall impact of an oil shock by its aggregate effect on output levels and (2) the distribution of that impact by its effect on relative output levels. However, the analysis of this section suggests that, in a wide range of circumstances, these measures are inadequate approximations of policymakers' utility.

Consider, for example, the problem of comparing the overall size of the adjustment burden in a noncooperative game setting with the size of the burden in a cooperative setting. The move from a noncooperative to a cooperative solution raises the utility of all players. However, if spill over is negative, this move also is associated with a greater output loss and lower long-run inflation for all players. Accordingly, the size of the output loss does not, in this case, provide a correct indication of policymakers' utility. In general, the relationship between output losses and social welfare will depend on the nature of the spill-over effects of policy, which, in turn, depend on the structural and institutional features of the countries involved.

The difficulty of accurately measuring the changes in social welfare following an oil-price shock is even more evident when the question of the distribution of the adjustment burden is addressed. If one allows for differences in the relative weights assigned to output and inflation across countries, no systematic relationship between social welfare and output can be established, even for a given macroeconomic structure. For example, compared to a country with a very high aversion to unemployment, a country with a very high aversion to inflation may suffer a substantial output loss and yet experience a lower overall utility loss.

Notes

1. The game-theoretic aspects of policymaking in an interdependent world have been recognized by a number of earlier writers. See, for example, Bryant (1980), Hamada (1974, 1976, and 1979), and Johansen (1980).

2. There is, of course, a voluminous literature devoted to the international transmission of monetary disturbances; however, explicit analyses of two-country models (or models with more than two countries) are relatively scarce. We are unaware of any set of publications that present just the analyses needed here, although many of the individual pieces of the desired framework do appear in various other publications. Mundell (1963) for example, develops symmetric-negative constraints in a model with fixed prices and static expectations. Mussa (1979) presents an excellent discussion of macroeconomic interdependence that includes an exposition of Mundell's results. Argy and Salop (1979) present a model very like the extension of the Canzoneri and Gray (1982a) model discussed in this chapter, although they postulate static expectation formation. Daniel (1981) presents a rational expectations model that is also very like our extension; her use of intermediate goods serves the function of our indexing. Bruno and Sachs's (1979) simula-

tion model has all of the ingredients necessary to derive the three sets of constraints employed here.

3. There exists a number of publications that explore the effects of an oil-price shock in a single-country context; see, for example, Blinder (1981), Bruno and Sachs (1979), and Findlay and Rodriguez (1977). A few publications address this question in a multicountry setting that explicitly models OPEC's short-run savings behavior. Examples include Caprio and Clark (1981), Krugman (forthcoming), Sachs (1980), and Schmid (1976). Unfortunately, none of these provides the analysis required here of both an oil-price shock and the spill-over effects of monetary policy. For further discussion of this point, see the publications referenced in footnote 1.

4. In calculating the postshock equilibrium, which must be done to solve the model, it is assumed that the real value of the original dollar increase in the price of oil is preserved. That is, the dollar price of oil is adjusted in the postshock period for any changes in the U.S. price level that occur subsequent to the preshock equilibrium. Thus, the real value of the oil-price increase can be only temporarily eroded during the adjustment period.

5. The level of real income in each country is defined to be nominal net national income deflated by the domestic consumer price index. Accordingly, Y and Y^* are given as:

$$Y = (P/PI)X - (Q/PI)O - rB$$

$$Y^* = (P^*/PI^*)X^* - (Q/PI)O^* - rB^*$$

Because consumption patterns are identical in the two countries, and because the law of one price holds, $(Q/PI) = (Q^*/PI^*)$; the real price of oil in the United States is equal to the real price of oil in the ROW. Log linearizing Y and Y^* around their no-shock equilibrium values yields equation 8.7.

6. The demands for the two goods (in levels) are given by:

$$X^d = (PI/P)(P^*E/P)^{\psi}(C + C^*) + \text{OPEC demand}$$

$$X^{*d} = (PI^*/P^*)(P/P^*E)^{\psi}(C + C^*) + \text{OPEC demand}$$

Equation 8.10 is obtained by log linearizing X^d and X^{*d} around their noshock equilibrium values, setting the change in OPEC's demand for both goods equal to zero and equating output demand to output supply. The term ψ that enters equation 8.10, then, is the negative of the own relative price elasticity of the expenditure shares of the two goods. The term $(1 + 2\psi)$ that enters equation 8.10 is the negative of the own relative price elasticity of the levels of expenditure on the two goods.

7. An unitary income elasticity of money demand means that each country's nominal money balances are effectively deflated by the price of domestic output in the equations describing money-market equilibrium. If this were not the case, valuation effects would be another source of spill over.

8. Attaining the solutions for equations 8.1 through 8.13 requires calculating the one-period-ahead expectation of the price of U.S. and ROW output. This expectation appears in equation 8.12 as a determinant of the nominal interest rate. To find δp_{+1}, we begin by differencing equation 8.13, substituting the result, along with equation 8.12, into equation 8.11, and updating the result by one period.

$$\delta m^s_{+1} - \delta p_{+1} = \delta x_{+1} - \lambda \delta r - \lambda(\delta p_{+2} - \delta p_{+1})$$

Because of the way we have chosen to specify output supply and demand, δx and δr are expected to be equal to zero in the postshock equilibrium. The term $(\delta p_{+2} - p_{+1})$ is simply the change in the expected rate of inflation in the postshock equilibrium, which is equal to the change in the rate of growth of money, or δg. The term δm^s_{+1} is the deviation of the money stock in the postshock period from the value it would have assumed in the absence of shocks. Because the postshock period is the second period in which altered money-growth rate is applicable, this term is equal to $2\delta g$. Substituting these values into the equation above and simplifying gives:

$$\delta p_{+1} = (2 + \lambda)\delta g$$

An exactly analogous expression for the postshock price of ROW output can be derived. Once these expressions are substituted into equation 8.11, the solution of the model is a matter of straightforward algebra.

9. The nominal exchange rate also depreciates, that is:

$$\delta e = (1 + \lambda)^2(\theta + \tau + \phi)(1/D_1)(\delta g - \delta g^*)$$

We use this result to define the fixed-rate regime (Canzoneri and Gray 1982b).

10. In fact, in the case of a fixed real price of oil, the ROW price level necessarily falls after a U.S. expansion.

11. Once again, the nominal exchange rate depends on the ratio of the money supplies, that is:

$$\delta e = (1 + \lambda)^2(\theta + \tau + \phi)(1/D_1)(\delta g - \delta g^*)$$

We also use this result in an earlier analysis (Canzeroni and Gray 1982b).

12. Remember that we are assuming that agents' expectations are rational given their assumptions about monetary policy. If their views about monetary policy (and the price of oil) are correct, then their price predictions will be realized.

13. It is clear from the money-demand functions that, at full-employment equilibrium, the rates of product-price inflation are g and g^*. Because the terms of trade are fixed at full equilibrium, the rates of inflation of the general price levels (pi and pi^*) are also equal to g and g^*.

14. With the utility functions (equation 8.21).

$$\partial u / \partial \delta g = -2(\delta x)(\partial \delta x / \partial \delta g) - 2(\pi_0 + \delta g) = 2\rho_3 \delta \bar{q} \rho_1 > 0$$

$$\partial u^* / \partial \delta g^* = 2\rho \delta \bar{q} \rho_1 > 0$$

when

$$\pi_0 = \pi_0^* = 0 \text{ and } \delta g = \delta g^* = 0$$

15. It may be interesting to note that some unemployment will remain as long as any weight is given to inflation in the utility functions. The conditions $U_{\delta g} = 0$ and $U_{\delta g^*}^* = 0$ (which define the Nash equilibrium) imply:

$$\delta x = -(\mu / \rho_1)(\delta g + \pi_0)$$

$$\delta x^* = -(\mu^* / \rho_1)(\delta g^* + \pi_0^*)$$

So if $\delta g > -\pi_0$ and $\delta g^* > -\pi_0^*$, then δx and δx^* are negative as long as μ and μ^* are positive.

16. With the Nash solution, $U_{\delta g^*} = 2\rho_2(-\delta x) < 0$ because $\delta x < 0$; see footnote 12. Similarly, $U_{\delta g}^* = 2\rho_2(-\delta x^*) < 0$.

17. See our earlier work (Canzoneri and Gray 1982b) for a demonstration that such a solution exists.

18. See our earlier work (Canzoneri and Gray 1982b) for a derivation of the contract curve.

19. Our model does have implications for the size of the adjustment burden that are independent of its game aspects. If, for instance, the oil-price shock raises the price of domestic output in the two countries, the adjustment burden will be an increasing function of the degree of wage and oil indexation. In contrast to most other models in which indexing has been studied, however, in our framework the oil-price shock does not necessarily raise output prices. Thus, the conclusions for indexing in the chapter are not clear-cut. We discuss this point and other implications of our macroeconomic structure in the one good case in an earlier work (Canzoneri and Gray 1982a).

References

Argy, V., and J. Salop. "Price and Output Effects of Monetary and Fiscal Expansion in a Two-Country World Under Flexible Exchange Rates." International Monetary Fund, DM/79/33, May 1979.

Blinder, Alan S. "Monetary Accommodation of Supply Shocks Under Rational Expectations." *Journal of Money, Credit and Banking* 13 (1981):425–438.

Bruno, M., and J. Sachs. "Macro-Economic Adjustment with Import Price Shocks: Real and Monetary Aspects," National Bureau of Economic Research Working Paper no. 340, April 1979.

Bryant, Ralph C. *Money and Monetary Policy in Interdependent Nations.* Washington, D.C.: The Brookings Institution, 1980.

Canzoneri, M., and J. Gray. "Oil Price Changes and Monetary Policy in a Three Country Framework." Manuscript, Board of Governors of the Federal Reserve System, June 1982a.

Canzoneri, M., and J. Gray. "Monetary Policy Games and the Consequences of Non-Cooperative Behavior." Manuscript, Board of Governors of the Federal Reserve System, November 1982b.

Caprio, Jerry, and Peter Clark. "Oil Price Shocks in a Portfolio-Balance Model." Board of Governors of the Federal Reserve System, International Finance Discussion Paper no. 181, June 1981.

Daniel, Betty C. "The International Transmission of Economic Disturbances Under Flexible Exchange Rates." *International Economic Review* 22, no. 3 (October 1981):491–509.

Findlay, Ronald, and Carlos Rodriguez. "Intermediate Imports and Macroeconomic Policy Under Flexible Exchange Rates." *The Canadian Journal of Economics* 10, no. 2 (May 1977):208–217.

Gray, J. "Wage Indexation: A Macroeconomic Approach." *Journal of Monetary Economics* 2 (1976):221–235.

Hamada, Koichi. "Alternative Exchange Rate Systems and the Interdependence of Monetary Policies." In *National Monetary Policies and the International Financial System,* edited by Robert Z. Aliber. Chicago, Ill.: University of Chicago Press, 1974.

Hamada, Koichi. "Macroeconomic Strategy Coordination under Alternative Exchange Rates." In *International Economic Policy,* edited by Rudiger Dornbusch and Jacob Frenkel. Baltimore, Md.: Johns Hopkins University Press, 1979.

Hamada, Koichi. "A Strategic Analysis of Monetary Interdependence." *Journal of Political Economy,* vol. 84 (August 1976):677–700.

Johansen, Leif. "The Possibility of an International Equilibrium with Low Levels of Activity." Manuscript, University of Oslo, May 1980.

Krugman, Paul. "Oil and the Dollar." In *Economic Interdependence and*

Flexible Exchange Rates, edited by J. Bhandari and B. Putman. Cambridge, Mass.: M.I.T. Press, forthcoming.

Mundell, Robert A. "Capital Mobility and Stabilization Policy Under Fixed and Flexible Exchange Rates." *Canadian Journal of Economics and Political Science,* vol. 29 (November 1963):475-485.

Mussa, Michael. "Macroeconomic Interdependence and the Exchange Rate Regime." In *International Economic Policy: Theory and Evidence,* edited by Rudiger Dornbusch and Jacob Frenkel. Baltimore, Md.: The Johns Hopkins University Press, 1979.

Sachs, Jeffrey. "Energy and Growth Under Flexible Exchange Rates: A Simulation Study." National Bureau of Economic Research Working Paper no. 582, November 1980.

Schmid, Michael. "A Model of Trade in Money, Goods and Factors." *Journal of International Economics* 6 (1976):347-361.

Comment

James M. Boughton

Matthew Canzoneri and Jo Anna Gray have developed an effective analysis of the costs that arise when national authorities do not cooperate in formulating monetary policies. This chapter is valuable for two principal reasons. First, the authors demonstrate that noncooperative solutions are unambiguously inferior to cooperative solutions, regardless of the nature of spill overs between countries. Second, they help to define cooperation more clearly than is usual in this context. Cooperation does not necessarily imply an explicit exchange-rate policy or that countries implement policies jointly; it only implies that countries define policy objectives in a cooperative setting so that the policies are understood clearly by authorities in other countries and, in some sense, further the joint interests of all.

The limitations in this analysis are primarily in the way that Canzoneri and Gray choose to model the interactions among countries. Specifically, there are two issues suggested by the Canzoneri-Gray model but not developed in the chapter. First, how important are the asymmetries and the positive spill overs depicted by Canzoneri and Gray? Is it possible for the United States to expand or contract its own money supply and make everyone better off? Second, if international cooperation is difficult to achieve, what other methods for reducing the costs of policy independence are available?

Suppose that the authorities in the United States decide to increase the growth rate of the supply of money in response to a contractionary external shock. It is very likely that this increase will make the U.S. economy better off in the sense that the country will enjoy a higher rate of domestic output and employment during the adjustment to a new equilibrium. The interesting question is whether the economies of the rest of the world also will be made better off in this sense. The traditional anwer is that the increase in U.S. output is expected to come at the expense of decreased output in other countries. In contrast, Canzoneri and Gray suggest that other countries may be made better off by the U.S. expansion if oil-price effects are asymmetrical or if there are positive spill overs. This conclusion raises the possibility of a locomotive approach as a second-best substitute for cooperation.

Canzoneri and Gray's analysis is carried out in the context of policy responses to an oil-price shock (such as occurred in 1973–74 or in 1979–80), and the authors are concerned primarily with expansionary policies designed to raise output. The analysis, however, carries over to a situation

The views expressed in this comment are those of the author and should in no way be interpreted as offical views of the International Monetary Fund.

221

in which countries implement contractionary policies in order to reduce inflation. For example, an antiinflationary policy in the United States tends to cause the real exchange rate of the dollar to appreciate. This, in turn, increases the cost of imports in the rest of the world, inflating consumer prices and, through indexation, inflating wages as well. This negative spill over could, therefore, lead to competitive revaluations as countries attempt to reexport the resulting inflation burdens by implementing monetary policies that are similarly restrictive.[1]

The negative-spill-over scenario does appear to describe the experience of the world economy following the 1979–80 oil-price increase, although, in fact, the range of spill overs has been much wider than the Canzoneri-Gray model suggests. In response to a tightening of monetary policy in the United States, real interest rates increased in the United States and the real exchange rate of the dollar appreciated. This appreciation was perceived in many other countries as contributing to imported inflation through the depreciation of their own exchange rates. Authorities in those countries reacted to the situation by tightening monetary policy in order to keep interest rates at high levels in real terms and thereby limit exchange-rate depreciation. In the absence of that type of policy response, the spill over would clearly have been negative. In practice, the United States and the rest of the world experienced a contraction of output in response to a general tightening of policy. The explanation for this, however, is not in the existence of positive spill over, but in the existence of sympathetic policy formation. This sympathetic policy arose not only because all oil-importing countries were subjected to similar external shocks but also because the exchange rate in many countries is an argument in the authorities' objective function. By simplifying the authorities' preferences to a quadratic function of domestic variables, Canzoneri and Gray limit the influence of the exchange rate to an indirect role and thus may omit an important part of the recent story.

When real interest rates rise substantially, as they did during the recent period, there is yet another channel through which positive or negative spill overs may arise. This channel is important whenever countries hold nonzero net financial balances compared with the rest of the world. Net creditor countries such as the United States and the major oil-exporting countries receive additional earnings on their external financial assets when real interest rates rise. These earnings increase the balance on current account, contributing to an expansion of gross national product (GNP). Many of the other industrial countries, as well as most oil-importing developing countries, hold negative external financial balances. For these countries, an increase in real interest rates reduces the balance on current account, contributing to a fall in output. The spill-over effects through this channel, therefore, are negative for surplus countries and positive for deficit countries.

Canzoneri and Gray claim that the effects of monetary policy on real oil prices are asymmetric whenever oil prices are denominated in U.S. dollars and are not indexed to changes in the U.S. price index. They obtain this result by assuming implicitly that purchasing-power parity holds continuously and that, therefore, real oil prices are the same in all countries.[2] In that case, an increase in the U.S. money supply directly decreases the real oil price in the United States by inflating prices of goods other than oil; by depreciating the value of the dollar, it leads to a decrease in real oil prices abroad as well. In contrast, an increase in the money supply of other countries has no effect on the real price of oil—except insofar as it affects the U.S. price level—because monetary expansion is assumed to have no impact on real exchange rates.

The problem with all this is that we know that changes in monetary policy do affect real exchange rates. For example, at various times during the late 1970s and early 1980s, Japan, the Federal Republic of Germany, the United Kingdom, and the United States all implemented restrictive monetary policies. Over periods of two to three years, these restrictive policies all resulted in very substantial appreciations of these countries' real exchange rates.[3] Even when real effective exchange rates did not change, bilateral exchange rates against the dollar changed markedly. For example, from the second quarter of 1978 to the fourth quarter of 1980, there was almost no net change in the real effective exchange rate of the U.S. dollar. During that same period, the pound sterling appreciated 53 percent in real terms against the dollar, the Italian lira appreciated 9 percent in real terms, and the Japanese yen depreciated 13 percent. These bilateral movements cannot be explained readily by differences in the stance of monetary policy, but they do illustrate the dangers of assuming constancy of real exchange rates.

An implication of this conclusion is that the asymmetries envisaged by Canzoneri and Gray are of minor practical importance. The other large industrial countries can reduce their own real oil prices by expanding their money supplies as well as by relying on expansionary monetary policy in the United States. The locomotive conclusion—that both the United States and the rest of the world would be made better off by a more expansionary policy in the United States (combined with a less expansionary policy in the rest of the world)—does not follow from the assumption that OPEC prices its oil in terms of U.S. dollars. An asymmetry may arise, however, if oil prices are indexed to changes in U.S. prices and if purchasing-power parity does not hold. However, then the Canzoneri-Gray conclusion is reversed: optimal policy requires a relatively tight monetary policy in the United States and a relatively expansionary policy in the rest of the world. That configuration would minimize real oil prices in the rest of the world, with little or no effect on real oil prices in the United States.

What actually happens to real oil prices when the United States implements an antiinflationary monetary policy? Consider the period from the end of the first quarter of 1981 to the end of the first quarter of 1982. During those four quarters, nominal oil prices declined about 4 percent in terms of U.S. dollars. Adjusted for changes in the GNP deflator, the real oil price in the United States declined by about 11 percent. In the rest of the world, however, real oil prices generally increased because of the depreciation of most currencies in relation to the dollar. For example, real oil prices in the other major industrial countries increased by amounts ranging from 2 percent in the Federal Republic of Germany to 7 percent in the United Kingdom. In this sense, then, a change in U.S. monetary policy acts as a supply shock on the other industrial countries. The tightening of policy in the United States leads to a medium-term increase in real oil prices in other countries, contributing both to inflation and declining output. The spill over, therefore, is positive in terms of output, but negative in terms of inflation.

Overall, the spill overs to other countries from a change in policy in one large country are more complex and possibly more negative than is implied by the Canzoneri-Gray model. The locomotive approach does not appear to be an adequate substitute for the implementation of cooperative coordinated policies. On the other hand, as the authors note with appropriate bathos, "the problem with cooperative solutions is that they require cooperation." One would have to be extremely optimistic to expect countries to achieve the kind of cooperation that would be necessary for the achievement of the optimum solutions described by Canzoneri and Gray. It is worth asking, therefore, what else individual countries can do in the absence of general cooperation. The following remarks are intended to be indicative of the ways in which this analysis could be expected; they are not intended as specific recommendations for policies.

There are at least three layers of policy coordination, of which international cooperation is the most general but not necessarily the most important. Internal coordination in each country's formulation of policies not only may be more central to the smooth functioning of the international monetary system, it may even be a prerequisite for the achievement of international cooperation. The mix of domestic policies—for example, the relative stance of fiscal and monetary policies—may, therefore, be regarded as a second underlying layer of policy coordination. The Canzoneri-Gray model, by focusing exclusively on monetary policy, is not able to cope with this issue, but it does provide a framework within which an analysis of the issue could be developed. Third, underlying the policy mix is the choice of instrument by which a policy action is implemented. Important examples of instrument selection include the choice between spending increases and tax cuts as a vehicle for fiscal expansion and the choice between interest-rate control or monetary-base control as a strategy for influencing monetary growth.

Manifold problems arise when the mix of domestic policies is severely unbalanced. For example, a country with a restrictive monetary policy and an expansionary fiscal policy is likely to experience unusually high real interest rates and a substantial appreciation of its real exchange rate. The spill-over effects of such a policy mix on other countries may severely aggravate the already difficult task of achieving international policy cooperation. Unfortunately, internal balance may be quite difficult to achieve. In countries where fiscal and monetary policies are determined independently, the fiscal and monetary authorities may disagree with respect to their assessment of the optimal setting for policy. Furthermore, once the policy mix becomes unbalanced, it may be difficult to balance again, even if the authorities think with one mind. Where fiscal policy has been relatively tight, an expansion nonetheless may threaten to produce large budget deficits that could be difficult to justify politically. Where fiscal policy has been relatively expansionary, retrenchment may be impossible politically unless the growth rate for output is extremely buoyant or unless the cutback is accompanied by an expansion of monetary growth. Monetary expansion, however, may rekindle inflationary expectations and weaken the credibility of the authorities. That type of revision would be expected to depreciate the real exchange rate, also. Depreciation might be welcome in that it would help restore external balance, but it also could aggravate incipient inflationary pressures.

Some of the undesirable side effects of efforts to balance the policy mix perhaps could be alleviated by the implementation of supplementary policies. For example, in cases where inflationary expectations are generated by expansion of monetary growth, but where the corresponding fiscal contraction eventually will offset any actual inflationary pressures, the imposition of an informal income policy might help to accelerate the restoration of internal balance. In cases where attempts to reduce fiscal deficits are expected to lead to unacceptable declines in output, restructuring government expenditures or tax policies in order to promote productivity and employment also could be valuable. The feasibility of incomes policies or structural policies varies markedly from country to country, but in all cases the range of options is much broader than is suggested by a model focusing on monetary policy alone.

The way that monetary policy is conducted can make a substantial difference in terms of the volatility of financial varibles. Rapid or unexpected financial innovation, for example, could lead to an unstable or volatile demand for money, in which case excessive emphasis by the authorities on the achievement of monetary targets or on control of the monetary base could destabilize both interest rates and exchange rates. The formulation of monetary-policy strategies that are realistic, flexible, and clearly understood by the public can contribute to financial stability and thereby help to create an environment in which international cooperation can take place. In addition, monetary authorities may be able to make use of supplementary policy tools. Examples of these supplementary tools include direct intervention in foreign-exchange markets as well as changes in banks' reserve requirements, ceilings on interest rates, and selective quantitative controls. For example, a decrease in reserve requirements—offset by contractionary open-market operations—may contribute to an increase in the yields on bank deposits, which could help to appreciate the exchange rate at a given rate of monetary growth.

The conduct of fiscal policy presents an even richer menu of options for the authorities. Tax-financed fiscal expansion has a smaller beneficial impact on output than does bond-financed fiscal expansion, but it also has the advantage of not raising the budget deficit. Whether a reduction in the budget deficit would necessarily contribute to a lowering of interest rates is perhaps not yet well understood, but it might well have a calming effect on market expectations and help to promote financial stability. More important, setting fiscal policy involves choosing not only the level of spending and the level of taxation but also the types of spending and taxes. These choices can have important effects on saving rates, investment incentives, and productivity.

Improvements in the conduct of monetary and fiscal policies are difficult to model and even more difficult to achieve. Nonetheless, it is very important to introduce these options into discussions of how to smooth the adjustment of industrial countries to external shocks. As indicated at the outset of this comment, it may very well be that expansion or contraction of monetary policy in one country improves the situation of that country at the expense of others. However, it is clear that an improvement in the efficiency with which policy is conducted in one country will benefit not only that country but its trading partners as well.

Notes

1. Canzoneri and Gray define spill-over effects in terms of their effects on output. This comment uses the term *spill over* more broadly to include effects of inflation as well.

2. Their equation 8.4 implies that the nominal exchange rate must always adjust to offset movements in relative consumer prices: $\delta pi - \delta pi^* - \delta e = 0$. Therefore, $\delta q - \delta pi = \delta q - \delta pi^* - \delta e$. That is, changes in the real oil price must be equal in the United States and the ROW. The model does permit movements in the real exchange rate defined in terms of domestic output prices.

3. The appreciations in real terms were as follows: 15 percent for the German mark over ten quarters following 1975, quarter (Q) 4; 28 percent for the Japanese yen over nine quarters following 1976, Q2; 28 percent for the U.S. dollar over eight quarters following 1979, Q3; and 65 percent for the pound sterling over eleven quarters following 1978, Q2. These figures are based on relative normalized unit labor costs, adjusted for effective exchange-rate changes, as reported in *International Financial Statistics,* various issues.

**Part III
Sectoral Issues and the
International Financial
System: The Role of OPEC
and the Impact of Industrial/
Trade Policies**

9

OPEC and International Financial Markets: Redistribution and Recycling

David Sternlight

The purpose of this chapter is to describe (1) the recent history of the Organization of Petroleum Exporting Countries (OPEC) oil prices, production, exports and imports, which has led to a surplus available for investment, and (2) the deployment of that surplus in the international community. OPEC reserves are discussed in the world-reserve context. Particular attention is paid to the recent tension among OPEC members caused by the revenue-seeking behavior of some members, who have sought revenues first through higher prices and then through price competition for higher volumes. Some future price paths that may result from the interaction of market conditions and OPEC behavior as well as future OPEC revenues are discussed to indicate the future impact of actions by OPEC countries on the international monetary system.

Price History

There has been a great deal of speculation about and research to uncover the mechanism behind OPEC pricing decisions. Without an understanding of this mechanism, if there is one, it would be difficult to forecast revenue and related financial variables.

One set of arguments about the underlying mechanism is political. These arguments are based on the speeches and explanations offered by OPEC leaders before, during, and after each OPEC meeting. The historical record is well documented in such publications as the *Middle East Economic Survey* and the *Petroleum Economist,* which have reported such rhetoric in detail. Some principal factors cited as affecting pricing decisions have been: an attempt to compensate for a decline in OPEC purchasing power due to a decline in the value of the U.S. dollar through both rising inflation and falling exchange rates; profligate U.S. consumption of energy, associated with bad energy policy; overt transfer of aid to developing countries by way of (implied) OPEC revenue sharing; the desire to transfer excessive oil-company profits to OPEC members; and U.S. policy toward

Israel. One would expect these factors, when they were most visible in the environment, to lead to OPEC price increases. A second set of factors also has been part of the OPEC litany. These include a desire for stable world markets; a desire not to damage the world economy or that of OPEC customers; concern regarding the effect of higher oil prices on developing countries; and the desire to reward customers for constructive energy policies (conservation promotion, development of alternative energy supplies) and antiinflationary policies. One would expect this set of factors, when operative, to lead to price reductions.

At each OPEC meeting, a pricing decision is taken. Because it is the real price of energy that affects the quantities of energy supplied and demanded, a decision to increase prices at a rate above that of inflation is a real price increase. A real price decrease, on the other hand, often has been implemented through freezing nominal prices of oil at a particular OPEC meeting. An attempt to correlate these pricing decisions with the causal factors cited reveals that there is zero correlation between the factors described and the price direction determined by pricing decisions.

If these factors do not explain OPEC pricing decisions, what does? Analysis has shown (Gately et al. 1977) that there is an extremely high correlation between OPEC pricing decisions at each meeting and the tightness or looseness of world oil markets in the six months preceeding each OPEC meeting. One useful way to measure this market condition is by examining the short-term rate of change of OPEC production. When it is increasing rapidly, in a time frame of fixed capacity, markets may be said to be tight. When production is level or declining, markets may be said to be loose.

This explanation seems to be related to the supply-demand balance for world oil. Yet something more is needed to fully explain price paths (see table 9-1), and that is the effect of stockpiles. The demand faced by OPEC is a derived demand, which is the residual of economic demand, stockpile demand, and indigenous supply in oil-importing countries. Furthermore, transportation-distance and cost differences, as well as specific gravity and sulfur-content differences between countries' crude oils, which lead to refining-cost differences, affect the value of these crude oils, creating differences between the market prices of different countries' crude. In some cases, these differences may cause some countries to have great difficulty selling any crude at all, particularly when markets are weak, excess oil-production capacity is high, and refinery-operating levels are well below their capacity.

A notable example of the effects of these operational factors is how price behavior reacted to the Iranian revolution compared to how it reacted to the Iran-Iraq war. In each case, lost production was made up, largely by Saudi Arabia. Yet, in the first case, prices rose sharply while, in the second, prices fell after a time. The difference was due to stockpiling. Prior to the

Table 9-1
OPEC Crude-Oil Official Sales Price
(U.S. dollar per barrel)

	1977	1978	1979	1980	1981	1/82	9/82	12/82	1/83	2/83
OPEC Average	12.88	12.93	18.67	30.87	34.50	34.29	33.69	33.43	33.44	33.15
Saudi Light	12.40	12.70	17.26	28.67	32.50	34.00	34.00	34.00	34.00	34.00
Iran Light	12.81	12.81	19.45	34.54	36.60	34.20	31.20	31.20	31.20	31.20
Iraq	12.61	12.62	18.56	30.30	36.66	34.93	34.83	34.83	34.83	34.83
Nigeria	14.45	14.07	20.86	35.50	38.48	36.47	35.42	35.42	35.42	29.87
United Arab Emirates	12.88	13.26	19.81	31.57	36.42	35.50	34.56	34.56	34.56	34.56
Kuwait	12.37	12.26	18.48	29.84	35.08	32.30	32.30	32.30	32.30	32.30
Libya	14.06	13.89	21.16	36.07	40.08	37.00	35.50	35.50	35.50	35.50
Venezuela	12.75	12.75	17.22	28.44	32.88	32.88	32.88	32.88	32.88	32.88
Indonesia	13.55	13.55	18.35	30.55	35.00	35.00	35.00	34.53	34.53	34.53
Algeria	14.37	14.14	19.65	37.59	39.58	37.00	35.50	35.50	35.50	35.50
Qatar	13.19	13.19	19.72	31.76	37.12	35.45	34.49	34.99	34.49	34.49
Gabon	12.80	12.80	18.20	31.09	34.83	34.00	34.00	34.00	34.00	34.49
Ecuador	12.90	12.33	22.41	34.42	34.50	33.35	33.20	33.20	33.20	33.20

Source: Data from *International Energy Statistical Review*, various issues.

Iranian revolution, stockpiles were low. Although the Saudis made up for lost supply, derived demand for OPEC oil increased beyond that level, due to panic stockpiling by oil companies and others, who were attempting to protect themselves against an unknown medium-term future. The Saudis were unwilling to compensate for this extra stockpile demand.

During the Iran-Iraq war, on the other hand, stockpiles were high, and the additional loss of crude oil could be handled easily. Subsequently, as demand fell (due to the higher prices resulting from the Iranian revolution as well as from previous price rises), oil markets became quite weak and prices fell. The observed price path was consistent with the operational factors' effects, once stockpile levels were taken into account.

Price Dynamics

On the basis of the analysis and experience referred to in the preceding section, the following explanation of price dynamics may be submitted. OPEC prices are set at each meeting in an exploratory way. They are based on the derived supply-demand conditions that OPEC members confront. The degree of price change is a function of the degree of market tightness, as measured by OPEC capacity-utilization rates. The ratio is nonlinear around a desired capacity-utilization figure. When OPEC capacity-utilization is in the vicinity of that desired figure, or target, the ratio of price changes to utilization changes is less than when OPEC capacity-utilization is further from the target. At full capacity, price increases are made in order to clear the market and can be quite steep. These price decisions are informed, however, by the medium- and longer-term effects of any particular possible price change. In particular, when a short-term price change could lead to production and revenue levels that would be unacceptable to Saudi Arabia within a few years, the change will be resisted strongly.

Two recent examples of how anticipated effects affect pricing decisions were the $32 ceiling adopted by the Saudis when a price overshoot by others would have led to significant demand reductions and production losses within a few years, and their subsequently attempted $34 floor when price drops by others in search of market share under weak demand could have led to a price war in OPEC, which, in turn, could have led to a significant revenue loss for all members, followed by sharp price rises as demand reached capacity and highly unstable markets that could have produced even further revenue losses. The pattern of production as a result of events since 1977 is shown in table 9-2.

Why do these price dynamics exist? Energy conservation, in the form of the increased efficiency of energy use (smaller cars, better-insulated homes, improved industrial processes), has a long response period to price rises

Table 9–2
OPEC Crude-Oil Production, Excluding Natural Gas Liquids
(*million barrels per day*)

	1973	1977	1978	1979	1980	1981	1/82	4/82
Total	30.989	31.278	29.805	30.928	26.890	22.624	21.285	16.725
Percent change from 9/73[a]		−5.46	−9.91	−6.51	−18.72	−31.61	−35.66	−49.45
Percent change from 12/76[b]		−8.61	−12.91	−9.63	−21.43	−33.89	−37.81	−51.13

Table 9–2 continued

	5/82	6/82	7/82	8/82	9/82	10/82	11/82	12/82
Total	17.08	18.845	18.45	18.045	18.515	19.41	19.395	18.986
Percent change from 9/73[a]	−48.37	−43.04	−44.23	−45.46	−44.03	−41.33	−41.37	−42.61
Percent change from 12/7[b]	−50.09	−44.94	−46.09	−47.27	−45.90	−43.29	−43.33	−44.52

Source: Data from *Monthly Energy Review*, various issues.
[a]Preembargo peak of 33.083.
[b]Postembargo peak of 34.224.

because it is essentially a capital-investment process. It takes ten or more years to turn over the stock of cars on the road; it takes forty years to turn over most of the housing stock. Some analysts believe that we are still experiencing demand reductions due to the 1973–74 OPEC price rise, with much more to come as a result of the significant price rises since then. Furthermore, as these investments are made, they are sunk, and subsequent price reductions by OPEC cannot reverse their demand-reducing effects, except in the longer run. Fuel-switching investments are similarly sticky, as are commitments to alternative energy supplies.

Thus, OPEC may be thought to have been probing for the market-clearing price of crude oil since 1973. In the opinion of some, they have slightly overshot it now. Errors of overshooting, if not corrected quickly, can produce irreversible price and revenue consequences for OPEC and, most seriously, for countries with longer-lived (larger) reserves of crude oil, most notably Saudi Arabia. This explains both the Saudis' caution and the strong attempts to contain the larger excesses of some other OPEC members.

OPEC Revenues and Their Distribution

Table 9–3 shows the sharp increase in the value of OPEC exports from 1973 to 1977, when prices were rising in response to the market-clearing probe and the change in quantities demanded more than offset the price rises, at first because the quantities demanded continued to increase, and later because they decreased less rapidly than did the prices. The postembargo production peak was in December 1976; production declined nearly 9 percent (see table 9–2) in 1977. Thus, exports rose from $39 billion in 1973 to $149 billion in 1977. In 1978, however they declined to $141 billion as production fell to almost 13 percent below the peak. In 1979, production rose slightly, to almost 10 percent below the peak, and export revenues increased to $210 billion as prices rose (see table 9–1). The sharp price rise in 1980 more than offset the loss of production, which declined to a level 21 percent below the postembargo peak, and, as a result, exports increased to a high of $296 billion. Since then, weak markets have been associated with weak prices, and export revenues have declined significantly. Prices (all in current dollars) declined from $34.50 in 1981 to $33.15 in February 1983, and the decline has continued since then. Real declines, of course, were sharper. Production declined from 22.6 million barrels per day in 1981 to 16.7 million barrels per day in April 1982, a level 52 percent below the postembargo peak. After April, lower prices raised production to about 19 million barrels per day by December 1982. Consequently, export revenues declined from the 1981 level of $270 billion to the most recently available (January 1983) estimated figure of $232 billion.

Table 9-3
OPEC Merchandise Trade Balance
(in billions of dollars)

	1973	1974	1975	1976	1977	1978	1979	1980	1981	1982[a]	1/83
Exports	38.894	119.267	111.620	135.558	149.030	141.67	210.35	296.15	270.43	253.142	232.092[a]
Imports	19.972	32.141	51.322	62.456	84.350	94.78	97.64	131.38	159.39	159.468	159.468[b]
Balance	18.922	87.126	60.298	73.102	64.680	46.89	112.71	164.77	111.04	93.674	72.624

Source: Data from *International Financial Statistics*, various issues.
Note: Excludes Ecuador and Gabon.
[a]Latest quarter annualized for Indonesia and Venezuela.
[b]Previous-period figure used.

Associated with this export picture is an import pattern reflecting OPEC members' increased expenditures on consumption and on internal projects. Because of planning and physical lead times, it is difficult to alter such a pattern quickly. As a result, as exports rose, imports rose (see table 9–3) from the 1973 level of nearly $20 billion to the 1980 level of $131 billion, which led to an increasing trade balance that rose from almost $19 billion in 1973 to almost $165 billion in 1980. Subsequently, as export revenues fell, imports continued to rise, reaching an estimated $159.5 billion in January 1983. This produced a sharply decreasing trade balance, which fell from the 1980 high of nearly $165 billion to slightly more than $72.5 billion in January 1983.

Table 9–4 shows the import-export picture since 1980 in more detail. (The trade figures differ slightly from those in table 9–3 because the data are from the Bank of England rather than from the International Monetary Fund.) Taking into account net invisibles and external borrowing, the OPEC surplus available for investment declined from $113 billion in 1980 to − $1 billion by the second quarter of 1982. OPEC countries are beginning to dip into reserves as well as borrow further. Table 9–5 shows the disposition of the surpluses, and table 9–6 shows the growth of international reserves. As is given in table 9–6, the rate of growth for the world rose from 2.5 percent annually between 1952 and 1962 to 12.5 percent annually between 1972 and 1977 to 9.9 percent annually between 1978 and 1981. From 1981 to January 1983, reserves declined at 0.4 percent annual rate. Most of the reserve growth came in OPEC countries and, in particular,

Table 9–4
Oil Exporters' Current-Account Balance and Cash Surplus
Available for Investment
(in billions of dollars)

			1982		
	1980	*1981*	*1st Quarter*	*2nd Quarter*	*3rd Quarter*
Exports	310	283	58	51	57
Imports	137	158	40	40	39
Merchandise trade	173	125	18	11	18
Net invisibles	− 67	− 69	− 17	− 18	− 19
Current balance	106	56	1	− 7	− 1
Net external borrowing, and so on	7	9	8	6	NA
Surplus available for investment	113	65	9	− 1	NA

Source: Data from *Bank of England and Quarterly Bulletin,* 1983, no. 1.

Table 9-5
Identified Deployment of Oil Exporters' Surpluses
(in billions of dollars)

| | | | | | | 1981 | | 1982 | | |
	1974	1975	1976	1980	1981	3rd Quarter	4th Quarter	1st Quarter	2nd Quarter	3rd Quarter
United States										
Bank deposits	4.00	0.60	1.60	-1.10	-2.10	-1.90	0.50	1.50	5.20	-1.00
Treasury bonds/notes	5.40	2.00	4.20	8.20	10.90	3.20	2.20	2.60	2.70	2.50
Treasury bills	0.70	0.50	-1.00	1.40	-0.60	-0.60	-0.10	0.80	-1.50	NA
Equity, and so on	1.00	6.90	7.20	5.60	7.90	2.00	3.00	0.30	0.80	0.10
Total	11.00	10.00	12.00	14.10	16.10	2.70	5.60	5.20	7.20	1.60
United Kingdom										
Sterling bank deposits	1.70	0.20	-1.40	1.40	0.50	-0.10	0.00	0.50	0.30	0.20
Eurocurrency bank deposits	13.80	0.20	0.80	14.80	7.90	3.40	-0.40	-0.90	-5.50	1.30
British government stocks	0.90	0.40	0.20	1.90	1.00	0.20	0.30	0.10	0.20	-0.30
Treasury bills	2.70	-0.90	-1.20	-0.10	0.00	0.00	-0.20	-0.10	NA	NA
Sterling equity, and so on	0.70	0.30	0.50	0.10	0.20	0.00	0.00	-0.10	-0.10	-0.20
Other foreign equity, and so on	1.20	4.10	5.60	-0.50	-0.60	-0.10	0.00	0.00	NA	NA
Total	21.00	4.30	4.50	17.60	9.00	3.40	-0.30	-0.50	-5.10	1.00

Table 9-5 continued

	1974	1975	1976	1980	1981	1981 3rd Quarter	1981 4th Quarter	1982 1st Quarter	1982 2nd Quarter	1982 3rd Quarter
Bank deposits—other industrial countries	9.00	5.00	7.00	26.20	-2.60	-2.10	-2.40	-2.00	-5.90	NA
Other investments—other industrial countries				17.00	21.70	2.50	3.40	1.00	1.40	NA
International Monetary Fund/International Bank for Reconstruction and Development	3.60	4.00	2.00	4.90	2.50	0.50	0.70	-0.60	0.30	NA
Loans to developing countries	11.60	12.40	10.30	6.70	7.20	1.40	1.80	1.20	0.20	NA
Total identified net cash surplus	56.20	35.70	35.80	86.50	53.90	8.40	8.80	5.50	-1.90	NA
Residual unidentified items				34.50	12.10	10.60	5.20	3.50	0.90	NA
Total net cash surplus				121.00	66.00	19.00	14.00	9.00	-1.00	NA

Source: Data from *Bank of England and Quarterly Bulletin*, various issues.

Table 9-6
International Reserves
(in millions of Special Drawing Rights at end of period)

	World	Industrial Countries	Percent	OPEC	Percent	Saudi Arabia	Percent
1952	49.4	38.5	78	1.7	3	NA	NA
1962	62.9	52.5	83	2.0	3	0.3	NA
1972	147.4	110.3	75	10.0	7	2.3	2
1976	223.6	123.3	55	56.1	25	23.3	10
1977	265.9	149.7	56	62.1	23	24.7[a]	9
1978	283.1	174.1	61	46.2	16	14.9	5
1979	307.0	180.8	59	56.3	18	14.8	5
1980	358.7	211.5	59	73.6	21	18.5	5
1981	375.8	212.7	57	81.4	22	27.9	7
1982	371.4	211.9	57	77.0	21	26.9	7
1/83	374.1	217.3	58	75.0	20	25.9	7
Annual percentage change							
1952–1962	2.5	3.2		1.6		NA	
1962–1972	8.9	7.7		17.5		14.9	
1972–1977	12.5	6.3		44.1		60.8	
1978–1981	9.9	6.9		20.8		23.3	
1981–1/83	-0.4	1.9		-7.3		-6.7	

Source: Data from *International Financial Statistics*, various issues.
[a]Changed basis.

Saudi Arabia. The annual rate of industrial-country growth in reserves rose from 3.2 percent in 1952 to 1962 to 7.7 percent in 1962 to 1972. The subsequent growth has been at an annual rate of 6.3 percent in 1972 to 1977, 6.9 percent in 1978 to 1981, and a low 1.9 percent in 1981 to the first quarter in 1983. In contrast, as might be expected from the previous discussion, OPEC growth went from the high annual rate of 44.1 percent in 1972 to 1977 to 20.8 percent in 1978 to 1981. The subsequent decline has been at a 7.3 percent annual rate. Saudi reserves did not escape the decline. From a high of 60.8 percent annual growth between 1972 and 1977, the Saudi Arabian annual growth rate dropped to 23.3 percent in 1978 to 1981 and has declined at 6.7 percent since then.

What of the Future?

Based on analytic work and on the public statements of Sheikh Yamani and others, who doubtless were informed by a Saudi world oil model that uses a market-clearing algorithm at its core, two possible oil-price scenarios for the future can be postulated (figure 9-1). The first, called Yamani, is based on the public statements and assumes a constant nominal oil price until about 1984, followed by a return to the 1981 peak in real terms. After 1985, the Yamani scenario assumes a constant real price until sometime in the late 1990s. Note that a constant nominal price until 1984 means that the real price will fall until then.

The second scenario, called Disorder, assumes the same real price decline, arrested in 1984. The price then remains constant in real terms until the mid-1990s, when OPEC once more nears production capacity as a result of the greater quantities demanded and the lower quantities supplied by other oil producers, a situation caused by the lower price. The price then quickly rises to clear the market and remains at the higher level.

Figure 9-2 shows the notional OPEC oil-export revenues resulting from the two scenarios depicted in figure 9-1. Interestingly, the discounted total revenue consequences of the Yamani and Disorder cases are roughly similar, with the amount of oil left in the ground at the end of each case nearly equal. As figure 9-2 shows, OPEC revenues decline to $250 billion in the near term and then increase, remaining near $300 billion (in 1981 U.S. dollars) through at least 1992 before rising to about $400 billion thereafter.

Conclusions

It would appear that, absent an unexpected major disruption that could significantly destabilize world oil markets, under the conditions specified, the

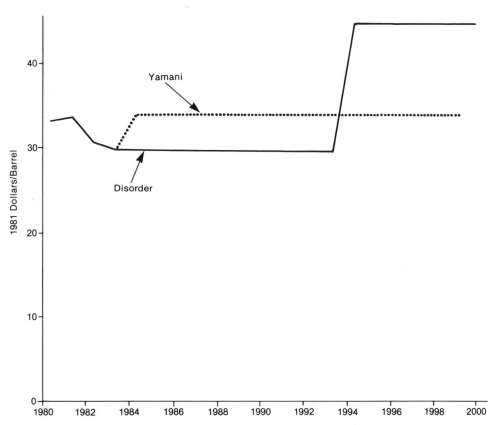

Figure 9-1. Real Market Crude Oil Prices Under Two Scenarios

revenue outlook for OPEC is for a reduction of less than 20 percent from 1982 until about 1984. Although this will present difficulties to some member countries, they can be expected to use a variety of mechanisms to handle the situation. In addition to national measures, such as reserve draw down and reduction in import and development expenditures (partly through the postponement of some projects), revenue transfers from Saudi Arabia and perhaps others to the more seriously affected OPEC countries might be expected. These transfers might occur in connection with mutually agreed-on price and production behavior so that a destabilizing, no-win price competition for market share would be avoided. In this case, the transfers are likely to be bilateral, removing them, in the first round, from intermediation. The transfers may be overt or covert and may include concessionary loans. Some of these measures are in use already. Perhaps some OPEC countries can balance their budgets further by reducing fund transfers to the

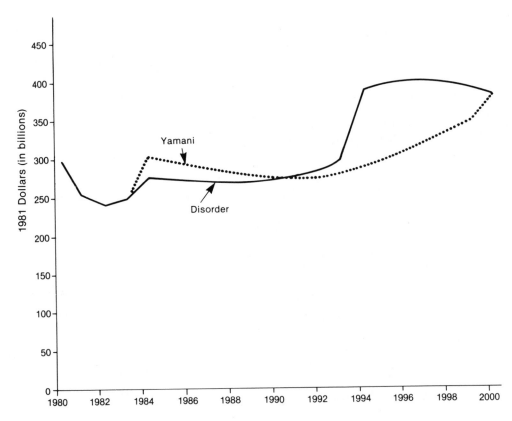

Figure 9-2. Notional OPEC Oil-Export Revenues Under Two Scenarios

Palestine Liberation Organization (PLO) for weapons purchases now that the circumstances of that organization have altered and it has announced a shift in its tactics toward substantial emphasis on diplomacy.

For some time after 1984, OPEC revenues are likely to present OPEC countries and others with an opportunity for stable planning, because it seems likely that the revenues will be roughly constant in real terms through the early 1990s. Thus, it is probable that the international monetary system will not be confronted by another major increase in OPEC revenues until that time.

References

Bank of England. *Quarterly Bulletin,* various issues, London.

Baumol, William J., and Richard E. Quandt. 1964. "Rules of thumb and optimally imperfect decisions." *American Economic Review,* 23–46.

British Petroleum. 1980. *Statistical Review of the World Oil Industry.*

Fischer, Dietrich, Dermot Gately, and John F. Kyle, 1975. "The prospects for OPEC: A critical survey of models of the world oil market." *Journal of Development Economics* 2:363–386.

Gately, Dermot. 1981. Modeling OPEC behavior, C.V. Starr Center for Applied Economics discussion paper series. New York: New York University, June.

Gately, Dermot, John F. Kyle, and Dietrich Fischer. 1977. "Strategies for OPEC's pricing decisions." *European Economic Review* 10:209–230.

Greenberger, Martin. 1983. *Caught unawares.* Cambridge, Mass.: Ballinger.

International Monetary Fund. *International Financial Statistics,* various issues, Washington, D.C.

Johany, Ali D. 1980. *The myth of the OPEC cartel.* New York: Wiley.

Pindyck, Robert S. 1979. "Energy demand and energy policy: What have we learned" In B. Kursunoglu and A. Perlmutter, eds., *Directions in energy policy.* Cambridge, Mass.: Ballinger.

Sweeney, James L. 1981. *World Oil: EMF6 Summary Report.* Stanford, Calif.: Stanford University, September.

U.S. Department of Commerce. *Business Conditions Digest,* various issues, Washington, D.C.

U.S. Department of Energy. 1980. *Energy Information Administration 1980: Annual Report to Congress,* vol. 3, Washington, D.C.

U.S. Department of Energy. *Energy Information Administration, Monthly Energy Review,* various issues, Washington, D.C.

U.S. Department of Energy. *International Energy Indicators,* various issues, Washington, D.C.

U.S. Library of Congress, *Document Expediting Project, International Energy Statistical Review,* various issues, Washington, D.C.

Comment

Tamir Agmon

The relative price of oil is one of the major variables in the world markets for goods, for capital assets, and for money. Therefore, David Sternlight's chapter dealing with the dynamics of the future relative price of oil is important input in a book that deals with the future of the international monetary system. The radical increase in the price of oil in 1973–74 and the periodic increments since then, activated a process of international financial intermediation that has shaped, to a great extent, the multinational banking system in the last decade. The effects of the transfer of real resources following the increases in the relative price of oil in 1973–74 and in 1979 were mitigated by an increase in the rate of inflation of the dollar, which affects the demand for money worldwide.[1]

Through its effects on the markets for goods, for capital assets, and for money, the relative price of oil is an input in the determination of exchange rates. Changes in exchange rates are explained partially by the relative inflation between the relevant currencies, by the relative change in the trade balances, and by capital movements. All these factors are affected by changes in the relative price of oil.

In this comment, the main factors that determine the changes in the relative price of oil are discussed. In the first part, the interchange between political and economic factors in the determination of the changes in the relative price of oil is presented and discussed. An example of this process in the markets for goods and for money is described in the second part.

The Interchange of Political and Economic Factors in the Determination of the Relative Price of Oil

The price of oil is not determined in a perfect market. This is not to say that the relative price of oil is divorced from the demand for and the supply of crude oil. It implies, instead, that the demand for oil and its supply, as well as the resulting price, are affected by many considerations not present in the paradigm of a perfect market.

The most obvious deviation from the perfect market is on the supply side, where the Organization of Petroleum Exporting Countries (OPEC) has operated as an effective cartel since 1973. This deviation, however, does not sufficiently explain the determination of the quantities supplied. OPEC

246

is organized around a price leader—Saudi Arabia. The decision maker is the Saudi government, and it has both economic and political considerations. The Saudi government has a strong interest in a stable world system and is particularly sensitive to the danger (from its point of view) of radical changes in the Persian Gulf region. In terms of the model presented by Sternlight, the Saudi government has an interest in the orderly Yamani scenario, rather than the Disorder scenario, even if the present value of the two scenarios is similar. The Saudi government has used its power to favor the preferred scenario by cutting back production or side payments to other countries. Decisions on the demand side also are made within a political as well as an economic context. The issue of independence (in the sense of minimizing the reliance of a given country on oil import from OPEC) is at least as much a political as an economic issue. Indeed, this is a real case of political economy.

Given the basic structure of its international relations, a certain country may decide to convert a substantial part of its energy-generating sector from oil to coal, even if the coal also is likely to be expensive in the long run. The decision is made because this country judges its relations with the coal suppliers to be more stable than its relations with OPEC members. The argument for the decision is even more persuasive when the alternative source of energy is present within the country itself. South Africa's decisions are an extreme example of this sort of policymaking, but even Western Europe (with regard to coal) and the United States (with regard to synthetic fuel) follow this route. If the political risk premium in the current and the future price of oil is considered, setting this policy may maximize some value function, but only if financial value is assigned to the reduction of political risk.

This policy is characterized by some degree of irreversibility. The cost structures of coal-fired power plants and coal liquefaction plants are such that, once they are installed, they will be utilized even if the price of oil is reduced quite substantially. Therefore, if sufficiently large countries follow such a policy, both the current and the future demand from oil will be affected and the demand curve will shift down to the left. The price of oil that reflects current and expected demand for oil and its supply is, therefore, determined by a mixture of political and economic factors.

Sternlight points out the well-known relationship between the revenues of OPEC members and their financial investments. A more complete analysis would include the three participants in the process of international financial intermediation. The three participants are the suppliers of the funds (OPEC members), the users (some of the non-OPEC less-developed countries, or LDCs), and the intermediaries (the developed countries and the banks).[2] A change in the relative price of oil starts a process that has a built-in financial hedge. A downward change in the price of oil, ceteris paribus, will reduce the flow of new short-term deposits into the world banking system. At the same time, it will reduce (again, given ceteris paribus) the import expenditure of the oil-importing countries and will reduce the demand for medium- and long-term loans to finance the trade imbalances. In Walrasian terms, there will be a simultaneous reduction in the excess demand for short-term deposits and long-term loans. (This is the financial reflection of the changes in the supply and the demand for oil that were analyzed earlier.) The ensuing exchange-rate system will reflect the changes in both the real factors (flow of goods) and the financial factors (capital movements).

As was mentioned earlier, exchange rates, as well as the whole nature of the international monetary system, are determined by the rate of inflation in the world. The most important component of world inflation is the rate of inflation of the dollar. The connection between the change in the relative price of oil and the dollar rate of inflation is presented and discussed in the next section.

Changes in the Price of Oil and Dollar Inflation

The phenomenon of inflation is the prime example of how political and economic factors intermingle with regard to economic policies. The following is a very partial analysis of the possible relationship between changes in the price of oil and changes in the rate of inflation in the United States (dollar inflation). The analysis is partial because there are many other considerations that affect the rate of inflation. Moreover, there is no explicit process by which the rate of inflation is determined by a policymaking body. Rather, the rate of inflation is the outcome of many decisions, some of them unrelated. These decisions are made by various agencies. Some decisions are made autonomously, and some are made in response to the autonomous decisions of others.[3]

For a clearer exposition, a stylized paradigm of two countries and two periods is employed. Assume two countries, A and B. A is an oil exporter, and B is an oil importer. A is producing only oil (denoted X), and B is producing only consumer goods (denoted Y). Assume one currency, issued by the government of B. In accordance with the classical free-trade model presented by Mundell (1968, pp. 8–15), the basic system is described as follows. Domestic expenditure in A in terms of X (oil) is:

$$D_a = X_a + PY_a - T \qquad (9C.1)$$

Domestic expenditure in B in terms of Y (consumer goods) is:

$$D_b = \frac{X_b}{P} + Y_b + \frac{T}{P} \qquad (9C.2)$$

In these equations, P represents the terms of trade (price of Y in terms of X) and T represents capital exports (lending) of A in terms of X. The demand for consumer goods in the oil-exporting country (A) is:

$$Y_a = Y_a(D_a, P) \tag{9C.3}$$

The demand for oil in the oil-importing country (B) is:

$$X_b = X_b(D_b, 1/P) \tag{9C.4}$$

The balance of payments is given by the ex ante relationship:

$$T = I_b(D_b, 1/P) - PI_a(D_a, P) \tag{9C.5}$$

where I_a and I_b are the import functions of A and B.

Given normal conditions for stability, it has been shown that a transfer will have a two-phase effect.[4] The first phase is the actual transfer, and the second phase is the change in the terms of trade. Such a change is required to restore equilibrium following the actual transfer.

Given imperfect competition, both on the demand side and on the supply side, the classic result may change by willful action. Let us start on the supply (of oil) side. Country A, the oil exporter, is trying to affect a transfer of real resources by increasing the relative price of oil. P will go up, and domestic expenditure in A and B will adjust. Now we add currency to the system. Due to limitations of absorptive capacity and portfolio considerations, the oil-exporting country is buying short-term deposits denominated in B's currency. In the paradigm employed here, these are one-period deposits. In other words, country A lends money to country B. (Thus begins the international financial intermediation described in the preceding section.) The deposits are denominated in nominal terms, giving country B some discretion with regard to the deposits' value in terms of the consumer goods (Y) and allowing the government of B to affect its price level in terms of its own currency (b).

This process is described schematically in figure 9C-1. The real price of oil, $P(Y/X)$, is depicted on the vertical axis, b_2, the price level in terms of b in period 2, is depicted on the horizontal axis. In the figure, P_1 is the initial price of oil (in relative price term). $E(b_2')$ is the expected price level in terms of b at the initial state. The oil-exporting country (A) is trying to affect a real transfer by increasing the real relative price of oil, using monopolistic power, to P_2, the initial transfer line. A possible solution is for country B to accept the transfer, in which case K is a possible equilibrium point. The transfer would then be carried out both by an increase in P and a decrease in b_2. A decrease in b_2 for nominal deposits that were negotiated given $E(b_2')$ would be equivalent to an increase in the real return on A's deposits. Thus, there would be a current and a future transfer.

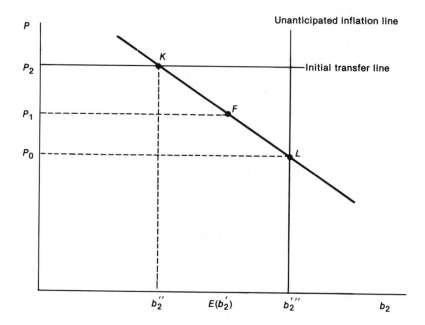

Figure 9C-1. The Real Price of Oil and the Price Level

Table 9C-1
Changes in the Price of Oil and the Dollar, 1973–1981
(percent)

Year	Changes in the Price of Oil[a]	Changes in the Dollar Price Level[b]
1974	316.7	11.1
1975	(15.6)	9.1
1976	4.3	4.6
1977	5.2	6.1
1978	(1.2)	7.8
1979	28.1	12.5
1980	47.7	11.5
1981	(10.7)	9.0

Source: *International Financial Statistics,* various issues.
[a]Changes in the price of oil relative to previous year's prices. Price is based on spot netback price of Saudi light crude in Rotterdam. Price is adjusted by the Wholesale Price Index.
[b]Changes in the U.S. Consumer Price Index.

The government of B has, however, a monopoly position in the currency market. A possible solution for B is to inflate at a rate higher than the one that is consistent with $E(b'_2)$. As long as the rate of inflation is higher than was expected at the time of the negotiation, the relative price of oil as well as the real return on the deposits would go down. This possible solution is depicted at point L. Neither K nor L are general equilibrium solutions. The final solution along the line KFL would be a matter of political and economic negotiation.

The stylized model presented in figure 9C-1 relates the relative price of oil to the rate of inflation. Clearly, this provides a very partial description of the relationship. However, the data on the actual relationship between the changes in the relative price of oil and the changes in the U.S. dollar price level over the period 1973-1981 (presented in table 9C-1) seem to be consistent with the model.

Notes

1. For the relationship between dollar inflation and demand for money worldwide, see chapter 4 in this book.

2. For a complete analysis of this system, see Agmon, Lessard, and Paddock (1979).

3. This issue is discussed by Canzoneri and Gray in chapter 8 in this book.

4. For the specific conditions and proofs, see Mundell (1968) pp. 11-15.

References

Agmon, T., D.R. Lessard, and J.L. Paddock. "Financial markets and the adjustment to higher oil prices." In vol. I, *Advances in the economics of energy and resources,* edited by R.S. Pindyck. Greenwich, Conn.: J.A.I. Press, 1979.

Mundell, R.M. *International economics.* London: MacMillan Co., 1968.

10 The New Nexus among Trade, Industrial and Exchange-Rate Policies

J. David Richardson

Interconnections among policies influencing trade, industrial structure, international payments, and exchange rates have long been a focus of development economics.[1] By contrast, these interconnections seem to be addressed rarely in developed-country analysis. Presumably, this is because they have been judged unimportant or quantitatively insignificant. Present trends in trade and payments policies, however, have generated new interest in these interconnections, which have been explored in several recent publications (for example, Blackhurst and Tumlir 1980, Bergsten and Williamson 1982, and McCulloch 1982).

This chapter is devoted to exploring these interconnections. Its title is a variation on the title of Richard Cooper's (1971) paper. Cooper's paper stands as a prescient exception to the usual dichotomous treatment of "real" policy and exchange-rate policy in developed countries.

One of Cooper's principal observations was that the absence of an adequate adjustment mechanism for international payments tempted nations to adopt distortionary trade and investment policies. These distortions were then justified on balance-of-payments or aggregate-employment grounds. Cooper's treatment of this observation was eloquent, but the observation predates his paper and has enjoyed a continuing popularity as an argument for exchange-rate flexibility. For example, in ascribing the view to Richard Blackhurst, L. Dudley (1981, p. 264) stated:

> Flexible exchange rates eliminate the balance-of-payments motive for tariffs and should therefore facilitate further rounds of negotiations to lower trade barriers.

I am indebted to Robert E. Baldwin, Robert Cornell, Rachel McCulloch, Clas Wihlborg, and John Williamson for their many insightful comments and corrections. They should be implicated in any appreciation but not in any dismay. I also gratefully acknowledge the support of National Science Foundation Grant PRA-8116459, awarded to the National Bureau of Economic Research (NBER). This chapter is part of the NBER's research program in international studies. Any opinions expressed, however, are my own, and not those of the National Bureau of Economic Research.

Isaiah Frank, Charles Pearson, and James Riedel wrote, in *The Implications of Managed Floating Exchange Rates for U.S. Trade Policy* (1979, p. 15):

> The great advantage of a floating exchange rate system was to have been that the adjustment would take place automatically through currency appreciations and depreciations, removing the need for otherwise undesirable trade and capital controls, and allowing governments to concentrate their policies on domestic economic needs. Thus if the adjustment process is working well, trade measures for balance of payments purposes are unnecessary and undesirable.

And, in a discussion of a paper by Charles Kindleberger, Milton Friedman noted (1969, p. 118):

> One of the major arguments for a flexible exchange rate system . . . is that it makes the case for free trade clear and simple. If you have a flexible rate and you reduce tariffs, movements in the exchange rate will automatically protect you against having any adverse balance of payments effects, and therefore you are not exporting or importing unemployment.

Today's payments adjustment is, arguably, as inadequate as when Cooper wrote his paper.[2] The characteristics of its inadequacy have changed, but not the fact, nor the source. Inadequacy now appears most dramatically as exchange-rate volatility. It used to appear most dramatically as balance-of-payments crises (official-reserve volatility). Exchange rates are still misaligned for long periods in the view of many commentators. And the sources of misalignment and volatility are still both government initiative and private speculative response. Distortionary trade and investment policies that used to be defended on balance-of-payments grounds are now defended by reference to today's increasingly sharp swings in international competitiveness, real exchange rates, and current-account balances.

On reflection, it may not be so surprising that pressures for aggressive trade and industrial policies are ultimately invariant to exchange-rate systems. Over long enough periods of time, ratios of wages, profits, and prices—in one sector relative to another and in one nation relative to another—are quite insensitive to exchange-rate and monetary fluctuations. These nonmonetary ratios are, ultimately, the real source of protectionist pressure. The monetary level of wages, profits, and prices does not really matter much. No worker, manager, shareholder, or creditor sees much inequity or need for government protection when his wages and income rise as fast as prices and when foreign wages, prices, and incomes rise at the same rate.

Over shorter periods of time, however, exchange-rate fluctuations can cause real adjustment and injury—in much the same way that monetary policy does. And when exchange-rate fluctuations are recurrent, sharp, and unpredictable, they can lead to recurrent, sharp, and undesirable signals to reallocate resources (see, for example, Artus 1982, p. 6). Unanticipated exchange-rate volatility has all the unfortunate features of unpredictable monetary policy. Both can send false, misleading, and wasteful price signals to economic decision makers. Thus, exchange-rate fluctuations are not irrelevant to trade policy, even though their long-run effects may be neutral. Changes in the level or even the trend of an exchange rate may be innocuous; changes in its variance or predictability are not.

Nor are trade and industrial policies irrelevant to exchange-rate and payments adjustment. Industrial policies aim at far more than just sectoral-share targets. They also aim at temporal targets that are important determinants of exchange rates and international payments. Among such determinants are growth rates (influenced by industrial policies toward research-and-development activities and high-technology industry) and the end-use production mix of consumption goods, capital goods, and education (C and parts of I and G in the familiar national-accounts breakdown). In practice, although not necessarily in principle, trade policies often aim for the same goals. Of course, their more narrow concern is with exports, imports, and foreign investment, all of which have obvious exchange-rate/payments effects. Both trade and industrial policies involve fiscal policy, debt management, and international transfer of rents, all of which, in turn, influence exchange rates, payments, and international indebtedness.

Little effort will be made here to differentiate trade policies from industrial policies, following W.M. Corden (1980, p. 167) and Richard Blackhurst (1981, p. 361). Blackhurst argues that, as governments become increasingly interventionist, much industrial policy is just a veil for trade policy. Conversely, the most potent political arguments for trade policy have almost always been industrial (maintenance of sectoral production and employment). As global markets for products become more and more integrated, it is harder to distinguish any motivation that is unique to one policy compared to the other. Indeed, in the United States, trade policy (which supposedly we have always had) is essentially the stalking horse for industrial policy (which supposedly we do not have, because of philosophical objections). The terms *trade policy* and *industrial policy* are used interchangeably in this chapter.

In practice, some of the most important links between industrial policies and exchange-rate adjustment are one part politics and one part economics. In principle, there need not be any links at all, political or economic. Some practical political/economic connections are discussed in the next section, and then the conceivable absence of any connections is discussed. The topics covered in the remaining sections of the chapter are less sweeping: one section is a compilation of ways that international monetary turbulence influences trade and industrial policies, and the final section reverses the causation. It sketches ways that trade and industrial policies influence exchange rates and international payments.

A number of conclusions are drawn in the chapter. (1) In a world of spatially mobile capital and reasonably accurate expectations, trends in international competitiveness and financial-asset yields are tightly linked. Volatility in one causes volatility in the other. Policies that affect one affect the other. Financial policy influences real exchange rates and alters the pressures for trade and industrial policies. Trade and industrial policies cause overshooting of financial variables and alter the pressures for financial policy. (2) Whatever the other goals of real and financial policies, any failure to make them stable, credible, systematic, and predictable generates volatile and costly signals to reallocate resources. The problems thus engendered are unpredictability (more than inefficiency) and resource disorder (more than resource misorder). The solution to such failure is to reorder resource allocation, not necessarily to reallocate resources. (3) Stable, credible, systematic, and transparent exchange-rate policy can allay resource disorder by limiting deviations around economic trends. Economic trends can be enhanced in the presence of well-defined market imperfections by stable, credible, systematic, and transparent trade and industrial policies. (4) To reduce the likelihood of global-resource disorder, real- and financial-policy options may involve retreating from multilateralism and from unrealistically binding rules. These should not, however, be replaced by the vacuum of policy anarchy. More sensible and timely replacements seem to be aggressive bilateral peacemaking, noninclusive coalition formation, and the formulation of credible conventions to govern government policy, both real and financial.

Political/Economic Policy Parallels and Proposals

Over the past fifteen years, one of the most fundamental parallels between exchange-rate policies and industrial policies is their common trend toward the laissez-faire ordering of interchange among governments. A familiar U.S. concept may help to explain this parallel. "Frontier justice" has seemed to increasingly order both trade and exchange-rate policy. Under frontier justice, whatever a government can get away with, it should do. Strong governments survive prosperously; weak governments, tenuously.

The problem with applying the concept of frontier justice in economic policy is unpredictability. More organized systems of justice regularize economic exchange, establishing boundaries for what qualify as voluntary transactions, rules governing the exploitation of market advantage, and sanctions to guarantee the enforcement of contracts. Frontier justice, by contrast, can destabilize economic exchange, becoming an irritant, rather than a lubricant, to the market.

Another way to describe governmental frontier justice is to call it policy anarchy and aggression. Tendencies toward anarchy and aggression have always been present, of course, and it may be unduly alarmist to forecast an increasing realization of them. Yet some of the constraints that check policy aggression have become looser. U.S. hegemony, however one defines it, has waned since 1945.[3] Undesirable though it was in some ways, it clearly checked the scope for policy aggression, much as the frontier sheriff or U.S. marshall checked the scope for frontier justice. U.S. influence was, roughly speaking, once sufficient to make other nations fall into line in trade policy, exchange-rate policy, and the international institutions that oversee them, but the United States seems less able and less willing to exercise that influence now. The awkward question this raises is: what happens on the frontier when the citizenry grows stronger and when the sheriff not only grows weaker but begins to act just like everyone else? The problem facing both trade policy and exchange-rate policy is how to avoid frontier justice in intergovernment relations—that is, how to reorder policy interchange.

Increasingly aggressive industrial and exchange-rate policies are to be feared more for their potential to disorder resource allocation than for their potential to misorder it. To put the problem starkly, the law of the jungle (pure laissez-faire) seems increasingly to dictate policy interchange among governments. Yet this is as haphazard a way of ordering policy transactions as it is of ordering market transactions. Even the most conservative economists have in mind some particular legal structure of common-law conventions when they favor free markets and liberal trade policy. The threat that presently confronts both industrial and exchange-rate policies is that long-standing legal structures and conventions governing government behavior will be abandoned. Conceivably, anarchy could begin to rule among governments. Uncertainty at best and chaos at worst could be the consequence for international trade and investment. To appreciate the danger of the worst case, consider what happens to everyday commerce during civil disorder, when legal systems crumble and vigilantism waxes strong.

Some recent history when this threat has been realized is easy to document. Policy initiatives to minimize the likelihood of its reemergence are more difficult to conceive.

Two events have played an important historical role. One was the aggressive exchange-rate initiative that encouraged aggressive trade-policy initiatives, and the second was the aggressive trade-policy initiative that reinforced the earlier abandonment of conventions governing exchange-rate adjustment. The first event was the United States's unilateral abrogation of its commitment to the gold-convertibility of the dollar in 1971, which was coupled with a swashbuckling invitation to the rest of the world to adjust exchange-rate parities. This event and its counterpart were enforced by an aggressive application of trade policy in the form of the infamous import surcharge of 10 percent. The second event, or set of events, was the mammoth multiplication of world oil prices in 1973–74 and 1979–80. Economically, this amounted to a repeated application of beggar-thy-neighbor export taxes by the Organization of Petroleum Exporting Countries (OEPC) governments. Many of the implied revenues from these export taxes were recycled successfully. Those that were not caused transfer problems in much the same way that reparations payments did following World War I. The important role of oil as an input caused stagflation problems. Only some of the resulting structural and supply stresses were alleviated by conventional aggregate demand policies; others were made worse. Sovereign governments naturally chose different macroeconomic policy mixes to reflect different menus of relief and endurance. These different policy responses often necessitated sovereign exchange-rate management.

The crucial question with regard to policy is whether there are any sensible alternatives to the mutually devolving vortexes of aggressive trade and exchange-rate initiatives. It is easier to describe what seem to be unlikely or undesirable alternatives. One is a return to hegemonic policy leadership in the fashion of the frontier sheriff. This seems to be out of the question for any government, barring a massive military realignment that might emerge from a world war. Also out of the question is an extensive (that is, global) set of new rules governing trade or monetary relations, such as the return to a gold-based adjustable-peg system or an exhaustive ordering of global industrial and commodities markets. Such alternatives are, at worst, unappealing and, at best, premature—in the same way that creation of the U.S. Constitution was premature before the country had a decade's experience with the more loosely binding, less-inclusive Articles of Confederation. Finally, the oft-repeated exhortations for more policy coordination beg the fundamental question of why such largesse would be in the narrow national interest of aggressive governments. Policy coordination is not a true solution; it is a safe haven only in the eyes of commentators without any stake in policy aggression.

Blackhurst (1981, p. 369 and throughout) addressed the fundamental question in his references to the national benefits of a return toward conventions in governmental policy initiatives. The conventions Blackhurst seems to have in mind would at least order, but not bind, trade and exchange-rate policies. Governments themselves would be the constituents. Mutually agreed-on conventions would protect governments from each other and also from domestic political constituents in narrow pursuit of trade and exchange-rate policies that serve their special interests at the expense of the interests of other constituents.

There are two important practical challenges in any such return toward conventions. One is to avoid overambitious promulgation of rules that, when broken, breed the now-familiar unpredictability, uncertainty, and incredulousness that disorders resource allocation. The second is to keep the resource and time costs of negotiation in check.

In the light of these points, it seems timely to consider reinforcing recent retreats from commercial and financial multilateralism. Multilateralism currently may be too ambitious and too costly to maintain. Bilateralism, trilateralism, quadrilateralism, and so on may be the cheaper, more promising, and most predictable route toward a new multilateralism. Initially, after all, the General Agreements on Tariffs and Trade (GATT), International Monetary Fund (IMF), and World Bank were upheld by small, nonexhaustive groups of nations. Another metaphor may strengthen the argument against multilateralism: small neighborhood gangs take on the obligations of turf-sharing agreements only after a conclusive demonstration of neighborhood peace and predictability, which stemmed from agreement arrived at within the exclusive club of larger gangs.

A practical alternative to multilateralism might be aggressive bilateral peacemaking—the formation of mutually advantageous coalitions with like-minded governments. For example, the United States and Japan seem likely partners for a bilateral but possibly non-Most Favored Nation (MFN) trade agreement that would order trade along lines that are held closely in common. A successful U.S.-Japan trade agreement might then encourage other trade-policy combatants to pursue peace. In another example, the United States, which currently seems to be in a position to bargain, might ask for European trade-policy concessions in return for a U.S. recommitment to exchange-market intervention. U.S. intervention might, at the very worst, have innocuous effects on microeconomic allocation and macroeconomic prosperity. At best, it might purge the economic system of large unanticipated exchange-rate variations that could be mistaken for resource-allocation signals. The case for avoiding resource-allocation mistakes and disorder through stable, predictable monetary policy ought to apply with equal force when the means is stable, predictable exchange-rate management.

The general goal of any return toward convention in government policy interchange is to reorder resource allocation or, perhaps more accurately, to allay the imminence of disorder. Stability, credibility, and predictability are crucial prerequisites for both new trade policy and new exchange-rate policy (Krueger 1981, p. 91, Grossman and Richardson 1982, pp. 20–27, Artus 1982, pp. 10–11). Stable, credible, and transparent trade policy influences trends in resource allocation. Stable, credible, and transparent exchange-rate policy influences deviations from those trends. Ideal trends with minimal divergences are the obvious targets. Trend mistakes are costly, not only for the usual reasons (because misallocated resources are continuously less productive than they would be if allocated correctly), but also because they often waste irreversible human and physical investment, so retraining and retooling costs are, ultimately, unavoidable. Divergence mistakes are costly, not only because of human aversion to risk, but also because temporary competitive imbalances can generate empty shelves and storage lots in one location, excessive inventories in another, and resource-diverting arbitrage for transfering the goods from the latter location to the former. The three respective resource-allocation costs associated with divergence mistakes are waste from rationing, waste from excessive stockpiles, and waste from unnecessary transportation and redistribution.[4]

In a peculiar way, the goals of stability, credibility, and predictability amount to making trade and exchange-rate policies more endogenous and less exogenous. In this context, endogenous simply means systematic policy. Policy still may be quite flexible and responsive to circumstance, but it will be governed by conventions and behavior that are stable, self-enforcing, and readily apparent to economic decision makers.[5] Exogenous policy, typical though it is in standard economic analysis, amounts to arbitrary, unsystematic, and unpredictable policy in this context.

Pure Analytical Approaches and Their Limitations

A familiar position in pure analytic approaches to trade and industrial policies is that exchange rates and payments adjustment are red herrings. In the most familiar general-equilibrium models, exchange rates are ignored and payments adjustment is taken for granted. Exchange rates are ignored because they are assumed to be the relative price of two moneys, both of which are "veils" that have no real effects. Money does not matter, and neither do exchange rates. They are all neutral. An exogenous change in their value has no ultimate impact on production or consumption and, therefore, no ultimate impact on trade or industrial policies. Trade or industrial policies may, by contrast, have some impact on exchange rates and monetary variables, but the real consequences of these real policies will be invariant to their monetary consequences. This seems to be what Richard Blackhurst and Jan Tumler (1980, pp. 3, 13) had in mind when they remarked, "The economic value of trade liberalization is not affected by increased variability of nominal exchange rates . . . exchange rate fluctuations in no way reduce the importance of efforts to liberalize world trade."[6] This also is the regime W.M. Corden (1980, p. 174) characterized as having a vertical long-run Phillips curve.

As to payments adjustment, pure analytic approaches to trade and

industrial policies assume implicitly that it will be maintained automatically. The automatic-maintenance mechanisms are exchange-rate flexibility,
stabilizing official or private trade in assets (as occurred under the gold
standard), or a combination of the two.[7] Obviously, trade and industrial
policies cannot cause exchange-rate or payments problems under such
assumptions. For that matter, nothing else can, either.

Thus, when applying conventional analytic approaches, it makes about
as much sense to write a chapter on industrial policy, floating exchange
rates, and payments adjustment as it does to write one on industrial policy,
variable tides, and shoreline adjustment. Purity rejoices and dichotomy
reigns supreme.

Fortunately for the mandate of this chapter, one need only add a few
elements of reality to draw richer conclusions about the interaction of trade
and exchange-rate policies. Some of these conclusions bear extended discussion and are treated in the following sections of the chapter. Other conclusions are very general and are treated briefly in this section.

To start, analysts agree, in general, that money can "matter" to real
economic decisions as long as some market failure persists. For example,
domestic wages and prices may adjust sluggishly to clear markets. Exchange
rates will affect real decisions during such wage-price sluggishness. Temporary but persistent undervaluation (relative to a currency's ultimate equilibrium value) can encourage exports and protect domestic-import competi-
tors, an effect that led Corden (1978) to dub the undervaluation "exchange-
rate protection." Temporary but persistent overvaluation can lead to
increased pressures from compensatory protectionist policy by injured tradables producers (Bergsten and Williamson 1982).

Furthermore, exchange-rate misalignments may be sharper, more frequent, and more enduring the longer wage-price sluggishness stands in the
way of market clearing because the exchange rate and other flexible variables must do the work of sluggish prices. Excess supplies and demands spill
over into unrationed markets such as the foreign-exchange market, causing
greater unpredictability in flexible prices there. Trade and industrial policies
may even aggravate this spill-over unpredictability of exchange rates (or of
official reserves or of exchange-control adjustments) if they ration suppliers
and demanders administratively. Administrative rationing is, of course, one
tool of production quotas, import licensing, voluntary export restraints,
and mandatory performance requirements. The counterpart to the policy-
induced rationing is increased spill overs of frustrated supplies and demands
into unrationed markets. Prominent among these unrationed markets are
the international markets that include and are mediated by the foreign-
exchange market.

Distortions other than wage-price sluggishness also can make exchange
rates and money matter. Take, for example, intertemporal and capital-mar-

ket imperfections that set practical limits to the losses consistent with any firm's continued survival. With such imperfections, an increase in unanticipated exchange-rate volatility may cause an increased incidence of financial insolvency for firms that are still viable in terms of underlying trends. If insolvency is a boon, implying only a transfer of ownership and a shaking out of the least viable operations in the still viable firm, then there is no cause for alarm. However, if insolvency is a bane, implying waste of resources through indivisibility or immobility, then greater frequency, amplitude, and unpredictability of exchange-rate deviations is a critical problem. Even governments can become insolvent due to the same capital-market imperfections. Increased incipient exchange-rate volatility can exhaust not only owned official reserves but borrowed official reserves as well. This leaves a government with no recourse except to abandon the foreign-exchange market entirely or to apply strict distortionary controls. Financial crises, then, do have real effects, as illustrated most recently by the Mexican dilemma.

Market failure is at the core of each of these illustrations of substantive interaction between trade-industrial policies and financial/exchange-rate policies. The first illustration rests on the failure of markets to clear at a moment in time. The second rests on the failure of markets to clear over time. In general, market failure in one domain can provide a presumptive case for remedial action in some other domain, albeit of a second-best kind. For example, real distortions in the intertemporal trade carried out in global capital markets can be reduced greatly by stable international banking and financial arrangements. The imperfections that remain in the global capital market may provide economically sensible grounds for infant industry protection (Baldwin 1969). They also may provide grounds for industrial policy aimed at avoiding the resource waste associated with unemployed immobile capital or that associated with missing insurance markets, which leads to the making of irreversible human-investment decisions (Grossman and Richardson 1982, pp. 7–8, 22–23, Eaton and Grossman 1981). Predatory trade and industrial policies provide another example. Such policies in one country create market distortions in others. The ideal retaliatory response (or threat) may lie in exchange-rate manipulation, in some other financial intervention, or in completely unrelated domains rather than in the threatened markets themselves. This is because the retaliatory response must be credible to be effective. It must, therefore, emanate from sectors or activities where the injured country has a strong market position rather than a vulnerable one.

In the next two sections, more detailed conclusions about the interaction of trade, industrial, and exchange-rate policies are drawn.

Some Impacts of International Monetary Turbulence on Trade/Industrial Policy

The confluence of increasing capital mobility and increasing recourse to floating exchange rates can be argued to have brought unique pressures to bear on trade and industrial policies.

Increasing spatial capital mobility can be an independent source of financial shocks to the real international economy. It also can transmit reverberations of real and financial shocks in one region to other regions. Financial markets tend to reflect news faster than goods markets or factor markets. And some bits of news encourage significant portfolio reallocations across boundaries and currency denominations.

That is where exchange-rate systems enter. When pegged exchange-rate systems are credible and work, international asset-market fluctuations have comparatively minor effects on competitive and comparative advantages. When pegged-rate systems fail, however, then fluid financial capital may force exchange rates to oscillate markedly from trends consistent with real-trade fundamentals, distorting and destabilizing real trade patterns. It is useful to recall some familiar features of exchange-rate systems in order to illustrate these points.

Under credible and successful pegged-rate systems, official reserves absorb a large portion of the fluctuations in mobile international financial capital.[8] That is to say, official reserves are volatile. Money stocks are potentially volatile as well, depending on the importance of official reserves in the monetary base and the potential for sterilization. By comparison, exchange rates and current-account balances are not volatile, although they may exhibit secular trends, for example, parities may creep or glide by small increments over time. Exchange rates and current-account balances also may exhibit misalignment (Bergsten and Williamson 1982)—protracted periods of departure from normal or long-run values. During such periods, official reserve stocks may exhibit secular trends as well as volatility.

Under floating and conservative intervention systems, exchange rates absorb a large portion of the fluctuations in mobile international financial capital. That is to say, exchange rates are volatile. Their volatility induces accommodating adjustments in trade flows or other capital flows. Adjustments of trade flows takes place for familiar reasons. Adjustment to capital flows takes place because of exchange-rate-related capital gains or losses and because of the reversal of speculative-asset positions as exchange rates change. Exchange rates almost certainly are more volatile under floating and conservative intervention than under aggressive and credible intervention. Exchange rates also may exhibit secular trends, and official resistance to the exchange-rate trends will create trends in official reserves. Otherwise, official reserves are relatively stable.

There obviously is a trade off across exchange-rate systems between official-reserve volatility and exchange-rate volatility. The former has little direct influence on trade and industrial policies; the latter, much.[9] It can be argued that the strongest political pressure for protection emanates from specific sectors of the economy. Each industry views itself as having very little influence over exchange rates. Corden (1980, p. 176) suggests that industries think of their movement as "acts of God." Yet industries are painfully aware of the effects of exchange-rate influences. Depreciation and appreciation due to asset-market flux cause ebbs and flows in competitiveness, cash flow, and long-term economic viability.[10] To the extent that there are intertemporal capital-market distortions that set limits to the maximum losses consistent with any firm's survival, unanticipated exchange-rate volatility may heighten corporate, sectoral, and, ultimately, collective political pressure for protection, especially of a quantitative kind. Quantitative trade and industrial policies shrink the variance of international competitiveness, as well as change its mean. Tariffs (more accurately ad valorem tariffs) affect only the mean.[11] The impetus for these sectoral protectionist pressures is, of course, the fluctuations in a sector's real exchange rate, the ratio of foreign to domestic commodity prices in comparable currency units.[12]

This argument suggests only that pressures for government intervention in trade and production will be greater given volatile exchange rates. It does not suggest that international trade will be discouraged by floating. Thus, the argument is consistent with the oft-quoted failure to find convincing correlation between exchange-rate volatility and international trade (Hooper and Kohlhagen 1978), referenced, for example, by Levich (1981, p. 15) and Artus and Young (1979, p. 682). The explanation for this consistency is that current trade and industrial policies are as likely to be protrade biased as antitrade biased. Examples of protrade-biased industrial policies include: export performance requirements, indirect export subsidies, export tax relief, concessionary export financing, disguised encouragements to dump, and the official cultivation of scale-intensive and technology-intensive industry that necessitates reliance on international markets. Increased export promotion and export protection move global production and trade patterns toward their free-trade norms and, potentially, even past them.[13]

Of course, some exchange-rate variation is welcomed by interventionist interests. Sometimes, for short periods of time, governments can protect tradables producers by discretionary leaning toward currency depreciation. This is euphemistically called replenishing depleted official reserves or building them up "for a rainy day." Corden (1978) and a number of subsequent writers have described this as exchange-rate protection. It is limited in scope by the credibility of the government's exchange-rate targets. Incredible targets generate ineffective intervention and no exchange-rate protection (as is described in note 8). Even with scope, the effectiveness of exchange-rate protection is limited in time to the period during which wages, prices, and other nominal magnitudes remain sluggish. Exchange-rate protection is not a viable policy, for example, when wages are indexed fully and quickly to prices and when commodity arbitrage causes prices to adjust rapidly to exchange rates.

An extension of the idea of exchange-rate protection, recommended by several recent commentators, is to use official-reserve intervention on both sides of the market to stabilize average (aggregate) real exchange rates around their trends. The idea has some appeal as a means of avoiding the unanticipated real exchange-rate divergences that destabilize and distort resource allocation. What this proposal comes close to when enacted in a world with spatially mobile financial capital and with reasonably accurate forecasting of expected inflation is simultaneous stabilization of the average real interest-rate differential. When nominal interest parity, Fisherian interest parity, and mean forecast accuracy all hold, the average (aggregate) time trend in real exchange rates is approximately equal to the average international difference in real interest rates:[14]

$$\dot{e} - \dot{p}_d + \dot{p}_f \approx r_d - r_f \qquad (10.1)$$

where

$\dot{e}$ represents the time rate of change of any exchange rate (domestic currency price of foreign currency).

$\dot{p}_d$, $\dot{p}_f$, represent average domestic and foreign inflation rates for goods, respectively.

$\dot{e} - \dot{p}_d + \dot{p}_f$ represents a measure of the average time rate of change of real exchange rates.

r_d, r_f represent measures of domestic and foreign real interest rates, respectively.

Thus, to stabilize real exchange rates around their trend is to stabilize international differences in real interest rates. This requires intervention policy aimed at moderating asset-market shocks and stochastic variation both at home and abroad. It is notable that, on the left side of the equation, such policy would look like trade (or industrial) policy but, on the right side, it would look like financial policy. With spatially mobile capital, the two types of policy are closely linked. That is an important characteristic of today's international economy.

The band of approximation around equation 10.1 is narrower the closer are the spatial links between financial and capital markets and the more accurate are the economic forecasts. When it is reasonably accurate, equation 10.1 serves several purposes. It demonstrates the linkage between what usually is considered a concern of financial policy—the divergence of real interest rates from global levels—and what usually is considered a concern of industrial/trade policy—trends in international competitiveness. It also demonstrates that small, financially open nations may have, on the one hand, little policy control over real exchange rates (so that the real-exchange-rate targeting suggested earlier would be infeasible) and, on the other hand, little need for such policy control. The volatility of real exchange rates for such countries may be quite small, and their mean value may approximate purchasing-power-parity norms, because international arbitrage probably would minimize divergences of home real interest rates from dominating global levels. Such real-interest arbitrage might be most likely to occur when a multinational corporate presence is prominent in the small, financially open country.

Equation 10.1 also serves to demonstrate how important trade issues can arise from the intertemporal considerations associated with real interest rates. Divergences between home and foreign real interest rates may be as significant an influence on trade as trade policy itself, especially in a growing economy. Trends in and shocks to real interest rates can change the commodity composition of trade because they alter real exchange rates and, subsequently, can shift the margin of comparative advantage among goods.[15]

The most widely appreciated illustration of this effect is, of course, the overshooting phenomenon, summarized and surveyed by Susan Schadler (1977) and Richard Levich (1981).

The sequence of overshooting linkages between financial and real variables is familiar. The sequence begins with an unanticipated shock to a financial variable (Dornbusch 1976, Kouri 1976) or to a real variable (Neary and Purvis 1981). Unanticipated shocks include announcements of future developments (Wilson 1979), which, once announced, become anticipated future developments, and unexpected revisions of previous announcements. These unanticipated shocks cause the rapid adjustment of financial variables—asset valuations, interest rates, and nominal exchange rates. The rapid adjustment of financial variables then becomes a shock, to which some real variables respond rapidly at first and with slow unwinding later. Most important for trade and industrial policies are the ways that real interest rates and nominal exchange rates affect trends in international competitiveness, as revealed in equation 10.1. Unanticipated changes in the level of a monetary stock, for example, cause oppositely signed changes in real interest rates (r_d); unanticipated changes in the rate of monetary expansion cause similarly signed changes in the rate of currency depreciation ($\dot{e}$). Both resultant changes cause sudden movement of real exchange rates and competitiveness, with subsequent slow unwinding.

Some aspects of overshooting linkages are less familiar than those just discussed. First, real exchange rates really overshoot in response to monetary/financial turbulence. Virtually any temporary divergence of real exchange rates from their real norms should be classified as overshooting if it is caused by a monetary shock, because the ultimate equilibrium values of real exchange rates, like all price ratios, are relatively insensitive to monetary variables.

Second, monetary-policy innovations are not the only shocks that cause overshooting in real exchange rates and sectoral competitiveness. Overshooting is just as readily a result of unanticipated shocks to money demand (Artus and Young 1979, p. 670, Levich 1981, p. 25) and to stock equilibrium in other financial markets. Among such unfamiliar causes of overshooting are bank and brokerage failures, unexpected features of default and rescheduling arrangements, unforeseen beginnings and ends to bubbles, unpredictable outworkings of international currency substitutability, and unanticipated portfolio shifts among official-reserve assets of different maturities and currency denominations.[16]

Third, real shocks themselves can cause financial-market reactions that, in turn, feed back on the real economy in the form of overshooting and volatility. Examples of such reactions include unexpected business failures, animal spirits in capital formation, and exogenous resource-price shocks that change the capital value of resource ownership.[17] Even unanticipated cyclical movements in real output can cause financial-market reactions and subsequent overshooting. Unforeseen recessionary shocks reduce the stock demand for liquid assets and real interest rates. These reductions will, in turn, cause overdepreciation of domestic money and even greater overdepreciation of the real exchange rate. With no further shocks, the nominal exchange rate gradually would return part way toward its former value, and the real exchange rate would return all the way to its former value.[18] Unforeseen expansionary shocks have, of course, symmetrically opposite influences.

Given the large inventory of sources for overshooting, it is no wonder that concern over the recent volatility of exchange rates and real interest rates has mounted. Proposals abound for improved exchange-rate management and increased policy stabilization of interest rates, especially on the part of governments in the largest financial markets.

The concern becomes even more credible when each source of overshooting is seen not as an isolated, unique event but as a set of recurring, unforeseeable stochastic impulses. In this case, financial variables overshoot unpredictably on both sides of equilibrium. Induced overshooting and volatility of real variables may be even more pronounced. Equilibrium may be less a position of rest than an entrepôt for real exchange rates, international competitiveness, and relative prices of tradables to nontradables or capital goods to consumer goods. This is a disquieting scenario. Stable equilibriums are assumed to always constrain the economic system at its extremes, tugging it back most aggressively when it is furthest away. But equilibriums also have been conceived as dwelling places. It is not clear what will happen in an economy with so much recurrent volatility that equilibrium has become just a transit point. The most dangerous potential answer is unpredictibility and disorder in resource allocation. Inefficiency and distortions might increase, too, but seem, by comparison, much less threatening.

Some commentators have observed how pervasive overshooting is among all economic markets and how it is deeply rooted historically in economic analysis (for example, Levich 1981, Neary and Purvis 1981). Their implicit or explicit message is that exchange-rate volatility is similar to the volatility in all asset prices and we should worry no more about one than the other. Although it is undeniable that exchange rates can be described as asset prices, the prescription to treat them in the same way other asset prices are treated seems dubious. Exchange-rate volatility seems, on the face of it, to affect more industrial decisions more dramatically and more immediately than does volatility in prices of equities, bonds, or commodities futures. The most important effects on variation in other asset prices seems to be on future resource allocation and investment.[19] Variation in exchange rates, however, seems to have important current as well as future effects.

The most compelling reason why volatility in exchange rates has comparatively more scope for pernicious real mischief than does volatility in other asset prices is that exchange rates are relative prices of media of exchange, not just stores of value. When the relative price of exchange media vary, so will the terms of any real transaction requiring those exchange media to be bartered.[20] Almost all current (as well as future) international transactions involve such a barter. There is no medium of exchange for the national media, no supermedium.

The point is that foreign-exchange markets serve more purposes than those served by all asset markets. This makes price variation in the former more important than price variation in the latter. Foreign exchange (spot claims in foreign money) is different from other financial assets for exactly the same reasons (whatever they are) that money (whatever it is) is different from other financial assets. Public interest in stock markets and futures markets would understandably and properly rise if legal tender were redefined as contracts for pork bellies or baskets of ownership certificates to Dow Jones Industrials. Concern over pork bellies and the Dow Jones Average might become fit fare for every family's dinner conversation. Opposition would spring up immediately to the capricious signals for resource allocation generated by the vagaries of pricing on Wall Street and in the pits of the Chicago Mercantile Exchange. "That's all very well for speculative financial instruments," people might be heard to say, "but this stuff bouncing around from hour to hour is legal tender!"

This discussion has been aimed at documenting the ways that international monetary turbulence elicits sympathetic real turbulence and pressures on trade and industrial policies. (The last section of the chapter reverses the causation.) Here, the chief goal for international monetary policy is that its credibility and predictability be enhanced. For this to be achieved, the credibility and predictability of domestic monetary policy must be increased. To do that successfully requires some change in monetary targets and technical procedures (to enhance predictability), but, more important it requires an improvement in the systematic will, transparency, and endogeneity that govern monetary control. Given improvement in these factors, any one of a number of international monetary reforms might succeed.[21] Without such improvement, all seem likely to fail.

Some Impacts of Trade/Industrial Policy on International Monetary Turbulence

It is obvious that trade and industrial policies aim at sectoral targets. They attempt to influence the commodity composition of output and trade. It is less obvious that trade and industrial policies aim at temporal targets. They attempt to influence current-account balances, capital formation, and growth rates. To achieve their sectoral and temporal targets, trade and industrial policies inevitably must employ not only budget-balancing taxes and subsidies but also fiscal, monetary, and debt-management policies.

Exchange rates and international payments are sensitive to the sectoral targets of real policy, but they are especially sensitive to the temporal targets. These targets and their corresponding instruments influence levels, trends, and volatility of exchange rates, official reserves, and payments balances on current and capital account.

The importance of temporal targets in trade and industrial policy is documented, for example, in Mutti (1982, pp. 9–15). In major countries, government capital subsidies to industry range from two to ten times larger than government operating subsidies. Without exception, industrial subsidies generate benefits on balance to employment of capital. Another example is government export promotion, which typically is a sectoral policy carried out by temporal tools, including concessionary loans, loan guarantees, and sometimes even equity participation. It should be no surprise, therefore, that such a hybrid sectoral-temporal policy has hybrid consequences.

Does export promotion really strengthen a currency and bolster reserves? The usual affirmative answer rests on sectoral incidence alone; however, the definitive answer also must rest on the policy's temporal incidence—how the export promotion is financed.

The effect of industrial policies on levels and trends of financial variables is almost always conditional. One important condition is the type of industrial policy being considered. Two types are often distinguished. One is a "pick-the-winners" or positive-adjustment policy; the other is a "protect-the-injured" or defensive policy (see, for example, Corden 1980, Blackhurst 1981). Many commentators (for example, Krueger 1981) identify export-development policies with the first type and import substitution with the second. However, there are enough counterexamples of successful import replacement and of threatened export sectors clamoring for protection to make the usual identification dubious.

A successful positive-adjustment policy will strengthen a country's currency. One of the most familiar reasons for its success is its ability to overcome intertemporal capital-market imperfections. These imperfections may be associated with imperfect information, risk that exceeds corporate-insurer or creditor ability to bear, and other causes of market failure. Over time, the wisdom of a successful pick-the-winners policy will be appreciated in the integrated global capital market. For as long as this learning process takes, financial investors, some of them foreign, will be adding to their portfolios assets that carry a stake in the winners' winnings. Domestic investors, foregoing some foreign investments that they might otherwise have made, will do the same. Those who add the assets earliest will realize the largest capital gains over the period of information diffusion. These will tend to be the best informed and/or most daring investors. When information about the successful policy is diffused sufficiently, extraordinary capital gains will cease. Only normal returns will be made from then on. However, this will not encourage divestment, and normally none will take place. The important implication here is that investors will end up holding a larger stock of claims on the country that picked the winners than they would otherwise hold. Increased stock demand for selected domestic assets will then lead to arbitrage for the country's other assets. Arbitrage will cause almost all asset prices, including the foreign-exchange-market value of local currency, to be higher than otherwise, too.

Thus, the ultimate monetary effect of a successful pick-the-winners strategy will be an indefinitely stronger currency and/or an indefinitely more favorable trend in official reserves. During the period of information diffusion, the exchange-rate and official-reserve effects will be even more marked quantitatively. This is, by definition, overshooting, and it must take place because transitional capital-account surpluses must be financed somehow during this period.[22] The transitional impacts will, of course, be tempered if the winner industries are biased toward exports or import replacement. Incipient current-account surpluses will be financed by even greater transitional official-reserve absorption, or they will be reversed by even greater transitional exchange-rate appreciation. Such appreciation would have to create the current deficit necessary in order to fund the transitional capital inflow.

A defensive industrial policy will have exactly the same effects as does a successful positive-adjustment policy—if it avoids temporary insolvency and capital losses in firms that are viable in the long run. However, a defensive policy that delays the demise of nonviable enterprises will have the opposite effects. So will an unsuccessful pick-the-winners policy, in which losers are mistakenly identified as winners. Industrial policies of these last two types will result in a permanently weaker currency and/or less favorable trend in official reserves. In the transition period during which the global capital market gradually assesses the bleak results of the government's policy, depreciation and official-reserve losses will be even greater than they would ultimately have been. The reason for these effects is symmetrical to the reasons for the effects discussed earlier.

Thus, raw industrial policies, whether successful or not, cause overshooting of exchange rates and of trends in official reserves. Because of this, the policies may contribute to exchange-rate and payments volatility as well as influence levels and steady-state trends. Yet industrial policies are not developed exogenously nor in a vacuum. Some are conscious attempts to vitiate structural adjustments that are themselves unanticipated real shocks that cause overshooting. Trade and industrial policies such as those that attempt to offset oil-price shocks, real-wage aggression, and stagflationary influences of social policies (such as higher payroll taxes, environmental standards, and occupational safety and health mandates) may make the international monetary system less, not more, turbulent.

To state the argument in another way, during the past decade the chief cause of international monetary turbulence may well have been the unanticipated stagflationary shocks, coupled with the unanticipatable government policy responses to them under apparently new rules of the game. Setting trade and industrial policies that are consciously counterstagflationary should reduce international monetary turbulence. Examples of such policies include supply-side policies aimed at stimulating modernization, research and development, and capital formation at the expense of consumer-goods production. Many such industrial policies are, however, unfunded, and their enactment would lead to larger government budget deficits. The resultant crowding out would then remove much of their intended counterstagflationary influence.

Even worse, many industrial policies are themselves stagflationary. Such policies are better described as counterproductive. By affording ever larger measures of protection to firms and workers in inefficient and declining industries, they reduce productivity growth in exactly the same way that technological regress reduces such growth. Worst of all, they often expose the privileged position that industrial policy provides to rent-seeking opportunists and others in pursuit of unconditional windfall gains. The consequence is resource diversion away from normal economic activity and toward, instead, rent seeking (Krueger 1974), lobbying (Magee and Brock 1981), and suits against the government for (industrial) injury. Counterproductive industrial policies are catalysts rather than cures for international monetary turbulence.

One conclusion is that, if trade and industrial policies are to alleviate international monetary turbulence, they must be motivated by economic dollars and sense. They must be either consistent with private-market assessments or persuasively corrective of them. Policies motivated by anything else—by politics, national prestige, or an irrational romantic attachment to industry (such as "high-tech")—will destabilize international trade and payments (Grossman and Richardson 1982, p. 22). Markets have an inexorable way of disciplining politicians, nationalists, and romantics. Concomitant with discipline, however, is turbulence.

Finally, it may seem doubtful that the impacts of trade and industrial policies on the international monetary system are large enough quantitatively to worry about. Recent empirical calibrations of mixed real and monetary models (Hool and Richardson 1980, Richardson 1982a and b, Deardorff and Stern 1980), however, suggest the opposite. Sometimes, at least, their impacts are large. The intervening variables that trade and industrial policies influence directly are: effective prices of imported and exported intermediate goods; international transfers of rentlike revenues associated with voluntary export quotas and orderly marketing agreements; and capital gains and losses on the equity value of domestic industries.[23] Changes in these variables are what directly and often significantly affect exchange rates and payments.

Notes

1. See, for example, Baldwin (1975) which reflects the work on trade and exchange-rate regimes done in the mid-1970s, as coordinated by Jagdish Bhagwati and Anne Krueger. See also Krueger (1978 and 1981).

2. Conversely, unlike Friedman and the others quoted, Cooper did not imply that broadly floating exchange rates would be more adequate. Cooper preferred a system of gliding parities with presumptive indicators or even a system of flexible uniform taxes and subsidies on trade.

3. See Gilpin (1977), Keohane (1980), Kindleberger (1981), and Kras-

ner (1976) for extended discussions of hegemony and international economics.

4. Stockpiles are costly both to maintain and, in a growing economy, to build up at steady-state growth rates. Inventories can be excessive in the sense that they waste resources on maintenance and in the sense that they force regular incremental additions to stockpiles that otherwise could be consumed.

5. In addition to the discussed resource-allocation benefits of stable, credible, and transparent policy, Richardson (1982 a and b) and Grossman and Richardson (1982, p. 24) observe that such policy has the potential for generating a kind of leading adjustment. Leading adjustment has the virtue of being controlled by expected prices, costs, and profits. All of these are flexible and able to contribute to market clearing. None of them seem likely to be distorted in any systematic or undesirable way. Thus, the resource-allocation adjustment costs that are associated with policy that can be forecast and that are transparent may, in general, be minimal. There appear, however, to be two important situations in which this generalization may be misleading. Market power on the part of sector-specific factors (for example, a strong union in an import-sensitive industry) may lead these factors to exploit systematically transparent policy to take further advantage of their monopolistic position (for example, to raise wages unduly). And foreign-policy authorities may, in retaliatory response, exploit systematically transparent policy to take advantage of any market power they have. Gaming situations such as these, however, suggest only that stable, credible, and predictable policy response should be developed to deal with domestic-market power and foreign-policy retaliation.

6. For a strongly dissenting view, based on less familiar general-equilibrium models, see Chipman (1978, 1980).

7. It may surprise some general-equilibrium trade theorists to learn that they, too, are macroeconomists, in that they always implicitly provide the rudimentary and convenient macroeconomic structure on which their real analysis is based.

8. Two problems are often said to confront any regular and significant government intervention in today's foreign-exchange markets. One is that official reserves are inadequate to cope with massive cross-boundary portfolio reallocations. The second is that, no matter how great the official reserves, rational market expectations of the government's intervention, based on knowledge of its policy-reaction behavior, would cause the intervention to be ineffective. It is rarely observed that both of these problems are caused by a fundamentally deeper problem: the incredulousness with which the market greets government exchange-rate targets and commitments. Suppose that the market really believed in the government's exchange-rate commitments, and that the government really took policy

action consistent with those beliefs in order to ratify them. Then the payments mechanism would work much as it did under the gold standard, although not necessarily with fixed exchange rates. Massive portfolio reallocation might indeed take place. And the government's policy reactions would indeed be transparent to rational forecasters. But any massive capital movements based on rational expectations would themselves stabilize the exchange rate around the government's credible target. Little actual intervention would be necessary. By contrast, if the target were incredible, no amount of government intervention would succeed. Thus, the real problem is the stability and credibility of government financial policy, as discussed in the second part of the chapter.

9. By contrast, official-reserve swings have considerable direct influences on financial markets themselves, altering money supplies, bond stocks, and asset prices. These may have indirect effects on trade and industrial policies, but they rarely have any important immediate influence.

10. Deardorff and Stern (1980) empirically estimate some of the sectoral U.S. effects of dollar appreciation. Marsden and Hollander (1981) show how, for Australia, flux in the nominal exchange rate overwhelmingly accounts for flux in sector-by-sector international competitiveness.

11. This may be a reason to expect relatively more recourse to quantitative protection under floating exchange rates, and relatively less resource to tariffs, than would be typical under pegged rates.

12. Some define real exchange rates as domestic ratios of tradables prices to nontradables prices (see, for example, Neary and Purvis 1981). Most of the observations in this section correspond straightforwardly to this concept as long as tradables prices follow exchange rates more closely or quickly than do nontradables prices.

13. Other explanations for the failure to find much discernible impact of exchange-rate variation on international trade or investment include: (1) possible encouragements to trade based on foreign direct investment, made vertically to avoid input-price variation and horizontally to exploit arbitrage of the produce-where-cheap, market-where-dear variety (Artus 1982, pp. 6, 8, McCulloch 1982, pp. 10–11); (2) the large proportion of modern international trade and investment carried out by genuinely multinational corporations with no strong currency habitat, whose real decisions are less affected by exchange-rate variation.

14. Real interest rates are defined as the difference between nominal interest rates and reasonably accurate forecasts of inflation. Nominal interest rates differ internationally under spatial financial capital mobility by reasonably accurate forecasts of the trend movement in exchange rates.

15. Trends in real interest rates can even change international competitiveness within sectors, such as automobiles and capital goods, because capitalization of borrowing costs accentuates the dollar value of natural price differentials.

16. See Roosa et al. (1982) and Multiple Reserve Currency Study Group (1982) for other ramifications of multiple-currency holdings of official reserves.

17. Examples abound in the literature on the "Dutch disease." References abound in, for example, Corden and Neary (1982) and Neary (1982).

18. Therein lies a possible contributing explanation for the well-known hypersensitivity of the trade balance to cyclical fluctuation. A nation's trade balance may vary countercyclically, not only for the usual reasons, but also because overshooting causes its international competitive position to vary in an exaggerated countercyclical way.

19. For example, variation in the ratio of the market value of capital to its replacement value (Tobin's q) has its most important effects on the future capital stock through cumulative effects on current investment.

20. Admittedly, the terms of the real transactions may be only temporarily altered. The period during which this happens is influenced, again, by the duration of sluggishness in the adjustments of wages, prices, and expectations.

21. See Bergsten and Williamson (1982), pp. 23 and following) for a number of suggestions, including unsterilized pegging, management of intervention by reference rates, and capital controls, including real-interest equalization taxes.

22. The details of those transitional and steady-state conclusions are discussed in a number of recent publications by Sachs (1982) and by Branson (1982).

23. See Johnson (1966), Deardorff and Stern (1980), and Eichengreen (1981).

References

Artus, Jacques R. 1982. "Toward a More Orderly Exchange Rate System." Paper given at a Wingspread Conference on Evolving International Monetary Arrangements, Racine, Wisconsin, July 29-31.

Artus, Jacques R., and John H. Young. 1979. "Fixed and Flexible Exchange Rates: A Renewal of the Debate." International Monetary Fund *Staff Papers* 26, December, 654-698.

Baldwin, Robert E. 1969. "The Case Against Infant-Industry Protection." *Journal of Political Economy* 77 (May/June):295-305.

Baldwin, Robert E. 1975. *Foreign Trade Regimes and Economic Development: The Phillipines,* Vol. 5. New York: Columbia University Press.

Bergsten, C. Fred, and John Williamson. 1982. "Exchange Rates and Trade Policy." Paper presented at a Conference on Trade Policy in the Eighties, Institute for International Economics, Washington, D.C. June 23-25.

Bhandari, Jagdeep S., and Bluford Putnam, eds. 1982. *Economic Interdependence and Flexible Exchange Rates.* Cambridge, Mass.: M.I.T. Press.

Blackhurst, Richard. 1981. "The Twilight of Domestic Economic Policies." *The World Economy* 4 (December):357–373.

Blackhurst, Richard, and Jan Tumlir. 1980. *Trade Relations Under Flexible Exchange Rates.* GATT Studies in International Trade no. 8. Geneva: General Agreement on Tariffs and Trade.

Branson, William H. 1982. "Exchange–Rate Policy After a Decade of Floating." National Bureau of Economic Research working paper no. 909, Cambridge, Mass., June.

Chipman, John S. 1980. "Exchange-Rate Flexibility and Resource Allocation." In *Flexible Exchange Rates and the Balance of Payments: Essays in Memory of Egon Sohmen,* edited by John S. Chipman and Charles P. Kindleberger. Amsterdam: North Holland.

Chipman, John S. 1978. "A Reconsideration of the Elasticity Approach to Balance-of-Payments Adjustment Problems." In *Breadth and Depth in Economics: Fritz Machlup—The Man and His Ideas,* edited by Jacob S. Dreyer. Lexington, Mass.: D.C. Heath.

Cooper, Richard N. 1971. "The Nexes Among Foreign Trade, Investment and Balance-of-Payments Adjustment." In Vol. II of *United States International Economic Policy in an Interdependent World.* Papers submitted to the President's Commission on International Trade and Investment (the "Williams Commission"), July.

Corden, W.M. 1978. "Exchange Rate Protection." Australian National Working Paper no. 60 (April). Appeared subsequently in *The International Monetary System Under Flexible Rates: Global, Regional, and National,* edited by Richard N. Cooper et al. Cambridge, Mass.: Ballinger, 1981.

Corden, W.M. 1980. "Relationships Between Macroeconomic and Industrial Policies." *The World Economy* 3 (September):167–184.

Corden, W.M., and J.P. Neary. 1982. "Booming Sector and De-Industrialization in a Small Open Economy." Institute for International Economic Studies Seminar Paper no. 195. Stockholm: February.

Deardorff, Alan V. 1982a. "The Effects of Exchange-Rate Changes on Domestic Prices, Trade, and Employment in the U.S., European Community, and Japan." Research Seminar in International Economics Discussion Paper no. 111. University of Michigan, May.

Deardorff, Alan V. 1982b. "The Sectoral Impact of the Recent Appreciation of the U.S. Dollar." A Report to the Office of the U.S. Trade Representative. Mimeographed, Ann Arbor, Michigan.

Deardorff, Alan V., and Robert M. Stern. 1980. "Tariff and Exchange-Rate Protection under Fixed and Flexible Exchange Rates in the Major

Industrialized Countries." Research Seminar in International Economics Discussion Paper no. 99. Ann Arbor, Michigan, University of Michigan, June 16. Also in Bhandari and Putnam 1982.

Dornbusch, Rudiger. 1976. "Expectations and Exchange Rate Dynamics." *Journal of Political Economy* 84 (December):1161–1176.

Dudley, L. 1981. "Review" of "Trade and Payments Adjustment Under Flexible Exchange Rates," by J.P. Martin and A. Smith. *Journal of Money, Credit and Banking* 13:262–264.

Eaton, Jonathan, and Gene M. Grossman. 1981. "Tariffs as Insurance: Optimal Commercial Policy When Domestic Markets are Incomplete." National Bureau of Economic Research Working Paper no. 797, November.

Eichengreen, Barry J. 1981. "Effective Protection and Exchange Rate Determination." Harvard Institute of Economic Research, Discussion Paper no. 822. Forthcoming in *Balance of Payments Adjustment and Exchange Rate Dynamics: The Portfolio Approach,* edited by P.J.K. Kouri and J.B. de Macedo. New York: New York University Press.

Frank, Isaiah, Charles Pearson, and James Riedel. 1979. *The Implications of Managed Floating Exchange Rates for U.S. Trade Policy.* New York University, Graduate School of Business Administration, Monograph Series in Finance and Economics no. 1.

Friedman, Milton. 1969. "Discussion" (of a paper by Charles P. Kindleberger). In *The International Adjustment Mechanism,* edited by Richard E. Caves et al. Boston: Federal Reserve Bank of Boston.

Gilpin, Robert. 1977. "Economic Interdependence and National Security in Historical Perspective." In *Economic Issues and National Security,* edited by Klaus Knorr and Frank N. Trager. Lawrence, Kans.: Regents Press of Kansas.

Grossman, Gene M., and J. David Richardson. 1982. "Issues and Options for U.S. Trade Policy in the 1980s: Some Research Perspectives." National Bureau of Economic Research, *Research Progress Report,* Cambridge, Mass.

Hool, Bryce, and J. David Richardson. 1980. "International Trade, Indebtedness, and Welfare Repercussions Among Supply-Constrained Economies Under Floating Exchange Rates." National Bureau of Economic Research Working Paper no. 571, October. Also in Bhandari and Putnam 1982.

Hooper, Peter, and Steven W. Kohlhagen. 1978. "The Effect of Exchange Rate Uncertainty on the Prices and Volume of International Trade." *Journal of International Economics* 8 (November):483–511.

Johnson, Harry G. 1966. "A Model of Protection and the Exchange Rate." *Review of Economic Studies* 33:159–163.

Keohane, Robert O. 1980. "The Theory of Hegemonic Stability and Changes in International Economic Regimes, 1967–1977." In *Change in the International System,* edited by Ole Holsti, Randolph Siverson, and Alexander George. *Change in the International System,* Boulder, Colo.: Westview.

Kindleberger, Charles P. 1981. "Dominance and Leadership in the International Economy: Exploitation, Public Goods, and Free Rides." *International Studies Quarterly* 25, no. 1:242–254.

Kouri, Pentti J.K. 1976. "The Exchange Rate and the Balance of Payments in the Short Run and in the Long Run: A Monetary Approach." *Scandinavian Journal of Economics* 78 (May):280–304.

Krasner, Stephen D. 1976. "State Power and the Structure of International Trade." *World Politics* 28 (April):317–347.

Krueger, Anne O. 1978. *Foreign Trade Regimes and Economic Development: Liberalization Attempts and Consequences.* New York: Ballinger (for the National Bureau of Economic Research).

Krueger, Anne O. 1981. "Interactions Between Inflation and Trade Regimes Objectives in Stabilization Programs." In *Economic Stabilization in Developing Countries,* edited by William R. Cline and Sidney Weintraub. Washington, D.C.: Brookings Institution.

Krueger, Anne O. 1974. "The Political Economic of the Rent-Seeking Society." *American Economic Review* 64 (June):291–303.

Levich, Richard M. 1981. *Overshooting in the Foreign Exchange Market.* Group of Thirty Occasional Papers no. 5. New York.

Magee, Stephen P., and William A. Brock. 1981. "A Model of Politics, Tariffs, and Rent-Seeking in General Equilibrium." Mimeographed, University of Chicago, August.

Marsden, J.S., and G. Hollander. 1981. "Floating Exchange Rates, Inflation and Selective Protectionism: Their Effects on the Competitiveness of Australian Industry." Paper presented at the Sixth Annual Conference of the International Economics Study Group, Sussex, England, September 20.

McCulloch, Rachel. 1982. "Unexpected Real Consequences of Floating Exchange Rates." Paper presented at a Conference on the Evolving Multiple Reserve Asset System, Winspread, Racine, Wisconsin, July 18–30.

Multiple Reserve Currency Study Group. 1982. *How Central Banks Manage Their Reserves.* New York: Group of Thirty.

Mutti, John. 1982. *Taxes, Subsidies, and Competitiveness Internationally.* Washington D.C.: National Planning Association Committee on Changing International Realities.

Neary, J. Peter. 1982. "Real and Monetary Aspects of the 'Dutch Disease'." Paper presented at an International Economic Association

Conference on Structural Adjustment in Trade-Dependent Advanced Economies, Yxtaholm, Sweden, August.

Neary, J. Peter, and Douglas Purvis. 1981. "Real Adjustment and Exchange Rate Dynamics." Paper presented at a Conference on Exchange Rates and International Macroeconomics, National Bureau of Economic Research, Cambridge, Massachusetts, November 20–21.

Richardson, J. David. 1982a. "Four Observations on Modern International Commercial Policy Under Floating Exchange Rates." In Carnegie-Rochester Conference Series on Public Policy 16, *Monetary Regimes and Protectionism,* edited by Karl Brunner and Allan H. Meltzer. Amsterdam: North Holland.

Richardson, J. David. 1982b. "Opaque and Transparent Trade Policy: Some Expectational Considerations." Mimeographed, University of Wisconsin, February.

Roosa, Robert B. et al. 1982. *Reserve Currencies in Transition.* New York: Group of Thirty.

Sachs, Jeffrey. 1982. "Stabilization Policies in the World Economy: Scope and Skepticism." National Bureau of Economic Research working paper no. 862, Cambridge, Mass., February.

Schadler, Susan. 1977. "Sources of Exchange-Rate Variability: Theory and Empirical Evidence." International Monetary Fund *Staff Papers* 24, July, 253–296.

Wilson, Charles A. 1979. "Anticipated Shocks and Exchange Rate Dynamics." *Journal of Political Economy* 87 (June):639–647.

Comment

Robert A. Cornell

J. David Richardson ordered the discussion in his chapter around what he described as four unifying descriptive propositions and four additional prescriptive points. This comment is structured in the same way.

Let us begin with the descriptive threads of analysis. They are:

1. The world has descended to a state where laissez-faire reigns everywhere in the choice and application of international economic policies by nation states. In this autarkic jungle, economic agents receive signals that produce a disordering in resource-allocation decisions, rather than the misordering that is the usual focus of economic analysis.
2. Capital markets are becoming spatially but not temporally more perfect. That is, their pace of efficient development in the spatial dimension has outrun that in the temporal dimension.
3. People see foreign-exchange-rate movements generated chiefly by capital flows as changes in international competitiveness. Industrialists facing such changes do not have sufficient liquidity to survive the exchange-rate-movement cycle that, for them, is exogenous.
4. Industrial and trade policies have exchange-rate effects.

Richardson's distinction between disorder and misorder in resource-allocation patterns, his sense of an emergent chaos in the system, represents, I think, the central insight of his chapter. Perhaps I think this because I agree with the diagnosis. I would suggest, however, that, if it makes any sense at all to describe a chaotic state by the use of an analytic model, Richardson's choice of a laissez-faire or "law-of-the-jungle" model might be improved upon with no loss, and perhaps some gain, in the power of the resultant conclusions. The chief drawback of this use of the idea of laissez-faire lies in its sure propensity to disturb those who, from their intellectual cradles, have been sustained by a vision of the efficiency and stability of that abstraction, the perfectly competitive model. Such a laissez-faire environment, then, ought to be the antithesis of the primeval jungle. Doubtless, at issue is the definition of *laissez-faire,* and Richardson has adopted a special definition, whose principal features is not free, unfettered international movement of goods, services, and factors, but rather a pestilential competition among governments to interfere with such movements in an autarkic way.

The problem of definition can be avoided while, at the same time, a more robust framework for describing the present world can be produced by considering a model of imperfect competition. Thirty years ago, it would have been a monopoly model in which, as Richardson points out, the United States could enforce a more or less free-trade, or traditionally laissez-faire, regime for the world, much as Britain was able to do for a few brief decades in the middle of the last century. Since the 1950s, however, that monopoly position has slowly eroded (for perfectly valid historical reasons that, I think, should not be labeled as either good or bad and the capitalist world has come to be dominated, but not ruled, by an oligopoly composed of the United States, the European Community (EC), and Japan. It is a jungle all right, but it is a jungle terrorized by a tiger, an elephant, and a snake (no particular association of any beast with any of the aforementioned countries is intended here)—each of which has great strengths and some weaknesses, and all of which are contending for a preeminent position.

This system has qualities of inherent instability, born out of the ability, based on economic power, of each of the big beasts to distress the others (and the rest of the world) in its pursuit of autarky in economic policy. Thus far, then, we are still on the road to genuine Richardsonian disorder.

"But why," one could ask, "is there no collusion? Clearly, two of the beasts could gang up on the third, creating a more stable environment that might even induce the third to join and, if not, might arguably increase world welfare." Indeed, such notions have occurred, in various situations, in Washington, Brussels, and Tokyo. The fear of such collusion is present with more or less force in the hearts of relevant officials whenever they get together for an economic negotiation.

Why then, do they not collude? The answer lies in another major disturbance that has come to the lively jungle. An extraordinarily intelligent and dynamic group of interlopers, called newly industrialized countries (NICs) and including Brazil, Mexico, South Korea, Taiwan, Singapore, among others, has arisen to challenge the three others. Contrary to a popular view, the NICs are not unified, because their policies have their own autarkic qualities. However, they possess the dynamic markets that the large contending powers need and they furnish a new source of competition in the home markets of those powers. In short, they present a disturbance that, so far, has prevented the big powers from acting in concert either with regard to the NICs or with respect to each other. Confusion and disorder in international economic policy can persist; the balance of forces is shifting and unstable. Thus, an analogue to a model of imperfect competition supports Richardson's central concept of disorder (as opposed to misorder). Furthermore, it provides a good framework for the analysis of many international economic policy actions that would otherwise confound us. Unfortunately, an elaboration of one such analysis would go far beyond the small space available for this comment.

Both of Richardson's second and third points seem sound empirically, and the fourth is resoundingly self-evident (although Richardson does a service by reminding us of it). One caution however: both the point about capital-market efficiency and that concerning the exogenous nature of exchange-rate movements for industrialists are accurate only up to a certain point. To the extent that truly multinational industrial firms can, in effect, diversify their operations across countries and, more important, across currencies, they have some ability to cope effectively with the exogenous effects of exchange-rate movements. As firms, they have survivability. The ones experiencing difficulty, of course, are the immobile factors and purely domestic firms in both exporting and import-competing industries that do have to face exogenous shocks and thus become the locus of demands everywhere for mercantilist solutions.

Richardson's four unifying prescriptive threads of analysis are:

1. We should worry as much about the price of money as about its quantity.
2. Trade and industrial policies had better solve market problems.
3. Trade and monetary policies need to be stable, predictable, and credible. Governments must cease to lie recurrently.
4. The era of multilateralism may be over, or at least far away.

If the first prescription is an argument for massive exchange-market intervention, I, as a U.S. Treasury official, certainly will not support it. In terms of Richardson's basic analysis, however, I can make a few useful comments about the issue. U.S. intervention policy does not preclude intervention to stabilize disorderly exchange markets. It does refuse to counter the broader directions that exchange markets may be taking, on the grounds that, in the long run, proper resource-allocation decisions in goods and factor markets can thus be most effectively promoted.

This leads me to the second of Richardson's prescriptive points, with which I do agree. In fact, I would broaden it to say that trade, industrial, monetary, and exchange-rate policies all had better be aimed at solving market problems. That is, they should be used judiciously and, above all, to correct problems of misorder (and not those of disorder) in the resource-allocation process—which, is as good an argument against neo-mercantilism as can be found today.

Who, also, could disagree with a plea for stability, predictability, and credibility in governments' international economic policies? To the extent that policies do not possess those attributes, they contribute to the very disorder that is the source of neo-mercantilist tendencies.

If Richardson's final observation about the demise of multilateralism is interpreted as a descriptive rather than a prescriptive point, I am tempted to agree with it. As a prescription, however, it is dangerous. In the first place, bilateralism cannot offer surcease from the tendencies toward disorder that arise in either Richardson's or my analytical jungle; it can only contribute to them and to fundamental misorder as well. This is not to say that an occasional descent into bilateralism may not be inevitable in a disorderly world. It is to say that the focus, the thrust, the context of policymaking must stick with the principles of multilateralism that were built into the postwar system. That systemic context is everything, and it is under mortal threat. We cannot forget the lessons of the first four and a half decades of this century, lest we repeat them. The basic insight of this chapter is excellent and we should take it to heart. However, remember, if disorder is bad, misorder is worse for the health of the world economy. Bilaterism, practiced as it was in the 1930s, produces the latter. It should not tempt us.

Comment

Clas G. Wihlborg

Economic theories of structural change and commercial policy usually do not include money and financial markets. Theories of exchange-rate determination, on the other hand, often do not deal with structural change; instead, they are concerned mainly with short-term adjustment of highly aggregated variables, such as inflation, employment, and the current account of the balance of payments. The goal of J. David Richardson's chapter is to bridge this dichotomy in economic analysis and address a number of policy issues on which economists remain mostly silent. The difficulty of this task can hardly be exaggerated.

Richardson divides his analysis of the nexus problem into three parts. He discusses: (1) the need for international rules of behavior for governments; (2) the transmission of monetary phenomena and exchange-rate disturbances into real effects on the allocation of resources; and (3) the transmission of real disturbances in the form of relative demand and productivity shifts into monetary phenomena such as inflation and exchange-rate changes. Although this approach is valuable and comprehensive, it has the disadvantage of making the chapter into something of a catalogue of possible transmission mechanisms. Because there are many, Richardson does not quite succeed in deriving general policy conclusions; and, when he does draw conclusions, the reader cannot be sure under which particular conditions they were derived. For example, Richardson argues that there are circumstances under which central banks should intervene to decrease the unpredictability of exchange rates, because otherwise, exchange-rate variability could cause a misallocation of resources. On the other hand, governments are urged to follow predictable money-supply rules so as not to contribute to the unpredictability of exchange rates. However, intervention to smooth out exchange-rate fluctuations depending on nonmonetary factors is bound to have money-supply effects. The predictable money-supply rule must, therefore, allow for such interventions in order that the two recommendations not be contradictory.

In the remainder of this comment, I will attempt to approach the analysis of the nexus problem in a more general way than Richardson has in the chapter. I will adhere to the traditional separation between allocation, distribution, and stabilization issues. A separate discussion of each of these issues does not imply that they are independent. However, the separation is convenient and allows a clearer analysis of the nature of the trade offs among allocational efficiency, equity in the distribution of income among countries, and employment and price-level stabilization.

Like Richardson, I assume that the nexus between allocation issues, such as structural change, and stabilization issues, such as unemployment and exchange-rate adjustment, depends on the fact that prices in some markets adjust very rapidly while those in other markets are more sluggish. It may, in fact, be worthwhile to distinguish among three kinds of markets, which are identified by the responsiveness of their prices and quantities:

1. Typically, financial markets are characterized by rapid price adjustment but slow asset-stock adjustment. Thus, asset prices tend to overshoot their long-run equilibrium values. Under a flexible exchange-rate regime, the exchange rate may be characterized by this kind of behavior.
2. In some markets, prices are relatively rigid while quantities supplied adjust quickly. The foreign-exchange market is of this nature when it is under a regime of pegged rates. Certain goods markets also can behave like this, when inventory behavior is taken into account (see, for example, Blinder 1982).
3. Labor markets may be characterized by sluggish price and quantity adjustment. The microeconomic foundations of this kind of market behavior are weak, although the behavior may be common in many markets (Gordon, 1981). The existence of inventories may explain why both output and prices adjust slowly in many goods markets.

Given the existence of different kinds of sluggishness in prices and quantities, spill-over effects between different kinds of markets are to be expected. Walras law can hardly be circumvented.

A detailed analysis of the nexus problem would necessitate a specification of spill-over effects between goods and factor markets on the one hand and money and financial markets on the other. Such a modeling exercise is far beyond the reach of this comment. Instead, some general implications of the existence of spill overs for the simultaneous adjustment of real and monetary variables are discussed. In particular, the following sections address the potential role of exchange rate and trade and industrial policies—after a structural demand shift—for the purpose of: (1) achieving an efficient allocation of resources (the allocation issue); (2) redistributing income among nations (the distribution issue); and (3) achieving full employment and shifting the burden of adjustment among countries (the stabilization problem).

The nonrigorous nature of the analysis implies that the conclusions drawn should be interpreted as hypotheses.

The Allocation Issue

A demand shift between the two sectors must lead to a change in the equilibrium-relative price and the allocation of resources. Changes in goods and factor prices may play an important role in inducing the resource shift. Neary and Purvis (1981) have developed a model for an open economy in which labor moves rapidly between an exportables and an importables sector. Capital moves slowly, however, because this factor of production is sector specific in the short run. This rigidity causes overshooting of the country's terms of trade in the adjustment process to a new equilibrium terms of trade.

The Neary-Purvis model describes a barter economy. It is not far-fetched to argue that the exchange rate could play an important role in the adjustment process if money was added to the model. Assume, for example, that, as in many international macroeconomic models, the country is a price taker on importables but not on exportables. Furthermore, assume that the foreign currency price of importables and the domestic currency price of exportables are rigid. Under these assumptions, exchange-rate changes could perform the role of terms-of-trade changes. As long as goods prices are rigid and supplies of goods are unchanged, an excess demand for importables could reveal itself as a demand for foreign money, thereby causing a depreciation of the exchange rate. The exchange rate could overshoot its long-run equilibrium value for two reasons. First, goods prices are rigid (compare Dornbusch 1976), and, second, exchange-rate changes may substitute for changes in the terms of trade, as in the Neary-Purvis model.

In this framework, the exchange rate performs an important role in the adjustment process. An attempt by monetary authorities to smooth out real exchange-rate changes would imply that resources would remain misallocated for a longer time. Intervention in exchange markets would force the adjustment back on prices in goods markets. One can hypothesize that the fact that the exchange rate bears a large part of the adjustment burden without government intervention in any market implies that any intervention to stabilize the exchange rate could lengthen the adjustment process, thereby contributing to a misallocation of resources.

Industrial policies designed to speed up quantity adjustment in factor markets naturally would decrease the time during which resources are misallocated. In this connection, Richardson brings up the important policy problem of identifying growth industries and the problem of resisting pressures to protect the status quo.

The Distribution Problem

It is obvious that structural changes such as demand shifts between the export industries of two countries will have income-distribution effects within and among countries. These distribution effects will take place whether the adjustment to the disturbance is induced by changes in goods prices or by changes in exchange rates.

The existence of a nexus between exchange rates and relative prices among sectors implies that the optimal-tariff analysis may be applicable to exchange-rate policies. There is a substantial difference, of course, between the use of tariffs and the use of exchange-rate policies for the sake of improving the terms of trade, because exchange-rate policies are likely to be effective only temporarily. Nevertheless, governments may be strongly tempted to use such policies because international agreements prevent the use of tariffs for the sake of improving a country's terms of trade.

Therefore, Richardson addresses an important point when he argues for international rules of behavior with respect to exchange-rate policies. It is hard to see, however, how individual countries with some market power over the real exchange rate could be induced to abstain from exchange-market intervention designed to improve the competitive position of their export industries. Rules and conditions for overt income redistributions may have to be agreed upon at the same time.

In this connection, I disagree strongly with Richardson in his assessment of the welfare effects of the current "frontier justice" among world governments as compared to the effects of the previous situation, in which the United States dictated the rules of behavior for the world by force of relative economic power. By frontier justice, Richardson refers to a system in which many self-serving governments conduct independent and contradictory exchange-rate and industrial policies. To argue that world welfare was greater in a system of U.S. hegemony, one must assume that the United States acted as a benevolent dictator without self-interest. The abandonment of the so-called orderly system under U.S. hegemony is, in my view, a precondition for the development of a system under whose rules of the game nations face a greater degree of equality under the law, to use a phrase usually applied to individual rights.

The Stabilization Issue

The stabilization issue is defined here as the problem of achieving full employment after a structural shift by means of the exchange rate and trade and industrial prices. This section discusses, in particular, the costs (in terms of allocational efficiency) of such stabilization policies. Unemployment is assumed to occur as a result of sluggishness in price and quantity adjustment in labor markets.

In order to compare this discussion with the discussion of the allocation issue, assume again that there is a demand shift from one sector's goods to another's. This discussion is limited to a closed economy. As a result of sluggish labor-market adjustment, unemployment may be a consequence of the demand shift. The government could then use industrial policies or aggregate policies to restore full employment. No matter what kind of policy is used, a serious problem occurs when governments promise full employment or near-full employment. The problem for a market economy is that, when stabilization of the employment level is expected, the degree of sluggishness in labor markets increases. The more sector specific the full-employment policy, the more serious becomes the sluggishness in terms of relative wages as well as labor mobility among sectors. Thus, within a country, there is a trade off between the speed with which allocational efficiency is reached and the level of its structural unemployment. I know of only one model that explicitly addresses this very important issue. This model was developed by Lapan (1976). He analyzes the adjustment effects in labor markets of wage subsidies in an open economy. The trade off between the speed by which allocational efficiency is obtained and the level of employment during the process is illustrated. (See also Wihlborg 1978.)

The trade off between allocational efficiency and employment stabilization becomes more complicated when the objectives of several countries are taken into account. Assume that a worldwide demand shift occurs between two goods produced in several countries. In all producing countries, some unemployment is likely to occur as a result of sluggish labor-market adjustment. The use of sector-specific employment policies in one country shifts the whole adjustment burden in production to other producing countries. Obviously, the efficiency loss of all countries conducting such policies is substantial. The incentive for each government to pursue such policies increases with the number of other governments pursuing sector-specific employment policies. Thus, efficiency considerations favor international agreements on the use of industrial policies for employment purposes.

Full employment also could be pursued by means of, for example, an expansionary monetary policy. Inflation and a depreciation of the exchange rate at rigid nominal wages could temporarily prevent unemployment from occurring in one country. In this case, the sector with decreasing demand would have to shrink, but less so than the extent of the original demand shift. Again, there would be some shifting of the burden of production adjustment to other countries. Also, the exchange-rate effect of the monetary policy could force some adjustment onto sectors that were originally unaffected by the demand shift.

The trade off between allocational efficiency and stabilization clearly becomes quite complicated in the international economy. Each country's use of trade and aggregate policies for employment stabilization after structural shifts forces other countries to bear a larger share of the adjustment burden. Thus, the trade off involves governments with different preferences with respect to allocational efficiency and employment stabilization. A distribution of the adjustment burden must be negotiated among many governments. It is hard to see what set of international rules could be created to achieve optimality in this respect.

Conclusions

Although my approach to the nexus problem differs somewhat from Richardson's, I agree with Richardson on some important points. Particularly, the need for international rules of behavior for exchange-market intervention seems important in order to avoid real exchange-rate wars. The argument for an expanded set of rules of behavior for governments can be extended beyond trade and exchange-rate policies to industrial policies and aggregate policies for the purpose of stabilizing the employment level.

As opposed to Richardson, I arrive at the hypothesis that exchange-market intervention for the sake of stabilizing exchange-rate fluctuations due to real structural disturbances cannot improve the allocation of resources. Rather, any intervention would cause misallocations because the exchange-rate adjustment is likely to help induce resource mobility.

This leads to my final point—the need for research. The complexity of modeling the nexus problem is likely to be very great because the nexus depends on differences in the nature of adjustments among financial, goods, and labor markets as well as on differences among countries. It is hard to see how any policy conclusions with respect to welfare could be derived without knowledge of the reasons for particular kinds of market sluggishness. Market intervention without such knowledge is not likely to be "first best" and might even be welfare decreasing. The design of first-best policies is impossible without further research into the reasons for market failures with macroeconomic consequences. Governments' policies could be directed at the particular kind of market failures the governments are facing, once the reasons for the failures are discovered.

References

Blinder, A. 1982. "Inventories and Sticky Prices: More on the Microfoundations of Macroeconomics." *American Economic Review,* June, 334–48.)

Dornbusch, R., 1976. "Expectations and Exchange Rate Dynamics." *Journal of Political Economy,* December, 1161–1176.

Gordon, R. 1981. "Output Fluctuations and Gradual Price Adjustment." *Journal of Economic Literature,* March, 493–531.

Lapan, H.E. 1976. "International Trade, Factor Market Distortions, and the Optimal Dynamic Subsidy.'' *American Economic Review,* June, 335–46.

Neary, J.P., and D. Purvis. 1981. ''Real Adjustment and Exchange Rate Dynamics.'' Paper presented at Conference on Exchange Rates and International Macroeconomics, National Bureau of Economic Research, Cambridge, Mass., November 20–21.

Wihlborg, C.G. 1978. ''Liberty and Labor Markets—Reflections on the Swedish Experience.'' *ACES Bulletin,* Winter, 85–100.

Index

Contributors

Robert Z. Aliber, University of Chicago

Edward M. Bernstein, The Brookings Institution

James M. Boughton, International Monetary Fund

Matthew Canzoneri, Federal Reserve Board of Governors

Richard N. Cooper, Harvard University

Robert A. Cornell, Department of the Treasury, United States

Carlos F. Diaz Alejandro, Yale University

José D. Epstein, Inter-American Development Bank

Jacob A. Frenkel, University of Chicago and National Bureau of Economic Research

Jo Anna Gray, Federal Reserve Board of Governors

Donald R. Lessard, Massachusetts Institute of Technology

Ronald I. McKinnon, Stanford University

Hyman P. Minsky, Washington University in St. Louis

Franco Modigliani, Massachusetts Institute of Technology

Hugh Patrick, Yale University

J. David Richardson, University of Wisconsin and National Bureau of Economic Research

Eisuke Sakakibara, Ministry of Finance, Japan

Anna Schwartz, National Bureau of Economic Research

David Sternlight, David Sternlight, Inc.

Clas G. Wihlborg, New York University

Leland B. Yeager, University of Virginia

About the Editors

Tamir Agmon, associate professor of finance and international finance at Tel-Aviv University, also has been a visiting faculty member at the Massachusetts Institute of Technology and the University of Southern California. Professor Agmon's research on international finance and economics has appeared in numerous journals, including the *Journal of Finance,* the *Journal of Banking and Finance,* the *Oxford Bulletin of Economics and Statistics,* and *European Economic Review.* He is the co-editor (with Charles Kindleberger) of *Multinationals from Small Countries* (M.I.T. Press, 1977). Professor Agmon received the Ph.D. from the University of Chicago.

Robert G. Hawkins is vice-dean of the New York University Graduate School of Business Administration, a position he has held since 1980. He is also professor of economics and finance. The author of numerous articles in the fields of international finance, international trade policy, and multinational corporations, and co-author or editor of six books, he has been a consultant to the International Economic Policy Association (Washington), the Port of New York Authority, the Organisation for Economic Cooperation and Development, the U.S. Information Agency, The Ford Foundation, and others. Professor Hawkins has lectured on international economic issues at many institutions in the United States and abroad. He is executive secretary and treasurer of the American Finance Association and president of the Academy of International Business. Professor Hawkins received the B.A. from William Jewell College and the Ph.D. in economics from New York University.

Richard Levich is associate professor of finance and international business at New York University Graduate School of Business Administration. He also is a research associate with the National Bureau of Economic Research in Cambridge, Massachusetts. Professor Levich has been a visiting faculty member at the University of Chicago and at Yale University and a visiting scholar at the Board of Governors of the Federal Reserve System. His research on international financial markets has appeared in the *Journal of Political Economy,* the *Columbia Journal of World Business,* and other scholarly publications; he is the author of *The International Money Market: An Assessment of Alternative Forecasting Techniques and Market Efficiency* (JAI Press, 1979) and co-editor (with Clas Wihlborg) of *Exchange Risk and Exposure: Current Developments in International Financial Management* (Lexington Books, 1980). Professor Levich received the Ph.D. from the University of Chicago.